Didactics of Military Ethics

International Studies on Military Ethics

THE SERIES IS EDITED UNDER THE AUSPICES OF THE INTERNATIONAL SOCIETY FOR MILITARY ETHICS IN EUROPE (EUROISME)

VOLUME 2

EURO ISME
International Society for Military Ethics in Europe

The titles published in this series are listed at *brill.com/isme*

Didactics of Military Ethics

From Theory to Practice

Edited by

Thomas R. Elßner
Reinhold Janke

With the assistance of

Antonia C. Oesterle

TUTA SUB AEGIDE PALLAS · 1683 ·

BRILL
NIJHOFF

LEIDEN | BOSTON

Cover photo on the left: printed with kind permission of Bundeswehr/Vennemann.
Cover photo on the right: printed with kind permission of Bundeswehr.

Library of Congress Cataloging-in-Publication Data

Names: Elssner, Thomas R., editor of compilation. | Janke, Reinhold, editor of compilation. | Oesterle, Antonia C., editor of compilation.
Title: Didactics of military ethics : from theory to practice / edited by Thomas R. Elssner, Reinhold Janke ; with the assistance of Antonia C. Oesterle.
Description: Leiden : Brill Nijhoff, [2016] | Series: International studies on military ethics ; volume 2 | Includes bibliographical references and index.
Identifiers: LCCN 2016006318 (print) | LCCN 2016006989 (ebook) | ISBN 9789004312128 (hardback : alk. paper) | ISBN 9789004312135 (E-book)
Subjects: LCSH: Military ethics. | Military ethics--Study and teaching. | War--Moral and ethical aspects.
Classification: LCC U22 .D47 2016 (print) | LCC U22 (ebook) | DDC 174/.9355--dc23
LC record available at http://lccn.loc.gov/2016006318

Typeface for the Latin, Greek, and Cyrillic scripts: "Brill". See and download: brill.com/brill-typeface.

ISSN 2214-7926
ISBN 978-90-04-31212-8 (hardback)
ISBN 978-90-04-31213-5 (e-book)

This book is printed on acid-free paper and produced in a sustainable manner.

Contents

From Theory to Practice: The Short Long Path

Thomas R. Elßner and Reinhold Janke

There is a beautiful mnemonic by Lao Tze which describes one of the main challenges of conveying knowledge and values:" "Tell me and I forget, teach me and I remember, involve me and I learn." So how can we teach ethical knowledge, anchor values and create the ability to judge morally, make correct decisions based on this judgment and act responsibly? This demanding capability first of all requires active knowledge about a complex system of legal foundations, models of legitimation and ethical principles. The dilemmas which particularly soldiers in extreme situations may face, up to a desperate aporia, lead people to the boundaries of their knowledge and possibly even their conscience. After all, it is your own conscience that remains the final authority when all other authorities are insufficient or have failed.

Acting or not acting – which is correct, which is wrong, which is the lesser evil and how do I deal with the resulting guilt?

For soldiers, real trust in a true spirit of fellowship and the feeling of security in a stable community is especially important in such situations. Particularly in difficult times, a culture of dialogue forms a main element of this kind of trusting interaction.

Where people are not afraid to talk about their fears and where they do not doubt that they can openly voice their misgivings, an atmosphere of trust is created in which everyone feels that they have the right and the obligation to address things which touch their innermost feelings.

A lot has been said and written about the particular responsibilities of superiors as role models in terms of attitude and the fulfilment of duty, as leaders and companions, teachers and advisers. But the following particularly applies to superiors: a culture of communication alone is not sufficient. It is only the congruence of word and deed, the credible example, the willingness to participate and share without reservations in a community without ulterior motives or duplicity and without tactical calculation which is the key to success. Telling, teaching and involving others form the main elements of the successful teaching of knowledge and values in such a community.

The following contributions which were delivered at the Euro-ISME symposium at the Zentrum Innere Führung der Bundeswehr (Leadership, Development and Civic Education Center) in Koblenz in May 2014 address experiences already made in this context, promising methodical and didactical processes and the challenges and limits of the art of conveying knowledge. The topic of the annual meeting "Theory to practice" strikes a nerve, it seems. The high number of participants, over 100 participants from all continents, which even surprised the organizers, shows this. The 163 program which was ample anyway was designed to accommodate numerous smaller workshops apart from presentations and plenary discussions which helped to deepen the topic of the year with its many facets and perspectives. One important finding resulting from all the presentations and discussions was that there are a satisfactory number of theoretical considerations and models about military ethics that reflect responsibility but regrettably few offers which process existing knowledge in a didactical and sensible manner in courses for all ranks from private to general/admiral and thus create curiosity and are a real support for the practically oriented teaching of this complex topic. The essays collected in this volume offer a representative excerpt of the topics presented at the 4th Euro-ISME symposium at the Zentrum Innere Führung der Bundeswehr (Leadership, Development and Civic Education Center) in Koblenz. Looking back it has become clear once more that we are only at the beginning of our joint task of finding viable solutions and developing sustainable models so that ethics can be put into practice.

Discours d'introduction de la 4ème conférence annuelle d'Euro-ISME

Benoit Royal

Permettez-moi maintenant, pendant quelques minutes, d'aborder le thème qui nous réunit et de vous livrer quelques réflexions qui, je l'espère, serviront à introduire les débats et alimenter les discussions sur le thème majeur que nous avons choisi : « L'étude de l'éthique militaire : de la théorie à la pratique ». Vous ne pouvez pas imaginer à quel point ce sujet illustre l'état d'esprit dans lequel je me trouvais, il y a quelques années, lorsque j'ai commencé à travailler sur l'éthique. Pour vous l'expliquer, permettez-moi de vous livrer ce petit témoignage.

L'évènement que je veux vous raconter remonte à l'année 2004, à l'époque où jeune colonel, je commandais mon régiment en Bretagne. Ce soir-là, j'avais rassemblé l'ensemble de mes chefs de section officiers et sous-officiers dans un lieu isolé à l'extérieur au régiment pour y conduire un séminaire de réflexion que j'organisais annuellement. Quelques semaines auparavant, l'armée de Terre avait eu connaissance d'un évènement qui s'était déroulé en Côte d'Ivoire. En effet, depuis la in de l'année 2002, plusieurs milliers de soldats avaient été engagés dans une operation d'interposition dans ce pays, entre des forces régulières d'une part et des forces « rebelles » d'autres part qui avaient tentées un coup d'état. C'est l'opération « Licorne ». La mission de nos troupes consistait à protéger une zone tampon entre les différents groupes armés, et permettre un règlement politique de la situation. Les faits auxquels je fais référence, révélaient que dans le nord du pays, un bandit de grand chemin avait déjà été capturé une première fois par les soldats français, et avait été remis à la police locale. Il avait ensuite aisément corrompu ses gardiens puis avait été rapidement libéré. Il avait alors repris ses pillages et ses violences avec sa bande. Il avait alors été de nouveau capturé, blessé à cette occasion et était décédé au cours de son transport à l'hôpital. L'enquête avait prouvé qu'il avait été en fait exécuté par étouffement avec un sac plastique par des soldats français au cours de son déplacement. Les militaires ayant avoué l'acte délictueux avaient déclaré avoir reçu l'ordre explicite de leur supérieur de faire en sorte que – cette fois- ci – le blessé ne parvienne pas en vie à l'hôpital. Révélée à la justice par le chef d'état-major de l'armée de Terre, cette affaire avait largement alimenté les conversations de ces dernières semaines.

J'avais donc décidé ce soir-là, de faire réfléchir mes chefs de section sur ce cas concret et de but en blanc, je leur posais donc la question suivante :

« si vous aviez été à la place de ce chef de section, dans ce véhicule, et que vous aviez reçu de votre supérieur l'ordre d'exécuter ce prisonnier, qu'auriezvous fait ? »

De longues secondes passent sans que personne ne réagisse. J'accroche alors le regard d'un jeune lieutenant, arrivé depuis une année au régiment, et je l'interpelle directement. Il me répond avec une certaine vivacité : « Je crois que j'aurai fait pareil, ce gars-là n'a vraiment eu que ce qu'il méritait. C'était un salopard »

Un peu choqué de cette première réaction spontanée, à l'opposé de ce que j'espérais, je m'abstiens de réagir et continue à solliciter les autres participants du regard. Un sous-officier se tourne alors vers ce lieutenant et lui répond : « Vous n'avez pas le droit de dire ça mon lieutenant, ce n'est pas à nous de régler le cas des salopards. Ce n'est pas notre boulot. En ce qui me concerne, je n'aurais pas exécuté cet ordre. »

J'attends alors de nouvelles réactions qui tardent car je sens bien que ma question dérange. Elle semble déranger car c'est visiblement une question que mes soldats ne se sont jamais posée…Je sollicite alors directement un autre lieutenant qui a les yeux un peu dans le vague. Il me répond : « je vous avoue, mon colonel, que je ne sais pas ce que j'aurais fait, j'aurais été bien embêté. »

La suite de la soirée me permettra de remplir mon rôle d'éducateur des consciences et de transmettre les messages que j'avais préparés à mes subordonnés. Pour autant, cette scène me laissa perplexe car je n'avais pas mesuré qu'il pouvait exister un tel manque de réflexion éthique chez mes jeunes cadres. Cet évènement fut le point de départ de ma demarche éducative sur le sujet de l'éthique et explique en grande partie ma présence devant vous aujourd'hui. En fait, ce que je pris pour un manque de réflexion éthique chez mes cadres, était en fait un manqué d'appropriation de l'enseignement théorique dispensé et une sorte.

Tous ces hommes avaient suivi un enseignement éthique théorique de qualité. Ils avaient appris les règles de la guerre et le droit, ils avaient lu les philosophes…mais ces lectures étaient restées prisonnières dans une zone du cerveau. Le seul qui avait bien réagi était un sous-officier d'expérience qui lui, avait déjà vécu sur le terrain des situations de conflits et des opérations militaires.

Nous voilà donc exactement dans le sujet de notre colloque : de la théorie à la pratique. Afin de ne pas être trop long, permettez-moi de synthétiser en trois grandes idées, l'état de mes réflexions et de mon expérience sur ce sujet.

1 Une armée se doit posséder un socle de référence théorique solide de plusieurs niveaux. En effet, deux types de documents sont absolument nécessaires

pour préparer les esprits et les consciences. Le premier est un document de portée philosophique qui fixe les grandes valeurs et les grands principes sur lesquels se fonde l'enseignement. Ce document est souvent le reflet de l'histoire des Nations et reprend les grandes valeurs historiques sur lesquelles elles se sont fondées. Chez nos camarades Britanniques, ce document est le « The Military Covenant ». Chez nos camarades Allemands c'est la directive décrivant le principe « d'Innere Fûhrunge » Chez les Français c'est « L'Exercice du métier des armes, fondements et principes » Je n'ai pas trouvé d'équivalent chez nos camarades américains. Cette approche intellectuellement est nécessaire car elle permet de fixer le cadre moral général dans lequel le militaire va évoluer. Souvent un peu complexes pour le niveau d'exécution, ces textes doivent être complétés par d'autres écrits, plus directement transposables en actions concrètes et que l'on retrouve dans les différents règlements des armées.

A l'autre bout, le soldat a besoin d'une autre forme de document beaucoup plus simple, rédigé sous forme de commandement ou de code (code de l'honneur, code du soldat, etc.). Cette approche est souvent rituelle, mais aussi directement compréhensible au plus bas échelon, par des soldats qui, sur le terrain, sont confrontés à la complexité de l'action. Le caractère de ces codes, inévitablement caricatural est particulièrement intéressant car il permet de mettre en exergue ce qui est considéré comme essentiel. Ces documents se réduisent à des listes de commandements simples et accessibles au plus grand nombre. Il existe dans toutes les armées : le Code du soldat de France, The soldier's oath britannique, the Soldier's Creed américain, etc.

2 Ces documents ne peuvent se suffire à eux-mêmes et l'enseignement éthique doit impérativement être complété par l'étude de cas concrets historiques et contemporain aux trois niveaux de la hiérarchie : officier, sous-officier et homme du rang. L'exemple précédent que je viens de vous raconter est un révélateur qui illustre ce principe. Il montre la nécessité de poser des questions sur des cas concrets de terrain, des situations simples et probables, qui prennent d'autant plus d'importance aux yeux de ceux qui les étudient que ces situations ont été vécues. Il s'agit de multiplier les exemples, de faire réfléchir pratiquement les hommes et les femmes sur ce qu'eux-mêmes auraient fait dans telles ou telles circonstances. A mon niveau, j'ai par exemple, récapitulé 10 cas concrets que j'expose à mes lieutenants en séance d'instruction. Je les fais voter sur telle ou telle solution. Je les implique tous, les force à choisir et ensuite, je leur présente la solution qui a été choisie dans la réalité. Je leur expose les consequences de ces décisions et nous en discutons. Ces séances sont essentielles, très formatrices et très bien acceptées. En France, elles sont d'ailleurs souvent réalisées au niveau

des officiers, mais elles manquent encore aux autres niveaux de commandement : sous- officier et homme du rang, alors qu'elles sont essentielles à leur niveau. Je pourrais développer davantage cet aspect mais le temps me manque.

3 L'enseignement éthique doit sortir des salles de cours…et irriguer tous les aspects de la préparation opérationnelle de terrain. Il est essentiel en effet, que la réflexion éthique prenne sa place dans les exercices de terrain. Elle doit sortir des salles de cours bien confortables où chacun peut réfléchir aux cas exposés en pregnant tout le temps de la réflexion, hors de toute pression opérationnelle. L'idée est qu'il ne doit pas exister un seul exercice de terrain sans qu'au moins un cas pratique éthique soit inséré dans l'exercice. Il s'agit ainsi d'habituer les soldats à intégrer en permanence ces réflexions à l'exécution des actes tactiques de terrain, dans la difficulté, sous la pression du temps, de la météo et dans un vrai niveau de stress. Il faut faire comprendre que le comportement d'un soldat au combat doit être en permanence irrigué par l'esprit et les valeurs enseignées, et qu'il n'y a pas de frontière entre la théorie et la pratique.

L'objectif n'est pas de donner des recettes types qui marchent à tous les coups. Il est illusoire de chercher à classifier les situations de terrain. Il existera toujours des cas concrets dans lesquels il n'existera peut être jamais de bonne solution, mais une solution sera la « moins mauvaise solution ». Il s'agit bien de faire en sorte d'armer nos militaires, de les préparer à affronter ces situations inextricables et de leur permettre de trouver des solutions dont ils seront capables d'assumer seuls les conséquences. Plus ils y auront été confrontés avant, mieux il aurons été entraînés, plus facilement ils trouveront un chemin pour choisir, en conscience, la décision à prendre.

En conclusion

Napoléon avait coutume de dire à ses hommes : « Au combat, la plus heureuse des initiatives n'est souvent qu'une réminiscence ». On peut décliner cet adage pour ce qui concerne le comportement éthique au combat. A la guerre, lorsqu'il faut prendre une décision dans l'urgence, la solution qui se dessine n'est souvent que la réminiscence des enseignements reçus, des entraînements effectués, des valeurs que chacun a cultivées en soi. Ces valeurs, ces piliers qui vont permettre d'armer la conscience des soldats, se construiront d'autant plus facilement s'ils s'appuient :

1 Sur un enseignement qui puisse s'inspirer d'une hiérarchie complète de documents de différente portée : philosophique, pratique et de codes simples d'exécution.
2 Sur un enseignement qui ne fasse pas l'économie de l'étude des cas historiques (et souvent des erreurs commises) ainsi que d'exemples concrets permettant la mise en application des principes théoriques.
3 Sur un enseignement qui se transporte sur le terrain, qui soit dispensé sous la pression des

évènements et qui s'inscrive dans le quotidien de la préparation opérationnelle des militaires. Dans ces conditions alors, la meilleure – ou quelquefois la « moins mauvaise » – des solutions arrive naturellement à l'esprit, comme la résultante des réflexions, des lectures et des expériences vécues en amont, pendant le temps de paix. L'histoire a montré que la force technique seule ne peut pas vaincre durablement. Le glaive nu ne suffit pas. Il faut que l'esprit anime le glaive. Cet esprit c'est celui de l'éthique au combat, des valeurs défendues. L'esprit du glaive c'est une façon de conduire une action de guerre en s'appuyant sur des convictions ancrées dans les consciences individuelles et qui se galvanisent dans l'action collective. Cet esprit repose sur un équilibre subtil entre les causes défendues, la solidité d'un groupe et les valeurs transmises et enseignées à travers l'éthique militaire.

Introduction to the 4th Annual Conference Euro-ISME

Benoit Royal

Permit me to begin by explaining my state of mind a number of years ago, when I first began to reflect seriously about the problems of fostering ethics in military service.

The event I recall took place in 2004 when, as a young colonel, I commanded a regiment in Britain. Once each year I would gather all my section chiefs, officers and NCOs, in a retreat setting outside of the regiment boundaries, in order to conduct a leadership seminar. A few weeks prior to my annual gathering in 2004, the French Army had learned of an incident that took place in the Ivory Coast, where several thousand of our French soldiers had been engaged since 2002 in a peacekeeping operation, mediating a conflict between the regular forces on the one hand, and "rebel" forces who had attempted a coup. This was dubbed "Operation Unicorn."

The mission of our troops in that country was to establish a buffer zone between the different armed groups, in order to allow for a political settlement of the situation. During this time, in the north, an Ivorian highwayman known as "Mahé" had been terrorizing the local population. Recognized as a murderer and rapist, he had already been captured once by the French soldiers, and had been handed over to the local police. He easily corrupted his guards, however, and was quickly released, whereupon he resumed looting and violence with his followers. He had subsequently been recaptured and injured, but on this second occasion had apparently died of his injuries during transport to hospital. A subsequent investigation of the circumstances of his death while in captivity, however, proved that he had actually been executed by suffocation with a plastic bag by French soldiers during his transport.

The military personnel who admitted the criminal act reported receiving explicit orders from their superior to ensure that – this time – the injured criminal should not reach the hospital alive. Proven beyond a reasonable doubt by the Chief of Staff of the Army, this case had provoked a great deal of controversy in the weeks leading up to my seminar. So I decided, then and there, to invite my section heads to reflect on this particular case. Out of the blue, I surprised them with the question: "If you had been in the place of the section chief in this vehicle, and received from your supervisor an order to execute this prisoner, what would you have done?"

Long seconds passed without anyone reacting. Then I caught the eye of a young lieutenant, who had just arrived to spend a year in our regiment, and I directed the challenge to him. He replied with some vivacity, "I think I would have done the same! This guy really got what he deserved. He was a bastard!"

I was a little shocked at first by this spontaneous reaction, the opposite of what I had expected. I declined to respond at once, and continued to seek the views of other participants. Then an NCO turned to the lieutenant and replied: "You have no right to say that, sir. It is not for us to resolve the case of bastards. It's not our job. In my case, I would not have carried out the order."

I then waited for new reactions from other participants, which came slowly, because I could sense that my question was disturbing. It seemed to bother everyone, because it was clearly an issue that my soldiers had never before been asked to consider. I then directly solicited another lieutenant, whose facial expression seemed vague and troubled. He replied: "I confess, sir, I do not know what I would have done. I would have been pissed!"

The remainder of the evening afforded me the opportunity to fulfill my role as an educator of consciences and to disseminate various lessons that I had prepared for my subordinates. That opening scene puzzled me, however, because I did not imagine that there could be such a lack of ethical reflection among my young professionals. This event marked the beginning of my approach to the subject of ethics education.

In fact, what I took initially to be a lack of ethical reflection among my cadres, was actually a lack of ownership or internalization by them of their theoretical teachings, and a kind of failure to translate the broad principles of moral behavior into everyday situations. All of these men had been exposed to a quality education in ethical theory. They had learned the rules of war and the law, they had read the philosophers. But these readings remained trapped in some remote recess of the brain. The only one who responded to my question was a sergeant, well experienced in the field of conflict and military operations, even if less formally educated in other respects.

This bears directly on the underlying purpose of this Handbook: namely, to understand the foundations of military ethics in the customs and best practices of military professionalism itself. On this topic, I wish to offer three observations.

1 Every military organization or service must have a solid foundation in fundamental theory at many different levels.

   Specifically, two types of documented theoretical reference points are absolutely necessary to prepare the minds and moral consciences of military personnel. The first is a document which sets out a philosophical understanding of the great moral values and principles that underlie military customs and practices. This document is often drawn from a reflection on the historical experience of many nations, and aimed at recovering and setting forth many of the fundamental values emerging from that historical experience. For our British comrades, the relevant document is "The Military Covenant," while our military comrades in Germany point to the directive describing their fundamental conception of "Innere Führung," or "Inward Leadership." In France, it is "The Exercise of the Profession of Arms: Foundations and Principles." I did not find any equivalent document for our American comrades.

This approach is intellectually necessary because it helps set the general moral framework within which the military will come to operate. Because such foundational documents are often a bit complex for the ordinary, practical level of performance, however, these texts must be complemented by other writings, more directly translatable into action in accordance with the different laws and regulations of our own respective nations, or that of a host government or nation within which we may operate.

From the opposite side, the ordinary soldier needs a different, much simpler and more straightforward document, written in the form of commands or codes (a "code of honor," or a "soldier's code"). This approach to inculcating moral values is often ritualized, but it is also directly comprehensible at even the lowest ranks, and by soldiers on the ground, facing the complexity of combat action. Sometimes, to be sure, the character of these codes seems almost like a simplistic caricature of the fundamental moral values they incapsulate. Nonetheless, they are of particular importance in allowing a military organization to highlight what is considered essential, "ground truth." These documents are generally condensed or reduced to lists of simple and accessible commands or principles comprehensible to all. We find these in virtually all armies: the "Soldier's Code" (France), the "British Soldier's Oath," the American "Soldier's Creed," and so forth.

2 The foregoing documents may not be sufficient in themselves, and ethics education must be supplemented by the study of historical and contemporary case studies at three distinct levels of the military hierarchy: the Officer, the NCO, and the enlisted rank and file.

The case I discussed above illustrates this principle. It demonstrates the need to ask questions about specific and realistic situations, which should prove to be important even in the eyes of those who think themselves to be experienced. There should be many such examples that encourage military personnel, both men and women, to reflect substantially on what they themselves might have done in the given circumstances.

In training my staff officers, for example, I typically provided summaries of 10 case studies and invited my lieutenants to discuss and vote among themselves on a particular solution. I provided all participants with the power to choose, and then showed them the solution that was chosen in reality. I then showed them the consequences of those decisions, and we would discuss the circumstances even further. These sessions constituted essential training, and were very well accepted. In France, we customarily provide such discussion sessions and case studies for our junior and senior officers, but we don't do nearly enough at the other levels of command (such as chief warrant officer and enlisted ranks) although such training is essential for them as well.

3 Finally, and perhaps of greatest importance: ethics education must be removed from the classroom in order to infuse and nurture all aspects of operational readiness on the ground.

It is essential that ethical reflection should takes place in the midst of field exercises. It must leave the comfortable classroom environment, in which everyone has the luxury to reflect on the cases presented, taking time to think apart from all operational pressure. Instead, the idea is that there should not be a single field exercise without at least one case study in ethics included within that exercise. The aim is to accustom military personnel to embedding these moral reflections within their execution of tactical actions in the field, in the midst of difficulties, under the pressure of time, weather and real stress. We have to understand that the behavior of a soldier in combat must be constantly influenced by the spirit and the core values we have taught them, and come to recognize that there is no boundary between theory and practice.

The goal is not to provide "typical recipes" that will work every time. It is unrealistic to attempt to classify field situations. There will always be specific cases in which a good solution can never be found, but in which a solution will be instead the "least bad solution." It is well to ensure that we have equipped our military to prepare for these tricky situations, and allow them to develop solutions or responses whose consequences they will be able to bear. The more they have confronted such situations in advance, the better they will have been equipped and trained to respond, and the easier they will find it to make a conscientious and appropriate decision when the time comes.

Conclusion

Napoleon used to say to his men: "In battle, the happiest initiative is often a reminiscence." We may, however, reverse this adage with regard to ethical behavior in combat. In war, when a decision is needed urgently, the solution that emerges is itself often reminiscent of the lessons learned, actions performed, and the moral values that everyone has cultivated themselves. These values, these pillars that will help to arm the conscience of soldiers, develop more readily if they are grounded in:

1. Education that refers to an entire hierarchy of documents of different scope: aimed at both philosophical understanding and practical implementation, as well as compliance with the established provisions of codes of conduct.
2. Education that does not fail to incorporate the extensive study of historical cases (and often mistakes) and other concrete examples that demonstrate the best possible application of theoretical principles; and:
3. Education that is carried out in the field, where it is conducted under the pressure of events, so as to fit into the daily operational readiness of the military.

Under these conditions, the best – or sometimes, at least, the "less bad" – solutions naturally come to mind, as the result of reflections, readings and prior experience.

History has shown that technical strength alone cannot defeat an enemy consistently. The "naked sword" is not enough. We need also the spirit that animates the sword. This spirit is the spirit of ethics in action, defending well-established moral values. The spirit of the sword is a way to conduct a war action founded upon beliefs that, in turn, are rooted in the conscience of each and every individual soldier, and which serve to galvanize their collective action. This spirit is itself founded on a delicate balance between the causes defended through the strength of a group, and the values transmitted and taught through military ethics.

List of Contributors

Babic, Jovan
Professor of Ethics at the University of Belgrade, and Visiting Professor at Portland State University, OR, USA

Bock, Veronika
Dr. Director, Center for Ethical Education in the Armed Forces (zebis; Hamburg)

Brake, Moritz
Dipl.-Ing. (FH) Lieutenant Commander (LtCdr), Youth officer ("Jugendoffizier")

Cook, Martin L.
Ph.D. Adm. James B. Stockdale Professor of Professional Military Ethics, Co-Editor of *The Journal of Military Ethics College of Operational and Strategic Leadership*

Demont, Florian
Dr. Phil. Research Assistant Leadership and Communication, Military Academy/ Defense Academy at the ETH Zürich

Elßner, Thomas R.
Dr., theol. habil. Professor of Old Testament at the Philosophical-Theological University, Vallendar; Catholic Military chaplain and a teacher of ethics in the German Armed Forces, Zentrum Innere Führung, Koblenz; Vice President of Euro-ISME

Graaff, Miriam C. de
PhD candidate; MA in Communication Studies as well as Psychology, Dutch Ministry of Defense

Gugerel, Stefan
MilOKur MMag. Director of the Institute on Religion and Peace (Vienna, Austria)

Janke, Reinhold
M.A., Colonel Head of design and development at the "Zentrum Innere Führung" of the German Armed Forces (Koblenz)

Jeftic, Zoran
Ph.D. University of Belgrade, Faculty of Security

Lober, George
Senior Lecturer Department of Defense Analysis Graduate School of Operational and Information Sciences Monterey, CA

Lupfer, Timothy T.
MA Modern History, Deloitte Consulting (US)

Micewski, Edwin R.
Mag. Dr. phil.; Brigadier General (retired), Austria

Mompesyssin, Patrice
Brigadier General (retired), France

Montrose, Jeff
Master's degree in Peace and Security Studies from the Institute for Peace Research and Security Policy at the University of Hamburg. Doctoral candidate at the "Universität der Bundeswehr" (Munich) and Lecturer at the Catholic University of Eichstaett-Ingolstadt, Germany

Tonn, Kristina
M.A. Project management didactics portal/Researcher, Center for Ethical Education in the Armed Forces (zebis; Hamburg)

Rokovic, Vanja
Ph.D. University of Belgrade, Faculty of Security

Royal, Benoit
Brigadier General Research. Associated Researcher at CREC Saint-Cyr, France; President of Euro-ISME

Schubert, Hartwig von
Dr. Protestant theologian and military dean at the "Führungsakademie der Bundeswehr" (Hamburg)

Stanarevic, Svetlana
Ph.D. University of Belgrade, Faculty of Security

Verweij, Desiree

Prof. Dr. Associate Professor for „normative and political dilemmas of multilateral peace operations "at the Faculty for Management Science at the University of Nijmegen. The Chair is supported by Pax Christi Netherlands; and Professor of Military Ethics at the Netherlands Defense Academy in Breda

Weigt, Jürgen

Dipl.-Päd. Generalmajor; Commander of the „Zentrum Innere Führung" of the German Armed Forces (Koblenz)

CHAPTER 1

Responsibility Towards Myself and my Conscience: Leadership Responsibility between Ethics and Purpose

Jürgen Weigt

Paris – Shrivenham – Amsterdam – Koblenz. All the people of Koblenz will be extremely flattered to see their city as a meeting place, as part of a tradition, as the venue for a conference that has dedicated itself to special topics and that brings together a group of people – soldiers and civilians – to address ethical issues associated with the military profession.

It is a pleasure for me, as the host of this year's conference, to welcome you here to the Zentrum Innere Führung (Leadership Development and Civic Education Centre of the Bundeswehr).

We see your attendance of the conference as an honour and a distinction and will try to make your stay here as pleasant and as interesting as possible.

The header of the 4th Annual Euro-ISME Conference is: Didactics of Military Ethics "From Theory to Practice". I have been asked to deliver the opening presentation. I am highly grateful to the organisers, notably Brigadier General Royal, for the choice of the topic for this year. I believe it is important, indeed indispensable, for moral and philosophical aspects of ethics and military ethics to be addressed academically.

After being a soldier for more than 37 years and holding an extremely wide range of posts, I have seen many, many examples of situations in which ethical decisions in the military profession have been guided above all by purposive rationality. Maybe it is due to my father – on account of what he had experienced – having urged me at a very early stage not to turn a blind eye to facts. And certainly not if I actually wanted to look at them more closely. Maybe this appeal to me by my father to always want to keep sight of reality played a part in my taking up the career I have. Whatever the case may be, I realized during my education that it is important to know what is right and what is wrong. It was a learning process I went through – sometimes by means of trial and error.

In retrospect, I would say it is very important that I had my own basic ethics to guide me when I became a soldier. The first time I entered a barracks – it was in the mid-1970s –, I had a number of moral standards and values in my head from civilian life, and from the very first minute onwards, I asked myself whether and, if so, how people can manage in a military community with ideas

 | DOI 10.1163/9789004312135_002

about morals and morality that are exclusively civilian in nature. I learnt quickly, very quickly that ethics based on principles, an unshakable belief in theoretical, mostly inflated standards of human action, at times make it difficult to live with others in a barracks in a way that is suitable for everyday life. To put it more simply, I knew very soon that I was not without sin. Why should the other soldiers I then lived with be?

As early as my days as a platoon leader – responsible for around 30 mostly young men who were serving their country as conscripts, some with great keenness, others with less –, I sensed the conflict that existed between the temptation to implement ideals in real life and what a military organization really did in the Cold War. Almost every day, I was confronted with questions and problems that my mind could not dismiss – even as part of a team, although they arose on the borderline of moral action. Initiation rituals involving the consumption of large amounts of alcohol are just one example of conflicts of this kind.

In my view, military ethics – more than any other area of ethics – concern the depths of what it means to be human – beyond all the links between developments that can be proven scientifically. My many years of experience of life, my profession and military operations have shown me that it does not help me to simply follow pre-set recipes and argue over philosophical concepts in complex situations that are difficult for humans to handle.

On the contrary, in difficult situations, for instance, when decisions concerning the Afghanistan conflict had to be made, I have lived from the inner disposition I brought with me. You will note that I say brought with me, for it developed without my having occupied myself with these topics ethically or philosophically in the true sense of the words. I particularly felt that I was expected to act morally while on operational deployment. More intuitively than knowingly, I tried to find out how I could do what was morally good, right and proper. I often succeeded, but sometimes I didn't. The difference in perception does not permit a final judgement to be made. But it was often more a case of trial and error on my own part than the result of conveyance from others.

Principles for a leadership or life style that is as "moral" as possible have been important, but they have not been the sole "source of strength" for what I have thought and done as a soldier and a human being. The search for compromises and the manner in which I have handled and used things that are all too human have frequently prevented me from becoming too theoretical in my ideas. This is why in my concept of leadership as a leader, educator and trainer, I have not primarily strove to find virtually absolutely binding solutions for ethical issues.

I have never seen my personal responsibility as a soldier myself and a leader of other soldiers as merely being a question of my following rules, no matter how reasonable they appear to be at first sight. I always have been and still am on the look-out for solutions that are suitable for everyday life – always aware of my personal responsibility. I have never had the feeling in this army, my army, that I am inescapably obliged to be obedient. I have never experienced a situation in which I have had to decide between legality and morality. Even so, I have made decisions in routine duty and on operations that have had different implications, more painful ones than I anticipated. And if the same situations arose again, I would decide on them differently – with the knowledge I have today. However, there has always been one crucial point. I have always felt a final responsibility towards myself and my conscience. I have always relied in a moral sense on my own free decisions.

There are many difficult situations in which this does not make things easier. On the contrary.

The purposiveness of many military decisions leads to dilemma situations, particularly on operations. I have to put some people at risk in order to protect others. I have to take lives in order to save lives. When real-life situations and values clash, it is often only possible to make mixed decisions or judgements. Also because everybody has to go on living with the results of decisions. I sum up:

> I have been a soldier, a member of the Bundeswehr, for almost 40 years; I have been formed by its mission and the demands that derive from it.
>
> My many years of experience have taught me that you have to reflect about the existential questions of what it means to be a soldier beforehand, before you are placed in extreme, existential situations.
>
> As a military leader, lives are entrusted in me; I decide on whether they are to be taken or saved.
>
> It is possible and wise to seek advice on the legality and purposiveness of some questions.
>
> In the matter of morality, everyone is responsible towards their conscience whenever they make a decision.
>
> It has always been the final and highest authority for me.
>
> It is on account of this personal conviction that I believe it makes sense for questions concerning military ethics to be addressed at such a conference.
>
> For reflections of this kind must be conducted well before situations arise in which they are required.
>
> I hope that the conference will be interesting.

CHAPTER 2

Didactics of Military Ethics: From Theory to Practice

Thomas R. Elßner

The Iron Curtain fell 25 years – a quarter of a century – ago. Before the fall of the Iron Curtain two military blocks equipped with a multitude of nuclear weapons had been facing each other in Europe. Fortunately, today many young soldiers who were born in 1982 or later only know about this from their history books, and for many older soldiers or contemporaries this has already become a war story. At that time there were fierce and justified discussions in the context of peace ethics and military ethics as to whether nuclear deterrence and a nuclear first strike would make sense and what consequences such a first strike would have. The individual soldier, both conscript and career soldier, either actively participated in the discussion or not, depending on his personal convictions and interests. However, one thing was obvious to most of them: Should there ever be a nuclear war, hardly anyone in Central Europe and especially in Germany would survive it. Quite a few soldiers assumed deep in their hearts that such a war would not happen although they were convinced that everything had to be done to preserve world peace. Even though the threat was very real, questions of war and peace were extremely abstract and belonged to the highest political spheres.

Today – 25 years later – there are no longer two opposing military blocks in Europe, but ironically, now that the Cold War is over, most Bundeswehr soldiers for instance have gained operational experience and have even taken part in combat operations. Some of them were killed in action, others severely wounded in many different ways. This also includes an insidious disease, which has been known in Europe since the outbreak of the First World War 100 years ago and which is today called posttraumatic stress disorder (PTSD). In the light of this, a completely new dimension is added to the ethical aspects of military service, especially when it comes to applying military force. Military operations, including the use of armed force, usually take place far away from the home country in the context of multinational missions abroad, yet they are present in our everyday lives. The political decision-makers who are responsible for determining the mandate and passing it in parliament are not anonymous because they can be reached in real time via Facebook and Twitter almost round the clock; however, the deployed soldiers – from the private up

 | DOI 10.1163/9789004312135_003

to the general – are the ones who might have to apply military force in extreme cases and who must answer to their personal conscience for this decision.

Therefore the question has to be: How can military ethics help to prepare soldiers for situations in which they have to take difficult decisions? Do military ethicists really know what is on the minds of soldiers and what difficulties they have to face? Can military ethics help to overcome moral speechlessness and trite truths?

This includes the observation that occasionally even military ethicists become speechless, which is something they try to cover up with many words. Sometimes this can be seen when they use the bellum-iustum theory or, to put it simpler, the "Just War Theory", which has in part experienced a renaissance for quite some time, also in the European context, to justify or explain military interventions. It is important to know this theory and to be able to place it in its *historical* context; however, it does not offer a great amount of help when it comes to developing a really pronounced ethically correct power of judgment and decision-making support for the military actions of soldiers. Although on a normative level the bellum-iustum theory is way better than its general reputation, it nevertheless falls short because it ignores certain questions and does not know questions like the following ones: How is an honest post- crisis and conflict analysis carried out? What needs to be considered in order to enable the setting up of just political and legal structures in the time after a military intervention? How can former enemies be reconciled effectively without sweeping guilt and crimes under the carpet? In addition, the criteria associated with the "ius in bello", the classical law of war, are basically implemented in international humanitarian law (e.g. the principle of proportionality, the differentiation between combatants and the non-involved civilian population), so every soldier should actually know them. It is also easily overlooked that the bellum-iustum theory has been and is mostly cited by those who feel superior to their opponent, both in terms of ethics and in terms of military capabilities. At times, when reference is made to the bellum iustum theory this is done very selectively, either with regard to epochs (Antiquity, Cicero, Late Antiquity, Augustinus, High Middle Ages, Thomas Aquinas, Premodern Era, Hugo Grotius etc.) or criteria (ius ad bellum, ius in bello). In addition it is hardly ever mentioned that the Spanish late scholastic Francisco de Vitoria (1480–1546) already pointed out the dilemma of a bellum-iustum ex utraque, i.e. not only in the past but also today, the respective opposite party can easily use the criteria of just war for its military actions and hence, these criteria and consequently the theory itself are taken ad absurdum despite their superficial plausibility. Furthermore, when people talk about the just war theory sometimes the impression is created that this theory is some sort of parallel right existing alongside the international humanitarian law. However, such an impression would be fatal and involuntarily reminds us of the proverb: Well-intentioned is often the opposite of well done. One could almost say that today, the bellum-iustum theory with all its individual criteria can be seen as a legal matter which is part of the international humanitarian law, particularly since its concepts are not very precise (how do you define war? How do you define just?). Despite their inherent fragility, laws apply to everyone, which is an inestimable advantage. This is suspicious to some of the advocates of the bellum-iustum theory. When it comes to laws, the feeling of moral superiority is usually irrelevant. Apart from the indispensable knowledge of the international humanitarian law, the soldier also needs ethical reflections and discussions. This can be implemented particularly intensively using practical examples in order to help the soldier with his learning process and to prepare him for real situations.

Let us take one example that illustrates both the difficulties and the necessity of military ethics. The international humanitarian law neither allows the application of military force against children nor does it mention children as combatants. At first, everybody agrees to that. However, Africa is more and more becoming an important place of deployment for European armed forces. In some regions you can find the so-called child soldiers. We are talking about real children, between eight and twelve years old, not about seventeen year olds who are interested in a military career. These children are ruthlessly trained to kill without constraints. They are a fierce weapon in the hands of warlords. How will for example a Bundeswehr soldier react if while being on patrol he suddenly encounters a child soldier, a girl who is approximately ten years old – a situation that can all of a sudden become a classic duel situation. In addition, the child soldier is on drugs, has been abused several times, has witnessed the killing of her mother – in other words, the child soldier will not hesitate to fire at the soldier, to kill him. Every time I point out this example during my ethics classes in the context of the ethical idea of a "clash of duties" (do not use violence against children, the right of self-defence) there are three classic reactions. Some of the soldiers remain silent; they show no reaction, others become pensive and others again – quite a few – smile at their ethics teacher in a friendly but slightly patronizing way. First, they start mumbling something and then they clearly articulate: "Of course this is a classic case of self-defence and I'm allowed to fire." I respond: "Yes! That's true." As a reaction I get a nod in the sense of "well, that's obvious". However, in the blink of an eye this seemingly self-confident mood is changing when I ask the soldiers: "And in which military training centre can I practice shooting at real child soldiers?" "Do you know exactly how you'll feel if you exercise your guaranteed right of self-defence?" The reaction is silence. Here you can quickly see a double learning effect. First, even if something is permitted by international law it is still hard to actually do it and second, even if my actions are in line with international law and therefore correct, I will be affected both emotionally and mentally by such a situation. I do not know the effects an experience like that will have on me. Precisely such an experience or something similar can eventually cause soldiers to be thrown off the track, even if they seem to be very robust.

Now how do military ethics come into play? First of all we need to be aware of the possibilities but also the limits of military ethics. Military ethics are not above all things to the effect that they offer *the* solution, the perfect solution, for everything, also because even with responsibly reflected military ethics a happy ending is not necessarily guaranteed. And such a statement would also be dishonest because almost no human life always runs a hundred per cent smoothly and because there is no guarantee that good and considerate actions will lead to success. This sobriety, which also knows the abysmal depth of human life, is one prerequisite in order to be able to reflect on the things that need to be considered and observed in such situations *together with* the soldiers. Sometimes the question is raised whether talking about it in a warm room while sitting at a table far away from the reality; the actual situation during the missions really makes sense. To the surprise of some people, the quick and easy answer to that is a clear yes, because the counter question would be: If not now, when? And after a situation like the confrontation with a child soldier has occurred, it is indeed too late to start with ethical reflections. Therefore the time and place to deal with such difficult and complex situations intensively but without any external stress are practical and ethically reflected classes. I think the soldiers are familiar with such an approach from other areas, because before a soldier is allowed to touch anything inside a tank for the first time or to work as an IT expert who looks after computers he has to undergo many training sessions and pass the respective tests. This goes without saying and nobody would question it. However, where problems related to military ethics are concerned – questions of life and death – this is not considered to be perfectly normal. Some even think that such hours of ethical reflection take up valuable time that is actually needed for marksmanship training. Those who support this opinion do not act in favour of their soldiers. Do not get me wrong: I am not saying that it is an either-or decision, either marksmanship training or ethics classes, but rather a both-and situation.

There is an old aphorism going back to the Greek fabulist Aesop which the great humanist Erasmus Desiderius of Rotterdam translated into the Latin version we know today: Hic Rhodus, hic salta, here is Rhodes, jump here. Or translated a bit more freely: Here in Koblenz, Euro-ISME is holding its conference, tell me how you reflect on ethical challenges together with the soldiers.

Let me briefly explain three methodological-didactical models.

1. We at the section responsible for intercultural competence and ethics of the Zentrum Innere Führung (Leadership Development and Civic Education Centre) have developed a training board "Taking the right decision – acting responsibly". With the help of this training board, soldiers can ethically reflect on their military service in small working groups. In *group sessions* they talk about the ideas, virtues and values guiding them during their everyday life as a soldier. *Jointly*, they have to solve certain tasks that neither try to change their personal point of view nor have predetermined results. What is remarkable in this context is that many soldiers who have been working together for quite some time start talking about ethical questions for the first time. Often they are surprised to hear how the comrade they think they know actually thinks and feels. This training board is a major component when it comes to self-reflection on their military service.

We are going to present the board in the German Pavilion during a workshop this afternoon.

2. The Centre for Ethical Education in the Armed Forces (Zentrum für ethische Bildung in den Streitkräften – *zebis*), which was founded by the Catholic Bishop for the Armed Forces in Hamburg in 2010, has developed a didactics portal for ethics education. This didactics portal provides the military chaplains with educational models by means of which they can enter into a structured discussion with the soldier, e.g. about general topics related to military ethics or about current issues like UAVs. These models give enough leeway for discussions tailored to each target group. The military chaplain on site usually knows *his* soldiers and their questions best. These models are a valuable aid to the military chaplain to such a degree that he does not have to develop sound models with a high methodical quality himself in addition to his numerous other daily routine tasks. However, it is easy for him to familiarize himself with new topics quickly and to react appropriately to new developments because of his university education, experience of life and professional expertise. Today nobody has to be a jack-of-all-trades, something that is no longer possible anyhow in an extremely complex, work-sharing professional world.

Dr. Bock, the *zebis* director, is going to present this didactics portal to us in detail.

3. Finally, the versatile experience of soldiers gained during the missions is still not sufficiently evaluated in a structured way so that it can be properly used for ethical reflections. Therefore this time during our annual meeting we have set up a panel where soldiers have the opportunity to report if and how

ethical reflections helped them to deal with the tasks and challenges that arose during their deployment abroad. This is crucial if only in view of the fact that usually ethicists – with the exception of military chaplains – usually do not go on missions abroad and therefore do not have the chance to directly witness the everyday life of soldiers there.

Conclusion: Military ethics, as applied ethics that are part of general ethics and therefore not special ethics cut off from the other fields of ethics, has the task of connecting three areas with regard to content, methods and didactics. First and foremost there is the personal ethical reflection. What guides and determines my ideas and actions as a soldier (training board)? How do I convey ethical standards and values in a way that the soldiers realize that this is relevant to them (didactics portal, zebis)? The soldier has to be able to say: "It is a matter that concerns me", freely adapted from the Latin poet Horace (tua res agitur). And finally: How do I use the experience gained by soldiers facing difficult situations in which they had to take decisions with ethical implications for a well-structured practical ethical reflection?

CHAPTER 3

'What I Have Learned'

George Lober

In the fifteen years I have been teaching ethics to the men and women attending the Naval Postgraduate School, I have made a few observations and drawn some conclusions from those observations that I'd like to share with you.

To begin with it's my observation that most of the military professionals I teach enter my class with one or more of the following preconceptions. The first is that for some of my students, military ethics instruction boils down to one simple admonition: 'Be Good!' Unfortunately, most of the officers I teach have heard this admonition ad nauseam, and unless I counter it in short order, their inclination by even the second day of class is to say, 'Got it, Check!' and then tune me out. Their preconception is that all military ethics classes are alike – mine couldn't possibly have anything new to offer – and they have all been to the Church of 'Be Good!' many times, heard the gospel, understand it, and really don't need to hear it again.

The subtext of that preconception is that the actual reason my students need to be good is so they won't embarrass the organization – a thematic variation of which is, 'Don't get into trouble and embarrass the organization by violating policy XYZ.' Within this subtext, my ethics class is transformed before my students' eyes into a series of organizational lectures on behaviour control. Once again, though, the military professionals I teach tend to be insightful.

They discern at warp speed the distinction between honest ethical analysis and discussion, and a veiled lesson on the need to adhere to policy XYZ for the sake of their organization's image.

A second preconception often held by students entering my class is that military ethics are black and white. The subtext here is that there is only one right institutional answer; as an ethics instructor, I know that answer. Eventually I will give my students that answer, and then they can then stop thinking about the issue under discussion and move on, which typically means returning to their laptop screens to check Google news or their email.

Thus, in short order, the military professionals I teach enter my class expecting to be told once more to be good, not to embarrass the organization or their fellow service men and women, and to be told eventually the 'right' answer on any given issue or question.

This leads to my second observation: in my experience, the military professionals I teach tend to be far more cynical than their civilian counterparts, and

 | DOI 10.1163/9789004312135_004

this cynicism, combined with the organizational pressures my students feel to fall in line with the proper institutional attitude and response, renders them far less open than civilians to participating in frank discussions. This is problematic for me, because I am interested in honest discussions of applied ethics in general and military ethics in specific.

My third observation is that despite their cynicism and the perceived pressure to toe the standard institutional line of the moment, my students actually want to talk. There are unresolved moral issues and questions running through them, especially after the last twelve years of asymmetric conflict and terrorist attacks, and they want to talk about those issues and questions and, if possible, come to some resolution.

This leads to my fourth and final observation. I believe the last twelve or more years of combat deployments have changed my students. The ones I taught before September 11th are not the same as the students I teach now, and interestingly, the students I am teaching now are actually different from their counterparts of only five years ago. I'll elaborate further on this observation in a moment. But what do I conclude from these four observations?

I've concluded that if I want to be a successful teacher and provide my students with sound ethical frameworks with which they can resolve present and future dilemmas – and if I want to motivate them to honestly re-examine their own ethical stance on a given topic – then I have to create an learning environment that encourages honest discussion. This means I have to walk a very narrow line. I have to provide my students with the opportunity for reflection, re-examination and self-discovery, while simultaneously avoiding the perception that I am little more than a marketing rep for positive military behaviour.

I have also concluded that many of the military professionals I teach are ethically conflicted. At any given moment, their personal ethics may place them at odds with the organization in which they serve. Correspondingly, the ethics of that organization may place them at odds with a segment of their own society, just as the personal need, or organizational requirement, to advance in their careers may place them in the position of declaring that "'Ethical Choice A' is not what I think is right – but if I want to be promoted, 'Choice A' is what I have to do." I've concluded similarly that the very asymmetric nature of the conflict of these last twelve years, has placed some of my students in ethical compromises from which they are still struggling. It has also foisted upon others a re-examination of their organization's values.

Let me give you an example of what I mean. The one staple of my curriculum for the past fifteen years has been Fleamotta's piece, 'Should Military

Professionals Be held to a Higher Moral Standard?'[1] In it, Ficarrotta suggests it's entirely possible for an individual to function within different sets of ethical values, depending upon the context. Thus, it's possible for an individual to be a completely squared away soldier at work, and still come home and be a lousy spouse, father, or neighbour, as well as a liar, a cheat, etc. When I first assigned this piece to my students in the years before September 11th, they inevitably thought that Ficarrotta was on crack. There was no way one could be ethically inconsistent and remain an effective military professional. However, as the past twelve years of conflict have worn on, the vast majority of my students now completely accept Ficarrotta's assertion as a given. Of course, they say, one can function on different ethical systems depending upon the context. They've seen it first hand. They've seen the incredible warrior and trustworthy brother-in arms who, although married, is having an affair or two on the side; or the stellar senior enlisted who goes home and beats his wife. And they themselves may have compromised their values for the sake of the mission while down range.

So as an instructor, I believe I need to recognize these four influences – my students' personal ethics, their branch or service's ethics, the values and ethics they perceive as necessary for promotion, and the perceptions and ethics they've acquired through combat – may at any time be running just below the surface of whatever ethical issue, framework, paradigm, lesson, or case study I introduce.

How then do I, as a teacher, broach such a cynical, wary, potentially conflicted audience? I enter the first class of every course with the acknowledgement that I am uncertain of exactly where my students are coming from. I recognize they will all have undergone some military training, and I assume most of them will display a default courtesy to my authority until I prove undeserving of it. But beyond that, I approach each first class of every course expecting it to be significantly different from the last, providing I allow it to be so.

I also anticipate that in any new section of my course, a few students will toe the standard line and never deviate from it. For any issue they will cite the Uniform Military Code of Justice chapter and verse. These are my Pentecostals. No matter what case study or issue I present, their answer will be a variation on 'Code of Justice, Chapter 6, Paragraph Four, Amen.' I also anticipate that, at the other end of the spectrum, one or more students in every class will take an openly contrarian position to any issue, just to provoke discussions or see if they can get a rise out of me. These are my chain jerkers. Their answer to any

1 Carl J. Ficarotta, 'Should military professionals be held to a higher moral standard?' (Fall 1997) 24, *Armed Forces and Society*.

issue or case study is intended to pull the chain of someone in the class. They don't necessarily believe the positions they assume, but these students love watching the knee-jerk reactions their positions evoke. Therefore, my instructional focus in every ethics course I teach centres on the students in the middle, those military professionals who are willing to openly engage in honest discussion. I build my lessons around them.

I begin each new class each quarter by introducing case studies based upon actual civilian events, rather than military – case studies, however, that I believe may parallel issues my students are struggling with, and cases which are sufficiently complex to allow for the possibility of more than one ethical resolution. Such cases provide a vehicle for my students to enter into a discussion of ethics simply as individuals, and not necessarily as military representatives. I believe that is important. My hope and goal in introducing such cases is to create an initial first impression of my classroom as a place where students are free to share their reflections on a variety of ethical issues, including those specifically related to their roles as military professionals.

My next step is to select cases from own experience as an educator. For example, in recent years, this lesson has involved the academic tradition of inflating letters of recommendation. The dilemma is simple: do I tell the truth about a genuinely good, but not necessarily exceptional student – and thereby risk jeopardizing his selection – or do I inflate the truth, so that he will appear competitive within a field of others whose letters of recommendation have been inflated? I've yet to share the dilemma of whether or not, as a professor, I should inflate a letter of recommendation in order to assist a deserving student, without at least one or more of my students immediately introducing the same dilemma in the filling out of Fitness Reports on their subordinates. Together, we then lament the current processes that place us both in the ethically compromising position of either inflating the truth, or punishing a good soldier or individual because of the practices in our respective institutions.

If I'm successful in these initial steps intended to establish an open, honest environment for discussion, the rest of my curriculum – the introduction of various philosophical frameworks and paradigms, the analysis of ethical theory, the discussion of military based case studies, etc. – tends to roll much easier. It's important to note, though, that throughout my course, I continue periodically to insert civilian case studies and case studies from my own experience into the curriculum.

In my lessons, I try to ask the hard questions, those for which there are no pat answers. I learned years ago the best questions to ask are the ones to which I do not know the answer; otherwise, I simply am playing 'Guess What's in My Head' with my students. Besides, the difficult questions are really the ones my students want to discuss and the ones that generate the greatest introspection and learning. They also prevent the class from degenerating into a pedagogical exercise in chant and response.

I strive to recognize my students' truths. My students are combat tested and scarred. They have acquired certain truths over the last twelve years. As their teacher, I need to recognize the reality those truths hold for them. I may not agree with those truths, but if my students and I are going to examine the ethical strength of any such truth, the least I can do is approach that discussion with a degree of respect for the circumstances and experiences under which it was derived.

In that regard, I try to listen openly and fully to what my students say. The ethical resolution to a case study dilemma, or the flaw in a student's thinking, may appear obvious to me, but unless I extend the courtesy of honestly hearing what they are saying, I risk exchanging proselytism for dialogue. And trust me, the military professionals I teach are sensitive to that distinction.

> I fully recognize things may go south. At least once a quarter I will teach a bad class, so bad that I'll go home that night and once again calculate my potential retirement income. At least once a quarter a discussion will take a turn I didn't see coming, but I recognize that teaching ethics to military professional is hard, very hard, at least for me. Every class is different. Every student is different. The world changes, and the issues confronting my students become different. I recognize that some of them will be resistant to my message, that some days I will be successful and some days I will bomb. I understand that every course is its own season and that my job in every class is to do my best. As uninspiring and utterly cliché as that may sound, it is that thought – to just do my very best – that sustains me and that I consider before every class begins.

CHAPTER 4

Ethics and the Changing Character of War*

Martin L. Cook

There are many forms of violent conflict among human beings. In the West, "war" has been a very specific form of such conflict. As it evolved since the last major shift in the Western international system at the Peace of Westphalia in 1648, the Western understanding of war has taken a very specific shape in international law and in the evolution of customary international law. The paper will explore the various ways the United States has used its military power since the terrorist attacks on it on September 11, 2001. It will suggest that, although the U.S. has been engaged in continuous military activity since that period, only a small part of that activity conforms to the established legal and customary forms of "war" as conventionally defined. We will explore the range and nature of those uses of military force and then proceed to examine the challenges and stresses to traditional ideas of "just war" as they have been defined in the Western tradition. Furthermore, much of U.S. defense planning, acquisition programs, and force structure presumes "war" is only one, and indeed one of the less likely, ways in which we envision use of military force in the coming decades.[1] The ethical implications of these changing patterns of the use of force are that, insofar as the ethics of war and just war theory have been worked out to guide conventionally defined "war" in the West, we may well find that those ethical rules and customs conform poorly to the actual pattern of use we have witnessed and may require supplementation or even fairly fundamental rethinking to forge consensus on the ethical standards that will guide future conflict. We will conclude with examination of the ways in which these uses of force foreshadow the kinds of uses of military force we can expect from the U.S. (and perhaps others) into the future.

* The views expressed in this article are those of the author and do not necessarily reflect the official policy or position of the Navy, the Department of Defense, or the U.S. Government.

1 One exception to this is important, perhaps especially in the context of this conference in Hong Kong. That is the still somewhat inchoate "pivot to Asia" and the idea that China's rising military power and increased assertiveness in Asia may set the scene for some form of future great power conflict that might indeed conform to conventional "war" paradigms. I won't explore that set of issues here because it requires speculation about the future rather than examining actual practice of the past thirteen years.

 | DOI 10.1163/9789004312135_005

'Modern War' in the West

Modern conceptions of war in the West emerged from the specific historical circumstance of the political shape of Europe in the aftermath of the Reformation and the wars of religion that followed it. Before the Reformation, Europe was notionally a single civilization more expansive than the nation states it contained. It was "Christendom" – the domain of the Christians, notionally under a single supreme authority – the Church in Rome – and a single leader – the Pope. Under that concept of civilization, the rules and ethics of war were grounded in a shared religious faith and a shared religious authority that could and to some degree did define the rules of war and even enforce them.

One of the causes of the wars of religion that broke out after the Reformation was the shared belief, dating back to the Roman Emperor Constantine, that religious unity was an essential element to political unity and stability: "One God, one Church, one Emperor." Except for the Anabaptists, all the other post-Reformation Christian sects would ideally like to restore that unity with their theological tradition as the unifying force.

Only when it because apparent that that unity would not be restored did the European states to accept the compromise of the Westphalian system. That allowed them to continue to preserve religious unity as a basis of political unity, but only at the reduced scale of national churches. The religious principle was that first proposed between Lutherans and Roman Catholics at the Peace of Augsburg in 1555: cuius regio, eius religio (his realm, his religion – i.e., the ruler's religion would be the official religion of the territory). This allowed a continued insistence on religious unity inside each territory and permitted mistreatment, persecution and even death to non-conformist religious minorities in each territory at the sole discretion of the ruler.

Now lacking a common normative religious framework and an overarching political order, a need for rules of war no longer relying on Christendom emerged. Thinkers such as Hugo Grotius stepped forward to offer new secular versions of just war, grounded in natural law and human reason directly that, he argued, are valid even "etsi deus non daretur" – even if God does not exist. This laid the foundation for International Law as we have it today: a product of the West's particular history, but for complex reasons notionally universal and global. What emerged was the so-called Westphalian state system of sovereign independent states possessed of the rights of territorial integrity (all states should respect each other's borders) and political sovereignty (each state was free to govern its internal affairs as it saw fit).

A distinct set of norms emerged from this evolution that provided a specific understanding of "war" as distinct from other forms of violent activity. War, by definition, is something states do to and with other states. Norms arise in two areas: when it is legitimate to initiate war at all (jus ad bellum) and norms for the actual conduct of war (jus in bello). As the tradition evolves, the legitimate causes for war are progressively restricted to response to aggression that has already occurred when one state has already attacked another. This evolution comes to full flower with the Kellogg-Briand Pact of 1928, which declares all aggressive war illegal,[2] and is enshrined in the Charter of the United Nations, which restricts legitimate military action to response to aggress, and Security Council authorized collective security action under Article VII of the Charter. International legal norms find additional articulation in the Hague and Geneva Conventions, and are incorporated into the military manuals of all U.S. armed services. They are reinforced by an annual refresher briefing on the Laws of Armed Conflict, given by military lawyers (JAGS) to all U.S. military personnel in accordance with Geneva treaty obligations.

In Just and Unjust Wars, Michael Walzer nicely sums up the jus ad bellum rules defining legitimate war in international law in what he calls "the legalist paradigm":

1 There exists an international society of independent states.
2 This international society has a law that establishes the rights of its members – above all the rights of territorial integrity and political sovereignty.
3 Any use of force or imminent use of force by one state against the political sovereignty or territorial integrity of another state constitutes aggression and is a criminal act.
4 Aggression justifies two kinds of violent response: a war of self-defense by the victim, and a war of law enforcement by the victim or any other member of the international society.
5 *Nothing but aggression can justify war* [italics mine].
6 Once the aggressor state has been militarily repulsed, it can also be punished.

The crucial point is the fifth: only use of force that is a response to aggression is legitimate. This understanding is also reflected in the language of the United Nations' Charter:

- All Members shall settle their international disputes by peaceful means in such a manner that international peace and security, and justice, are not endangered.

2 This becomes the legal basis for War Crimes trials after World War II for the category of war crimes called "crimes against peace."

- All Members shall refrain in their international relations from the threat or use of force against the territorial integrity or political independence of any state....
- Nothing contained in the present Charter shall authorize the United Nations to intervene in matters which are essentially within the domestic jurisdiction of any state or shall require the Members to submit such matters to settlement under the present Charter; but this principle shall not prejudice application of enforcement measures under Chapter VII.

This last principle, of course, contains a crucial ambiguity that will become critical as we think about the nature of U.S. military action in the past thirteen years: what matters are "essentially within the domestic jurisdiction" of states, and what kinds of actions internal to a state might warrant Chapter VII enforcement actions, authorized by the Security Council? But at a minimum, clearly the Charter preserves the core of Westphalia's intent to leave internal matters to the political sovereignty of states and to restrict interference to actions that cross the high bar of Security Council authorization.

Let's sum up the concepts essential to this conception of the international system and of "war." Again, by definition "war" is restricted to things states do to and with each other. "War" is only legitimate when it is in response to aggression that has already occurred by one state's attack on the political sovereignty or territorial integrity of another, or when it is an act of UN authorized collective security. The welfare of human individuals and human rights are matters that fall "essentially within the domestic jurisdiction" of states.[3]

---

3 These issues having to do with the status of human individuals, their lives, their welfare, and their rights were not even considered in the original Westphalian system. Since WWII there have been steady efforts to address their exclusion in International Law, beginning with the Convention on Genocide from the then-brand new UN in 1949, running through various treaties and UN rights declarations subsequently, and culminating in the "emerging norm" of Responsibility to Protect, unanimously adopted by the largest number of heads of state ever convened at the 2005 World Summit of the United Nations. Despite the significance of these efforts and the gravity of the concerns regarding human welfare that drive them, they all harmonize poorly with the older emphasis on the sovereignty of individual states and their "essentially domestic" jurisdiction. The intervention in Libya was a Security Council authorized intervention, justified by appealing to Responsibility to Protect. But since both China and Russia consider the mandate for Libya to have been grossly exceeded as the operation unfolded, it is unlikely R2P authorizations will get through future Security Councils without veto for the foreseeable future.

United States' Use of Force After September 11, 2001

Al Qaeda's attacks on the United States raised novel challenges for the United States and for the world community.[4] To state the obvious: al Qaeda is not a state, nor is it an agent of any state. Al Qaeda "central" is located inside a sovereign state, Afghanistan, with which the United States is not at war, and toward whom no legitimate causus belli exists.[5]

In the aftermath of the 9/11 attacks, the U.S. did recognize a distinction between its attackers, al Qaeda, and the de facto Taliban government of the country of Afghanistan, which it did not recognize. It issued demands that that government turn over all al Qaeda members to the U.S. (among other demands it made as well).[6] These demands were sufficiently onerous that it is doubtful anyone in the U.S. government entertained any serious hope that the Taliban would meet them. Furthermore, the U.S. government declared them to be non-negotiable, since it didn't want to appear in any way to legitimate the Taliban government. Nevertheless, the "fig leaf" of an appearance of recognition of Afghan sovereignty was maintained, making the U.S. decision to attack inside Afghanistan for the purpose of routing out al Qaeda at least legally murky. Still, legally murky doesn't mean clearly legal "war," since the intervention not only drove al Qaeda from its camps but also effected expulsion of the Taliban government and regime change in Afghanistan.

In 2002, the Bush administration codified its approach to what it imagined to be an ongoing and global "war on terror" that would be required for sustained attempts to disrupt and destroy al Qaeda and affiliated groups wherever they might be. It did so in issuing the 2002 National Security Strategy (NSS) of the United States of America.[7] In one sense, this document is a routine product of the American government. The President issues an NSS every four years, and it provides the highest-level guidance to the government about the security priorities of the government. It is instrumentalized by a second document: the

4 It is important to recall that these were not the first al Qaeda attacks on the U.S. Previous attacks included those in Saudi Arabia in the bombing of the Khobar Towers facility, embassy bombings at Tanzania and Kenya, the first attempt at a World Trade Center bombing in 1993, and the attack on the warship USS Cole in 2000. For a full list see: http://en.wikipedia.org/wiki/Timeline_of_al-Qaeda_attacks.

5 For a good discussion of the difficulty of justifying the U.S.'s attacks into Afghanistan under settled understandings of International Law defining "war" see: http://www.globalresearch.ca/did-9-11-justify-the-war-in-afghanistan/19891.

6 See http://www.bbc.co.uk/history/events/the_us_refuses_to_negotiate_with_the_taliban for details on these demands.

7 http://www.state.gov/documents/organization/63562.pdf.

National Military Strategy of the United States of America (NMS) which spells out the implications of the NSS's guidance in terms of practical military matters such as the size of U.S. military forces, weapons systems to be procured, and so forth. This NSS, however, while in one sense routine, broke novel ground regarding the legal and ethical understanding of how the U.S. would use its military power. It essentially opened the door to using military forces well outside the settled legal and ethical understanding of legitimate "war" as understood by the international community and international law. Part of the NSS reads as follows:

> We will disrupt and destroy terrorist organizations by: defending the United States, the American people, and our interests at home and abroad by identifying and destroying the threat before it reaches our borders.
>
> While the United States will constantly strive to enlist the support of the international community, we will not hesitate to act alone, if necessary, to exercise our right of self defense by acting preemptively against such terrorists, to prevent them from doing harm.
>
> For centuries, international law recognized that nations need not suffer an attack before they can lawfully take action to defend themselves against forces that present an imminent danger of attack. Legal scholars and international jurists often conditioned the legitimacy of preemption on the existence of an imminent threat – most often a visible mobilization of armies, navies, and air forces preparing to attack.
>
> We must adapt the concept of imminent threat to the capabilities and objectives of today's adversaries. The greater the threat, the greater is the risk of inaction – and the more compelling the case for taking anticipatory action to defend ourselves, even if uncertainty remains as to the time and place of the enemy's attack. To forestall or prevent such hostile acts by our adversaries, the United States will, if necessary, act preemptively.

A number of aspects of this are remarkable and fundamentally move enunciated U.S. doctrine away from the "war" paradigm understood as Walzer's legalist paradigm. It takes a generally acknowledged exception to the legalist paradigm in existing understanding of just war and international law known as (as Walzer calls it) "anticipations" or as international lawyers call it "anticipatory self-defense" and expands its scope and range dramatically.

Traditionally, anticipatory self-defense has been defined very narrowly so as to limit its use to justify war to situations of clear imminence of attack combined with increased risk for the threatened state if it were to wait any longer or wait to absorb the attack before responding. The 2002 NSS stresses the fact that terrorist plots will be kept as secret as possible until they actually occur and couples that observation with the fact that the attacks planned may be mass terror attacks, such as 9/11, or perhaps and still worse attacks with weapons of mass destruction. That combination of uncertainty and magnitude of risk warrants attempting to find and eliminate groups that may make such plans and their capabilities preemptively. This is legally legitimate, the NSS argues, as a mere expansion of the already-recognized exception to the Legalist Paradigm of "anticipatory self-defense."

In reality, the proposed emendation of International Law is not a small expansion, but a radical revision of it. If treated as a generalizable statement of customary international law valid for the use of all states, it says every state may act unilaterally when, it its sole judgment, it believes there exists a threat to it. It would, at least in some cases, replace the clear visibility of response to aggression, publically seen, as a legitimate basis for the use of military force. Instead, states would be acting militarily – including intervening inside the territory of other sovereign states – to eliminate what they claim to be threats against them. It would make it difficult if not impossible for the international community to judge the legitimacy of the claims at the root of those actions.

It was, of course, this revised understanding of anticipatory self-defense that underlay the "weapons of mass destruction" (WMD) rationale for the invasion of Iraq. Those WMDs turned out not to exist, and historians will debate for a long time how valid the intelligence that was the basis of the belief that they did truly was.

Anticipatory self-defense in this revised sense also has been used to justify U.S. attacks places like Yemen, Pakistan and other places in pursuit of al Qaeda-affiliates. Further while the two subsequent NSS documents (the second one from the Bush administration and Obama's first) have dropped the language of the 2002 NSS in explicitly stating the revision of anticipatory self-defense, actual practice of both administrations has continued to act on it.

This continuing pattern of U.S. practice raises deep questions about the modern Western understanding of just war. It clearly represents a significant departure from relatively stable and settled understanding of legitimate war as they had evolved since Westphalia and as they were progressively codified in international institutions such as the United Nations. There is reason to worry that the U.S.'s loss of the "moral high ground" in defending international law opened space for actions such as Russia's in Crimea in the sense that it is harder for the West and the U.S. in particular to draw a sharp contrast between Russia's actions and the U.S.'s respect for settled international law.

Where does this trend lead us? It's hard to be sure at this juncture. But it is clear that the principles of the 2002 U.S. NSS, if (to put it in Kantian terms) universalized, are fundamentally destabilizing to the already and always fragile framework of international law. That said, the threat posed to not only the U.S., but much of the international system, by terrorist groups driven by deeply held utopian visions of alternate futures and willing to engage in attacks of the largest possible scale of which they are capable is real. Some more stable and internationally agreed legal framework for dealing with the threat they pose is required.

Of course, traditional "war" between sovereign states with conventional weapons is still possible, so the old paradigm is not entirely dead. But in what follows, I will argue that the U.S. is reconfiguring its military and intelligence systems in ways that suggest traditional war is not what it considers the most likely use of military force in the future.

One significant and troubling shift has occurred in the relationships between the conventional U.S. military, the Central Intelligence Agency, and the US Special Forces Command (USSOCCOM). Traditionally, of course, war fighting has been the primary domain of the conventional U.S. military (U.S. Army, U.S. Air Force, U.S. Navy, U.S. Marine Corps). The same is true for all other countries. The ethical and legal frameworks for containing and regulating war are all premised on the assumption that wars are conducted between such forces. Traditional just war debates about combatant/noncombatant status, legitimate targets, discrimination/distinction between military and civilian personnel and objects and so forth all work within that set of assumptions. They assume that war is a publically visible activity, conducted between such forces, and providing the world community with a basis for making moral and legal judgments about the legitimacy of what they do.

In the aftermath of the Watergate scandal of the 1970's, it emerged, however, that the U.S. was using covert forces, especially the CIA, in a wide array of activities in the international arena. Those activities included assassination of foreign leaders, destabilizing governments, and interference in foreign elections.[8] After a series of hearing by the U.S. Senate, chaired by Senator Frank Church, the Congress passed a law prohibiting the CIA from assassination. It reined in the CIA's covert activity by requiring an explicit "finding" from the President authorizing specific operations, and established a system of Congressional oversight over the CIA. The general thrust of these reforms was to dramatically reduce CIA covert action and to focus it more on intelligence gathering.

8 See Tim Weiner, Legacy of Ashes: The History of the CIA (New York: Doubleday, 2007) for a detailed, if depressing, account of these activities.

One quiet but significant shift in U.S. uses of force since 9/11 has been the return of the CIA to direct involvement in lethal operations. It was the CIA, rather than conventional U.S. forces, that first weaponized the Predator drone and conducted the first attack with it in Yemen. Weaponized drones are now operated by three different U.S. organizations: the conventional military, the CIA, and USSOCCOM. Of those three, only the military operates in the open and fully constrained by the Law of Armed Conflict (LOAC). Simultaneously, while the CIA has gotten back into the lethality business, the U.S. military's intelligence collecting capabilities has expanded enormously as well. Mark Mazzetti's excellent book, The Way of the Knife: The CIA, a Secret Army, and a War at the Ends of the Earth chronicles these developments. The upshot of these development is this: in the past thirteen years, a great deal of military-like U.S. activity is being conducted "under the radar" by covert U.S. intelligence agencies which, by definition, are not governed by LOAC or international law generally because much of what they do is inherently illegal.

In addition, the CIA (and at some points, the U.S. regular military) were engaging in "enhanced interrogation techniques" that many believe violated both U.S. law and international treaty obligations. Recently, the former senior lawyer for the CIA has written a book in which he lays out the path by which he was persuaded to deem those activities legal. See John Rizzo, Company Man: Thirty Years of Crisis and Controversy in the CIA.

Another development that promises to redefine how the U.S. uses military force in ways that will look much different than the established Western ideas of "war" is the continuing expansion of USSOCCOM.[9]

These forces comprise the U.S. Army's Delta Force and Green Berets, Navy Seal Teams, Air Force Special Operations Command, and Marine Corps Forces Special Operations Command. These forces are deployed in small units very widely across the globe. These forces do many things. Some of them are quiet, but not covert, such as assisting and training non-U.S. forces (what is generally called "capacity building"). But they also engage in "night raids" and special missions (most famously attacking Bin Laden's compound in Pakistan).

When used operationally, Special Forces often fail to conform to established international norms for combatant status. They often don't wear a fixed sign visible at a distance – indeed, they often wear indigenous garb to blend in with the society where they are deployed. When used on a raid inside a sovereign territory of a country with which we are not at war, since what they are doing is illegal, the are "sheep dipped" for the duration of the operation out of the U.S. military so that technically they are under the command of the CIA. But of

9 USSOCCOM's website is here: http://www.socom.mil/default.aspx.

course that means they're not legal combatants, and that they are no more entitled to Geneva Convention protections than are spies or other covert operatives. Suppose, for example. Seal Team 6 had been captured inside Pakistan. How would that eventuality have been assessed in international law and in terms of existing just war frameworks?

As the chart of the growth of USSOCCOM has grown and is planned to continue to grow, clearly the U.S. government is indicating that, even as the regular Army and Marine Corps are scheduled for dramatic reductions in end strength, it expects the USSOCOM will remain extremely busy.[10] This development, coupled with the shifting role of the CIA, means that U.S. military activity will look much less like Westphalian War. It will be covert, conducted by small units, and often in ways that are legally gray at best.

The last significant change in the U.S.'s approach to military matters I want to discuss has equally large potential impact on how the U.S. uses its military. Deep in the DNA of the United States is an aversion to standing and professional militaries. The U.S. Constitution provides for only two military forces in peacetime: a Navy, and the militia citizen-soldiers who, in peacetime, work for the state governors and are typically used for disaster relief, civil disturbance, and other non-combat like purposes (we call them the "National Guard" today). There is provision for creation of an Army if the Congress determines it must go to war – but money for the Army can only be appropriated for two years. The expectation, and the actual practice of the United States for most of its history, was to reduce military forces (except the Navy and the National Guard) to practically nothing after every major war. The motive for this suspicion was the Founders' belief that standing military forces were a threat to democratic government. In addition, however, they wanted their Army to be largely comprised of citizen soldiers who came from and went back to civilian life after the war. That, they thought, maintained a vital connection between the citizenry, the political process, and the military forces.

After WWII, as the Cold War was beginning, President Eisenhower realized that, for the first time in history, we would need permanent military forces and a permanent arms industry to be in a state of constant readiness because of the threat posed by the Soviet Union. In one of the best speeches in American history, in his farewell address to the nation as he left the Presidency, he warned of the grave dangers to our economy and our democracy posed by this development.[11]

10 Congressional report on planned reduction in the Army's end strength here: http://www.fas.org/sgp/crs/natsec/R42493.pdf.

11 The video of the speech can be found in full here: https://www.youtube.com/watch?v=CWiIYW_fBfY.

Even though that standing force was required, however, a tight connection to the citizenry and political process was maintained because for the first few decades, it was a draftee force. Consequently, most American men experienced at least a period of military service, and most American families had children in the military whose welfare concerned them greatly. It was that connection that served to keep the nation focused on its wars and it military personnel and when they felt the war was fooling or the risk to their families was not warranted, the withdrew political support (as happened in Vietnam, for example).

However, in 1973, President Nixon, largely for political purposes, moved away from a conscript force to an all-volunteer (or all-recruited force). Nevertheless, the assumption still was that if we entered any major conflict, we would return to the draft, and young men are still required to register for that possible draft eventuality.

It did not work out that way. Fewer and fewer Americans have any experience of the military whatever. In the past thirteen years, only one-percent of Americans have served in the military, and one-half of one-percent have seen combat. Our professional military has been deployed over and over again. In Vietnam, individuals did one "tour" and came home. It is not unusual to meet American military personnel who have deployed to Afghanistan or Iraq three or more times – some many more times.

The consequences of these developments are great. Former Chairman of the Joint Chiefs of Staff, Admiral Mullen, said toward the end of his tenure regarding the military, "We are less than 1% and we are living in fewer and fewer places and we don't know the American people and the American people don't know us."

A consequence of this is that, whereas Westphalian war assumed war was a national engagement in struggle with other nations, increasingly average U.S. citizens feel little or no connection to the military apart "thanking them for their service" in restaurants and airports and putting "support the troops" magnets on the back of their SUVs. It is politically possible to engage in long wars of dubious value abroad, at least in part, because they are largely invisible to average citizens. Their children are not being drafted to go. Their taxes have not gone up to pay for them. Congress avoids serious engagement such as declaring war and having to raise an army. Increasingly, the U.S. military can be treated as almost a foreign legion, free to be deployed by a President who faces little political risk no matter how badly it turns out.

Needless to say, this is not healthy in a democracy. But it permits precisely the hyper-militarized foreign policy the Founders intended to make impossible by not having standing armies in the first place.

Conclusion

Little of what the U.S. has been doing with its military in recent years is "war." Consequently the rules and laws that govern war as it has been understood in the Western tradition in the past three-hundred and fifty years apply imperfectly at best. Increasingly we are using covert forces against non-state actors inside the territories of sovereign states with which we are not at war. We use weapons systems such as drones that reduce risk to our forces to almost negligible levels. We are configuring our future force in ways that suggest we intend to operate in these ways to an even greater extent in the future. All of these things put pressure on inherited traditions, ideas, and laws regulating just war.

On the other hand, the threats posed by non-state actors that fully intend to continue attacks on the existing civilization of the world are real. There can be no doubt that they are seeking the most destructive weapons they can put their hands on. There is no doubt that if they have even the most awful weapons of mass destruction in their possession, they will attempt to use them. Further, unless they are on the high seas, they have to be inside what is at least notionally a sovereign state – even if often very weak or "failed" ones.

The unilateral reinterpretations of international law the U.S. has made since 2002 cannot be a stable basis for a shared international understanding of the appropriate use of force to cope with this threat. But neither can the particular shape just war thinking and international law has taken to define the Westphalian international system in it post-United Nations form. Novel and creative international collaboration is clearly in order to define legitimate uses of military force to cope with this changing environment.

CHAPTER 5

Why Address the 'E'-Word in Military Ethics Education?: The Role of Emotions in Moral Judgement and Decision-Making

Desiree Verweij

Introduction

Teaching applied ethics, especially in a military setting, comprises more than informing people about the most important theories of moral philosophy, starting with Aristotle's teleological approach in virtue ethics, followed by Kant's deontology, expressed in his categorical imperative, and Bentham's utilitarianism and his motto of the 'greatest happiness of the greatest number'. One might add Tronto's care ethics and the 'embeddedness' of the moral agent and of course all the present-day elaborations on these different theories, contexts, and related themes. It goes without saying that teaching moral philosophy from both a historical and systematic approach is important and forms *a conditio sine qua non* for laying a sound basis for applied ethics. In that sense applied ethics cannot be disconnected from fundamental ethics. If it is disconnected, applied ethics seems to be no more than drivel and dilemma training becomes an exchange of opinions never leading to the vital reflection, necessary for adequate moral decision-making.

Yet, applied ethics, rooted in fundamental ethics, branches off into many different directions and, in that respect, teaching applied ethics also demands knowledge of, and insight in the different disciplines and contexts these branches touch upon, both at a theoretical and a practical level. With regard to military ethics things are even more complex. As a form of applied ethics, it touches not only on different disciplines and branches related to military practice, but it also touches on different forms of applied ethics and is, as such, also related to these practices. For instance, both military ethics and medical ethics play a crucial role in the practice of military physicians and military medical personnel. This also holds for military ethics and business ethics, or organisational ethics, and the practices of military accountants and controllers.

Notably, teaching applied ethics, and especially teaching military ethics, adds one more complicating factor. There should also be knowledge of, and insight in the way people learn and in the possibilities and impossibilities of

© KONINKLIJKE BRILL NV, LEIDEN, 2016 | DOI 10.1163/9789004312135_006

teaching morally responsible behaviour, or specific military virtues, as armed forces aim to do, given their codes of conduct and mission statements. In a nutshell: teaching military ethics in an adequate and effective way, is a multi-dimensional enterprise, and as such, it is far from easy.

In this article I want to focus on, what seems to me, a crucial yet underexposed topic in teaching military ethics: the role of emotions in moral judgement and decision making. My aim is twofold:

1 With reference to Aristotle, but also with reference to neurosciences,[1] and moral psychology,[2] I aim to address the relation between emotions and morality, or to be more precise, the ability to experience emotions as a condition of possibility for experiencing a value as a value. In other words, when people have no emotions, when there is no sensitivity, or when people are dispassionate or numb, values will have no meaning to them and are perceived as unfamiliar words on paper that other people seem to fuss about. Obviously, this may have far-reaching and undesired consequences in military practice, for soldiers in these circumstances easily cross moral barriers. This is not only to the detriment of the people these soldiers are confronted with but often also affects the soldier himself, as studies on PTSS and 'moral injury' indicate.
2 My second aim is more practical and it implies the transference from the first part of the article to the military context. With reference to the work of Molewijk *et al*[3] on moral case deliberation in a medical setting, I will focus on the implications of the relation of emotions and morality for the didactics of military ethics. This seems important, given the connectedness between emotions, thoughts and actions. Emotions determine the way we think and act, yet, at the same time there is a mistrust of emotions or at best an ambivalent attitude towards these so called 'irrational aspects', or 'blind forces' as they are often perceived, not only in a military setting, but by many philosophers as well. 'Blind forces' is a quote from

1 Damasio, A, *Descartes' Error: Emotions, Reason and the Human Brain*, (London Vintage, 1994); Damasio, A, *Het Gelijk van Spinoza. Vreugde, verdriet en het voelende brein*, (2003, Wereldbibliotheek); Damasio, A, Looking for Spinoza. *Joy, Sorrow and the Feeling Brain*, (Harcourt, Orlando/New York 2003); Boer, den, J A, *"Neurofilosofie. Hersenen, Bewustzijn en Vrije Wil,"* (Boom, 2003); Malabou, C, *Que Faire de Notre Cerveau?*, (Bayar, 2004).

2 Haidt, J, 'The Emotional Dog and Its Rational Tail: A Social Intuitionist Approach to Moral Judgement', in (2001), vol.108, no. 4, *Psychological Review*, 814–834.

3 Molewijk, B, Kleinlugtenbelt, D, Widdershoven, G, The Role of Emotions in Moral Case Deliberation: Theory, Practice and Methodology, in (2011) vol. 25, no. 7, *Bioethics*, 383–393.

Kant,[4] who as a rationalist of the Enlightenment, has influenced generations of philosophers and ethicists with regard to the 'e-word'.

Emotions and Morality: Aristotle

Aristotle has already referred to the relationship between emotions and morality in his discussion of the virtues in the *Ethica Nicomacheia*.[5] He states that virtues are related to actions and feelings and he subsequently distinguishes three psychological phenomena: emotions, abilities and disposition. The term 'emotions' refers to desire, anger, fear, envy, joy, love, hate (etc.), in short all perceptions and sensations that are accompanied by pleasure or pain. The term 'ability' refers to 'phenomena that make it possible for us to experience these emotions; for example that make it possible for us to experience anger'. The term 'disposition' is describes as 'the phenomena that make that we relate to these emotions in a good or bad way.' And Aristotle continues: 'Our disposition with regard to anger for example is wrong when we experience this feeling in a way that is either too violent or too weak. However, when we experience anger in a moderate way our disposition is right. This also holds for the other emotions'.[6] In Aristotle's view, virtues of character are directed at 'the mean', as are their accompanying emotions and actions. They choose 'the mean' as opposed to excess and a deficit. Too much, as well as too little fear, or anger or desire is wrong. Experiencing these feelings at the right moment, for the right reason, for the right person, with the right intention and in the right way, is what distinguishes virtue.[7]

It may be clear that this is not as easy as is sounds. What is important to note, and what Nussbaum extensively discusses in her book *The Therapy of Desire*[8] is the fact that in Aristotle's ethical thought emotions are intelligent and discriminating parts of one's personality, closely related to beliefs. They should not be extirpated, but modified and cultivated. Emotions are forms of intentional awareness directed at an object; they are closely related to beliefs and can be modified by a modification of the related belief. Emotions can in fact be created and taken away by discourse and argument. In his study on Aristotle's *Rhetoric*,

4 Kant, I (2011) *Groundwork for the Metaphysics of Morals*, edited and translated by M. Gregor and J. Timmermann, Cambridge University Press.

5 Aristotele, *Ethica Nicomachea*, at 1104b15–18, (Historische Uitgeverij, 1999) (vertaald, ingeleid en van aantekeningen voorzien door Ch.Pannier en J.Verhaeghe).

6 *Ibid*, 1105b21–28.

7 *Ibid*, 1106b15–25.

8 Nussbaum, M C, *The Therapy of Desire. Theory and Practice in Hellenistic Ethics*, (Princeton University Press, 1994), 78–96.

Garver convincingly shows that emotions are continually at work in good decision-making; they have a 'constitutive role in good praxis and good character'.[9] In order to have emotions such as fear and grief one must first have beliefs of this kind. Fear implies an intentional awareness of its object and is based on beliefs and judgements. If the judgement changes, for instance because there is actually nothing to be afraid of, the feelings change. Emotions are not irrational in the sense of non-cognitive. On the contrary, they have a cognitive structure; they are discerning ways of viewing objects and are based on beliefs about the worth of things. Anger, for example is a necessary motivation for defending things of which we acknowledgement the importance. Nussbaum[10] rightly states that emotions, in Aristotle's view, are not always correct, anymore than beliefs or actions are always correct. They need to be educated. As indicated above, virtue is a 'mean disposition' with regard to both actions and passions. Being able to find this mean disposition is what the education of emotions is about.

Notably, Aristotle is not the only philosopher who discusses the importance of emotions and their cognitive status; it is also discussed in present-day philosophy and neurosciences. It is interesting to note that in neurosciences philosophy continues to play an important role since many authors refer to the relevance of philosophy or specific philosophers in this context.[11] William James,[12] Merleau-Ponty[13] and neuroscientists like Damasio[14] and Edelman,[15] all point to 'the embodiment of the mind' or 'embodied cognition' and the cognitive aspects of emotions. Den Boer[16] underlines the relevance of a dialogue between the hermeneutic approach and the neurobiological approach. (I will come back to the importance of hermeneutics in the second part of this article.)

The Plasticity of the Brain

With his book *Neurofilosofie: Hersenen, Bewustzijn en Vrije Wil,* den Boer,[17] aims to contribute to the dialogue between neurosciences, psychopathology and

9 Garver, E, *Aristotle's Rhetoric. An Art of Character*, (The University of Chicago Press, 1994), 108.

10 Nussbaum, *supra,* footnote 9.

11 Den Boer, *supra,* footnote 2.

12 James, W. (1950) *Principles of Psychology*, Dover, New York.

13 Merleau Ponty (1965) *Phenomenology of Perception,* translated by C.Smith, London, Routledge and Kegan Paul.

14 Damasio, *supra,* footnote 1.

15 Edelman, G.M. (2006) *Second Nature; Brain Science and Human Knowledge*, Yale University Press.

16 Den Boer, *supra,* footnote 2.

17 Den Boer, *supra,* footnote 2, p. 36.

philosophy. He maintains that if specific philosophical questions are not addressed by the neurosciences, they run the risk of inconsistent theory development and unfounded premises. Building on Churchland's insights,[18] den Boer's neurophilosophy combines results from neurosciences with conceptual analyses of the mind-brain discussion. He examines the 'plasticity' of our brain, which makes clear that genes are not the only determining factors. The brain of a person develops in a dialogue with his/her surroundings, implying a different view on the 'nature – nurture' debate. There are only a small amount of innate dispositions; the biggest part of a person's brain develops in the interaction with the surroundings of this person. Den Boer calls it a complex choreography in which genes can even be turned off.[19]

The plasticity of the brain is also underpinned by Malabou.[20] As a variant on Marx's statement that people make their own history, Malabou maintains that people make their own brain. The second part of Marx's statement, that they don't realize that they in fact do make their own history, also holds true with regard to our brain, as Malabou points out. We hardly realize how revolutionary developments in neurosciences have been during the last decennia. Moreover, we don't realize the role we play with regard to the development of our own brain, which is unfortunate since the activity of the brain determines our history as individuals, and we ourselves are the ones who influence this activity. Like Den Boer, Malabou describes this as 'plasticity', which is contrary to rigidity and genetic determination. Plasticity implies adaptability and the capacity to develop. With reference to the Greek 'plassein', Malabou distinguishes two aspects of plasticity:

1 the capability to receive a form (as 'clay' and 'loam' are able to), and
2 the capability to give a form (as is done in visual arts and plastic surgery).

This thus implies that the brain is changeable, 'formative and formable'.[21] Neural connections can be modelled, changed and repaired. Malabou points out that plasticity also implies the ability to nullify the form that is received or created. In that sense, she calls plasticity explosive as well, for it can imply the destruction of existing forms. It is important to note that Malabou explicitly states that one can ascertain with certainty that the ability to learn, to develop new capabilities, is possible as long as we live. Several other authors also

18 Churchland, P S, *Neurophilosophy. Toward a unified science of the mind/brain*, (MIT Press, 1986).

19 Den Boer, *supra*, footnote 2, p. 151.

20 Malabou, *supra*, footnote 2.

21 *Ibid*, p. 5.

discuss the lifelong ability for structural and functional brain reorganisation.[22] Of course this ability differs from one individual to the other, since upbringing, experience and practice make every brain unique. Yet, genes do not solely determine this uniqueness. The plasticity of our brain shows a form of freedom, that we can benefit from, however, we can also hold ourselves captive in the structures of our brain, by telling ourselves that we can't change, can't be free from perceived determining factors and are doomed to mental inertia.

Malabou makes a distinction between plasticity and flexibility. Being flexible implies being able to receive a certain form, the ability to make one fit in. It implies tractability and not the explosive energy to create, as is the case with plasticity. Malabou seems to come close to the 'Art-of-Living' philosophers Nietsche and Foucault when she describes the 'making of one's own history', or, 'becoming the subject of it' and understanding the relationship between the share of the 'genetic non-determinate' in the forming of the brain and the 'possibility of a new freedom'.[23] The possibility of our brain to learn and change and thus to form 'the self' and help people form their selves in an educational setting implies a new form of responsibility that one should be aware of, according to Malabou. The extent to which changing and learning are possible is convincingly illustrated by Malabou's discussion of the concept 'resilience' as recuperative power in the work of Boris Cyrulnik.[24] The concept 'resilience' is derived from material-physics and refers to the capacity to resist, or stand up to, shocks to a greater or lesser extent. Resilience manifests itself as a psychological process aiming at reconstructing and re-modelling of the self. Cyrulnic studied several cases of Romanian orphans who managed to constructively survive the traumatizing institutes of the Ceausescu period. With the help (care) provided by their foster families they managed to heal the 'tracks' in their brain, the 'markers' of their premature affective neglect and the contempt of society. As these children show, brain tracks can in fact be healed. According to Malabou, these examples, extreme as they may seem, apply to all of us, since the construction of every identity implies some sort of resilience, in the sense of a construction of opposites, a 'synthesis of remembering and forgetting'.[25]

Researches on the neuronal networks comprising the brain demonstrate that the brain is not a machine, unified, predictable and rigidly predetermined.

---

22 May, A, 'Experience-dependent structural plasticity in the adult human brain', in *Trends in Cognitive Sciences*, (October 2011), vol. 15, no. 10, 475–482; Pascual-Leone, A, *et al*, 'The Plastic human brain cortex' in (2005), vol 28, *Annu. Rev. Neurosci*, 377–401.

23 Malabou, *supra*, footnote 21, p. 26; p. 120–123.

24 Cyrulnik,B., (1999), *Un merveilleux malheur*, Paris, Odile Jacob.

25 Malabou, *supra*, footnote 2, at p. 122.

Given it's plasticity it is open to change. Plasticity in this sense implies the 'ability to change one's destiny, to inflect one's trajectory, to navigate differently, to reform one's form and not soley to constitute that form as a closed meaning'.[26] Plasticity operates on three levels:

1. the modelling of neuronal connections (developmental plasticity in the embryo and the child);
2. the modification of neuronal connections (the plasticity of synaptic modulation throughout life); and
3. the capacity for repair (post-lesional plasticity).

Against this background, Malabou quotes Jean Pierre Changeux who maintains that 'the discovery of the synapse and its functions was as revolutionary as the discovery of DNA'.[27]

Emotions and Moral Judgement

As is indicated by both Den Boer[28] and Malabou[29] stressful circumstances can have a detrimental effect on the micro architecture of the brain. For instance the perception of one's surroundings can be influenced by the changing amount of cortisol, which can also effect moral judgement. With regard to the connection between morality and the structure of the brain Damasio[30] was one of the firsts to underline the role of the brain in moral judgement. On the basis of the well-known example of Phineas Gage, a railroad construction foreman who's frontal lobe was severely destroyed by a large iron rod during an explosion, Damasio describes the change of character that took place after the accident. Phineas Gage changed from a responsible and socially minded person in an irresponsible and asocial individual, impolite, restless, without respect for his fellow beings, unreliable, indifferent and rude. His morality seemed to have eroded. The Phineas Gage case formed the basis for further research disclosing the prefrontal cortex as the area of the brain in which information from the body and the surroundings of the body come together, which makes it possible to make 'morally responsible' decisions.

26 *Ibid,* p. 17.

27 *Ibid,* p. 8.

28 Den Boer, *supra,* footnote 2.

29 Malabou, *supra,* footnote 2.

30 Damasio, *supra,* footnote 2.

Damasio developed his ideas further in his book *Looking for Spinoza. Joy, Sorrow and the Feeling Brain* (2003). According to Damasio, Spinoza, whom he calls a predecessor, played an important role with regard to our insights in human emotions and feelings. Body and mind are parallel attributes or manifestations of one and the same substance. Spinoza considered emotions, or affects as he calls them, as a central aspect of humanity and joy and sadness as the most important concepts in that respect. Emotions and their related reactions belong to the body, feelings belong to the mind. In line with the old Stoic philosopher Epictetus, Damasio maintains that thoughts produce emotions and physical emotions change in the kind of thoughts that we call feelings. Emotions thus precede feeling and feelings, in turn, are closely related to emotions, so closely related that we often make no difference between them. It starts with an emotion and ends in a feeling. To give an example: The emotion 'sympathy' (a social emotion in Damasio's categorisation) changes in a feeling of empathy. When you hear for instance that a person is heavily wounded in a car accident you might feel a twinge of pain. It feels as if you are the victim. The neurons that bring about this experience in a person's brain are present in the frontal cortex of primates and human beings and are known as 'mirror neurons'.[31] They do exactly as is indicated by the name: they 'mirror' the experience. Notably when this part of the brain is absent the mirroring does not work, as will be discussed further on. There is yet another distinction between emotions and feelings. Emotions are visible; they can be seen in the face and the behaviour of a person, heard in the voice, and detected in the blood and hormones. Feelings, on the other hand cannot be perceived or detected in this way. They can remain hidden.

As already indicated before, Damasio also underpins the connectedness of body and mind. He calls it 'a seamless interwoven human organism',[32] and states that 'feelings are interactive perceptions'.[33] They are 'mental manifestations of harmony and balance and of disharmony and dissonance'.[34] He discerns three sorts of emotions:

1 background emotions (for instance enthusiasm, nervousness and tranquillity);
2 primary emotions (or basic emotions). These are the emotions that often come to mind on hearing the word 'emotion': fear, anger, surprise,

31 Damasio, *supra*, footnote 2, pp. 107–108.
32 *Ibid*, p. 15.
33 *Ibid*, p. 84.
34 *Ibid*, p. 127.

aversion, sorrow, and happiness. Notably, primary emotions can be found in different cultures and also in non-human species.
3 Social emotions. These are: sympathy, shame, embarrassment, indignation, contempt, envy, gratitude and pride.

Social emotions like primary emotions can also be found in non-human species.[35] They are of crucial importance in the complex cultural interactions of any society and they are thus of crucial importance with regard to ethics. Damasio considers ethical behaviour a subcategory of social behaviour. It is important to note that research shows that damage to those parts of the brain that form a necessary basis for emotions and feelings has far reaching consequences with regard to adequate functioning in society, as was already suggested in the Phineas Gage case. People with these forms of brain damage miss the accompanying social emotions. They are unable to feel empathy, shame or fear and thus beak up social contracts and violate rules; they miss a feeling for what is socially 'right' and 'just'. When a person is not able to experience sympathy, shame, or quilt, his or her social behaviour is affected. This is illustrated by the case of a fifteen months old baby who suffered brain damage after a car accident. She recovered within a few days, but her parents noticed that she didn't react to verbal and physical punishment. This continued in her later years. She violated social rules (lying, stealing), displayed risky sexual behaviour, was unreliable, unable to hold a job, unable to take care of her child etc. etc. Yet, there was never a sign of remorse, no feelings of guilt, and no sign of sympathy for others.[36]

Damasio maintains that it is beyond dispute that a good functioning of emotions and feelings is necessary for social and humane behaviour, which implies behaviour in accordance with ethical rules that can be called 'just'.[37] Ethical principles are 'imprinted' by means of punishment and reward, which cannot take place when there is prefrontal brain damage at a young age. Consequently, when there is no 'imprint', feeling pain, which forms part of punishment, is disconnected from the action that caused the punishment. This disconnection implies that there is no memory of the relation between the action and the punishment that the person in question can use in the future. In other words, the brain does not inform the person that similar actions lead to similar punishment. Thus the social and ethical learning process cannot take place. Joy and sadness cannot be connected to the categories of personal and social

35 *Ibid*, p. 45.
36 *Ibid*, p. 139.
37 *Ibid*, p. 142.

knowledge that are crucial with regard to ethics. In Damasio's words: 'the categorisation of situations and of adequate and inadequate reactions and the mapping and linking of conventions and rules is deformed'.[38] Notably, the blocking of emotions and feelings also blocks the development of ethical principles and behaviour.[39]

The importance of emotions with regard to moral judgement is also underlined from the perspective of moral psychology, by Haidt.[40] He shows how rationalist models of moral judgement, focussing on reasoning and reflection, have long dominated moral psychology, as is for instance the case in the work of Kohlberg. The alternative Haidt proposes is the social intuitionist model, which holds that moral intuitions and moral emotions cause moral judgement. Although Haidt sees moral intuition as a kind of cognition,[41] it is not the same as reasoning. We think we are objectively reasoning; yet our reasoning is a construction of *post hoc* justifications.[42] With reference to the Scottish philosopher Hume, Haidt illustrates that reason can let us infer that particular actions may lead to the death of people, yet, unless we have sentiments that value human life, reason alone cannot advise against taking the action.[43] The social intuitionist model implies that moral judgement is caused by quick moral intuitions and is followed, when necessary, by slow moral reasoning. It is important to note that the contrast between intuition and reasoning is not the contrast between emotion and cognition. Intuition, reasoning and the appraisals contained in emotions are all forms of cognition, according to Haidt, who can thus be put on a par with the philosophers and neuroscientists discussed in the sections above. Notably, Haidt and Joseph[44] call Aristotle a forerunner of the current neural network theory as developed by for instance Churchland. The mind is seen as a 'network that gets tuned up gradually by experience'.[45] Virtue theories are considered the most psychologically sound approach to morality, since they 'fit with what we know about moral development, judgement, and behaviour'.[46] Virtues are cultural achievements built on and sometimes constrained by 'deeply rooted preparedness to construe and respond to

38 *Ibid*, p. 141.

39 *Ibid*, p. 144.

40 Haidt, *supra*, footnote 3.

41 *Ibid*, p. 814.

42 *Ibid*, p. 815.

43 *Ibid*, p. 816.

44 Haidt, J. and Joseph, C, 'Intuitive Ethics: How Innate prepared Intuitions Generate Culturally Variable Virtues' in (Fall 2004), 133, no. 4, *Daedalus*, ProQuest Central, 55–67.

45 *Ibid*, p. 62.

46 *Ibid*.

the social world in particular ways'.[47] Moral intuitions are defined as a subclass of intuitions in which we experience feelings of approval or disapproval with regard to things we see or hear, or with regard to choices we have to make.[48] With regard to these moral intuitions Haidt and Joseph, distinguish four universal patterns (or modules): suffering, hierarchy, reciprocity and purity, which undergird the moral systems of cultures. There are probably more patterns, of which 'ingroup' is mentioned as a fifth.[49] Thus, the human mind 'comes equipped' with these innate patterns or modules that we experience as 'flashes of affect', that as such form the basis for the development and construction of virtues.[50] Cultures differ in their use of the patterns and modules mentioned and in their appreciation of the related virtues. In that sense morality is socially constructed. Haidt and Joseph found for instance that American Muslims and American conservatives value virtues of kindness and respect for authority and spiritual purity, whereas American liberals value virtues of equality and rights.[51] Moreover, patterns can be used to trigger certain reactions. For instance, the pattern or module 'purity' and 'reciprocity' can be used to trigger 'disgust' and 'anger' with regard to certain groups (Christians, infidels, Muslims, Jews, women, homosexuals) and thus stimulate and proliferate racism, sexism and other forms of discrimination.[52]

Both Damasio and Haidt underline the importance of their insights with regard to education. Haidt[53] maintains that a correct understanding of the intuitive basis of moral judgement is useful in helping decision makers avoid mistakes and in helping educators to improve the quality of moral judgement and behaviour.[54] It comes as no surprise that Damasio also maintains that knowledge of emotions, feelings and the working thereof is important for the way we live.[55]

Learning about Emotions

The preceding sections have illustrated that feelings and emotions play an ineluctable role in social behaviour and thus with regard to ethics and moral

47 *Ibid*, p. 63.
48 *Ibid*, p. 56.
49 *Ibid*, p. 63 at footnote 15.
50 *Ibid*, p. 63.
51 *Ibid*, p. 64.
52 *Ibid*, p. 63.
53 Haidt, *supra*, footnote 3.
54 *Ibid*, p. 115.
55 Damasio, *Looking for Spinoza*, *supra*, footnote 2, p. 252.

responsibility. This also implies that our emotional system plays a crucial role in our moral judgement and thus with regard to the questions and dilemma's soldiers are confronted with. It has also become clear that the presence of emotional responsiveness is a good predictor of morally responsible behaviour. In other words, without empathy moral judgement is flawed. Subsequently the question arises: what are the implications of these insights for the didactics of military ethics? This question brings me to the second part of my article and thus to the transference from the first part to the military context. The work of Molewijk *et al* on moral case deliberation in a medical setting can be relevant in this respect.[56] In Medical Ethics, one of the oldest forms of applied ethics, ethicists have developed 'clinical ethics support services', abbreviated as CESS, which refers to 'all institutionalized services within healthcare organisations which support healthcare professionals and institutions in dealing with moral issues.'[57]

There is a European Clinical Ethics network that currently consists of clinical ethics experts from fourteen countries. One of its aims is to further improve the quality and professionalism of CESS (*ibidem*). A recent form of CESS is the so-called 'Moral Case Deliberation' (MCD), which resembles the Socratic dialogue in some ways, yet is different in others. MCD is a facilitator led collective moral inquiry into a moral question that plays a central role in a concrete case taken from a specific practice. It is a constructive dialogue in which professionals reflect on a moral question taken from their practice. These are often question about the 'right' thing to do in a specific context. However, also questions about the more abstract concepts behind practical questions may be addressed: such as the question: what is integrity? The goal of MCD is to critically investigate a moral issue and at the same time investigate the way the participants feel and reason about this issue, which leads to better reflection on moral issues as such, and improves the quality of the actions taken in the professional practice. It thus helps to develop, stimulate and sustain a professional attitude and enhances moral competence,[58] or moral professionalism. In MCD a distinction is made between the emotions a person experienced during a particular situation and the attitude of this person with regard to this emotion. The attitude towards the emotion and the way it is dealt with helps to explore the thoughts

56 Molewijk *et al, supra,* footnote 4.

57 Schildmann,J, Molewijk, B, Benaroyo, L, Forde, F, Neitzke,G,(2013) 'Evaluation of Clinical Ethics Support Services and its Normativity' in (Nov. 2013) vol 39 (11) *Journal of Medical Ethics*, published online 10.1136/medethics-2012-1000697.

58 Abma, T, Molewijk, B, Widdershoven G, 'Good Care in Ongoing Dialogue. Improving the Quality of Care Through Moral Deliberation and Responsive Evaluation' in (2009) 17, *Health Care Analysis*, p. 217–235.

and the moral judgement that are involved. Molewijk and his colleagues have extensively written on MCD and also focussed on the role of emotions therein. Molewijk *et al*[59] not only argue for a rehabilitation of the role of emotions in MCD, but also introduces an Aristotelian method for MCD that specifically focuses on the reflection on emotions, or rather on the 'rightness' (i.e. the adequateness) of the expression and the reliability of an experienced emotion in a particular situation. The method relates emotions to personal values and judgements. That is already useful in itself, but it may also be useful for teambuilding processes in which negative emotions disturb good cooperation. The method consists of five steps, which are described in detail in the appendix at the end of this article. Participants of MCD sessions in which emotions are addressed report that the quality and the thoroughness of moral inquiry was increased and that they experienced a deeper and more personal learning process (Molewijk o.c. p. 391).[60] However, it should be taken into account that addressing emotions presupposes a certain level of self-reflection and a feeling of security within the group. Also, the facilitator needs to be experienced and qualified, not only in order to prevent emotional harm and potential conflicts in the group, but also to facilitate and stimulate the actual learning process. This requires knowledge of the theoretical background of MCD: hermeneutics.

Hermeneutics and Teaching Ethics

That there is a close relation between ethics and hermeneutics is also underlined by Van Tongeren,[61] who defines ethics as the hermeneutics of the moral experience. Hermeneutics as the 'art of interpretation', (the Greek 'hermeneuo' means to translate or interpret), is focussed on gaining in-depth understanding by interpretation and explanation. Philosophers like Heidegger, Gadamer, and Dilthey are often mentioned with regard to hermeneutics, but obviously hermeneutics is not restricted to the works of these philosophers. It is not my intention to probe into the different yet adjacent philosophical contexts of hermeneutics and the hermeneutic approach, but I do want to underline the importance of this theoretical basis and specifically the insights of Gadamer,[62]

59 Molewijk *et al, supra,* footnote 4.

60 *Ibid,* p. 391.

61 Tongeren van, P, 'Ethiek als Hermeneutiek van de Morele Ervaring' in Wills, J P (ed), *Ethiek en Hermeneutiek*, (Damon, 1999).

62 Gadamer, H. G, *Wahrheit und Methode. Grundzuge einer Philosophischen Hermeneutik*, (1960, J.C.B. Mohr (P.Siebeck), Tubingen).

whose work and insights are widely acknowledged. Weinsheimer[63] for instance calls Gadamer's *Wahrheit und Methode* a book of unrecognized significance that reaches far beyond the discipline of philosophy, since hermeneutics is also important with regard to methodology in social sciences and in education. The goal of hermeneutics is to seek understanding, or as Jardine[64] maintains: to educate understanding. According to Gadamer understanding (*Verstehen* in German) is crucial in all interpretation.[65] In Gadamer's words: '*Alle Rede und aller Text sind also grundsätzlich auf die Kunst des Verstehens, die Hermeneutik, verwiesen*' (All discours and all texts are thus basically dependent on the art of understanding).[66]

Understanding implies three things that seem fundamental with regard to ethics education. In the first place, understanding the other, his or her way of reasoning and worldview. Yet, as Gadamer points out, understanding also implies understanding one another, coming to agreement ('*Verstehen heißt zunächst sich miteinander verstehen. Verständnis ist zunächst Einverständnis*').[67] And in the end, thirdly, understanding implies understanding oneself ('*Dass alles solche Verstehens am Ende ein Sichverstehen ist*').[68] These three aspects are part of a trajectory, in fact an experience, in which one's own ideas, worldview, preconceptions and presuppositions, one's 'horizon' as Gadamer calls it, form the start of a dialogue in which the discovery of another 'horizon' (ideas, worldview, preconceptions and presuppositions of the other, one's dialogue partner) eventually leads to a new way of understanding and self understanding. This new, or transformed, way of understanding is called a blending of horizons ('*Im Vollzug des Verstehens geschieht eine wirkliche Horizontverschmelzung*').[69] However, this three-step trajectory is not as easy as it may seem, for there is a paradox involved. One starts with 'openness' in which one's preconceptions and presuppositions are 'turned off' ('*Ausschaltung aller Voreingenommenheit*').[70] The openness is necessary in order to actually understand the other (or the text of the other), yet, the openness also implies a relation, possibly a confrontation,

63 Weinsheimer, J C, *Gadamer's Hermeneutics. A Reading of Truth and Method*, (1985, Yale University Press).

64 Jardine, D, *To dwell with a boundless heart: Essays in curriculum theory, Hermeneutics and the Ecological Imagination*, (1999, Peter Lang).

65 Gadamer, *supra*, footnote 63.

66 *Ibid*, p. 176.

67 *Ibid*, p. 168.

68 *Ibid*, p. 246.

69 *Ibid*, p. 290.

70 *Ibid*, p. 170.

between the ideas of both dialogue-partners.[71] The openness implies the willingness to listen to the other and suspend one's judgement. As Gadamer puts it with regard to texts: *,'Wer einen Text verstehen will ist vielmehr bereit sich von ihm etwas sagen zu lassen'*.[72] However, suspending is not cancellation. One's preconceptions and presuppositions are brought in; they become part of the dialogue. Gadamer calls it, *'Ins-Spiel bringen der Vorurteilen'* (Bringing the preconceptions into play).[73] This implies that one's ideas are at stake. Notably, Gadamer stresses the *'Verstehen'* (understanding) separate from our presuppositions[74] and at the same time he acknowledges the fact that there is no understanding completely free from presuppositions and preconceptions: *'Es gibt kein Verstehen das von alle Vorurteilen frei ware'*.[75] Acknowledging this paradox seems the first step to take on the road to understanding as *'Verstehen'*. It will preclude the feeling that one is confronted with a contradiction that opposes the 'understanding' Gadamer refers to. Adequately dealing with the paradox implies acknowledging it as such and trying to deal with it. When this can be learned, the blending of horizons (what understanding ultimately is) becomes possible and new insights are generated both with regard to the other and with regard to oneself. For understanding brings the self-understanding that will eventually lead to transformation of ideas. That is why Gadamer's maintains that understanding is not reproductive but productive.[76] It is productive in the sense that it helps us to better handle things; it helps to create practical knowledge, or what the Greeks called 'phronesis'. It can do this because understanding leads to a fine-tuning of our preconceptions and pre-understandings.

Conclusion

On the basis of the foregoing sections we can indeed conclude that teaching military ethics in a way that actually is effective and thus leads to morally responsible behaviour, or specific military virtues, is a multidimensional enterprise, and as such a job for skilled professionals. It implies first of all knowledge of and insight in the role emotions play with regard to ethics and moral responsibility. As was indicated by both Aristotle and Damasio: a good functioning of

71 *Ibid*, p. 253.
72 *Ibid*, p. 253.
73 *Ibid*, p. 289.
74 *Ibid*, p. 441.
75 *Ibid*, p. 465.
76 *Ibid*, p. 280.

emotions and feelings is necessary for social and humane behaviour. It also implies knowledge of and insight in the way people learn and in the possibilities and impossibilities of didactics, goals and methods. On the basis of the theoretical background presented in the first part of this article and the work of Molewijk and his colleagues in a medical context, which was presented in the second part, one can conclude that addressing emotions and the role of emotions in military ethics courses in an adequate and competent way (adequate and competent both from a theoretical and practical perspective) is highly relevant for a sustainable and effective learning process. The focus on the relation between emotions and morality in military ethics is crucial, since, as indicated earlier; the ability to experience emotions is a condition of possibility for experiencing a value as a value. The importance of emotions with regard to moral judgement is clearly illustrated by Haidt's reference to Hume who maintains that reason can let us infer that particular actions may lead to the death of people, yet, unless we have sentiments that value human life, reason alone cannot advise against taking the action. As indicated before, when people have no emotions, when there is no sensitivity, or when people are dispassionate or numb, values will have no meaning to them. Obviously, this may have far-reaching and undesired consequences. It can lead to 'moral disengagement' on the one side, and PTSD and 'moral injury' (in the literature often referred to as the emotional wounds of war) on the other, for stressful events can result in physiological and neuro-endocrine changes and changes in behaviour, which have a detrimental effect on the cognitive as well as the social and emotional level.

Addressing emotions and the role of emotions in morality might imply a change in the perception of emotions, since emotions are often still perceived as irrational and a sign of weakness. With regard to the irrationality of emotions, the forgoing sections have shown that emotions are intelligent and discriminating parts of one's personality. They are forms of intentional awareness, closely related to beliefs; they contain intuition, reasoning and appraisals and are in that sense cognitive. The philosophers as well as the neuroscientists and psychologists that were discussed in this article all point to the cognitive aspects of emotions and the embodiment of the mind or 'embodied cognition'.

The perception of emotions as a sign of weakness might prove more difficult to change. All cultures, with a few exceptions, construct images of tough, emotionless men, who can endure extreme pain, both physically and psychologically.[77] Moreover, the preconception of rationality, inherent or more fully

77 Goldstein, J *War and Gender*, (Cambridge University Press, 2001).

developed in men, is a concept with classical roots omnipresent in Western culture,[78] and not solely in Western culture. Thus changing perceptions with regard to gender and emotions will be an educational challenge. However, the discussion of the plasticity of the brain made clear that 'plasticity' implies the ability to learn, to develop new insights and capabilities. We have a lifelong ability for structural and functional brain reorganisation. Contrary to popular books with regard to our brain, neurosciences reject a simplistic mechanistic view; they show that we can learn and change the patterns in the landscape of our brain to a much larger degree than we have often thought possible.

As indicated before, there are some important implications with regard to teaching military ethics in a theoretical and practical way. The discussion of the moral case deliberation (MCD) has underlined the important role of the facilitator. He or she needs to be experienced and qualified also with regard to the stimulation of the actual learning process. This requires knowledge of the theoretical background of MCD and, I would like to add, any other form of dialogue in an educational setting (f.i. the Socratic dialogue), aimed at 'phronesis' (practical wisdom). Hermeneutics informs us of what understanding actually is: an experience in which our preconceptions and presuppositions (our horizon) forms the starting point of a trajectory in which the confrontation with another horizon (worldview, preconceptions and presuppositions of our dialogue partner) leads to a blending of horizons in which we come to a better understanding, including a better self-understanding, which leads to the transformation of ourselves and of the ideas we generate. Learning about emotions and feelings, and learning to reflect on them, and subsequently deal with them in an adequate way, implies that Aristotle's statement with regard to experiencing feelings 'at the right moment, for the right reason, for the right person, with the right intentions and in the right way' can actually be put into practice. This will be a blessing in any context, especially one in which the use of violence is at stake.

Appendix

Aristotelian Method for MCD (Molewijk *et al,* 2011)

Step 1: All participants describe a situation in which they experience a strong emotion. They subsequently describe three ways of dealing with this emotions (two extremes and the mean) on the basis of the following

78 Foxhall, L. and Salmon,J. (eds), *When men were men. Masculinity, power and Identity in Classical Antiquity*, (Routledge, 1998).

questions. (1) What would you do if the emotion leads you completely? (2) What would you do if you neglect the emotion, or put it aside? (3) What would you do if you had found the right attitude toward the emotion?

Step 2: Addressing the emotion and understanding the factual situation. One of the situations (described in step 1) is chosen (by the participants) for further moral inquiry. The participants ask questions about the facts of the situation and the emotion in order to be able to imagine themselves in that situation. It is important not to judge the situation, or the emotion and not (yet) to explore the thoughts behind the emotions. They should only ask for the facts in the concrete situation.

Step 3: Participants take part in a moral inquiry with regard to the emotion. Participants reflect upon the three notes that were written during the first step by the person whose situation and emotion were chosen in the second step. They reflect upon the 'right' attitude with regard to the emotion by searching for the virtue that makes the expression of the emotion in this (positive and constructive) way possible.

Step 4: Each participant formulates his/her 'right' attitude towards the emotion. Participants imagine themselves in the situation and define their 'right' attitude with regard to this situation (emotion, thoughts and virtue). They share their thoughts and reflect upon each other's judgements.

Step 5: What should I/we do (based on this moral inquiry)? What is needed in order to deal with the situation in the 'right' way and with the 'right' attitude towards the emotions involved? What are the lessons learned (for future situations like this)?[79]

79 For a comprehensive description of the method see Molewijk *supra*, footnote 4, at p. 392–394.

CHAPTER 6

Values – Attitude – Education: Military Ethics Education Formats at ZEBIS

Veronika Bock and Kristina Tonn

Introduction

The *Bundeswehr* is transforming itself from a conscript army into a volunteer and professional army, from a defense army into a combat force (German Federal Ministry of Defense 2006: 18), which not only safeguards immediate national security but also operates in various missions around the world under international mandates.

Soldiers today face enormous challenges and demands. Confronted with new forms of warfare, other cultures and in some cases a different understanding of international and human rights, soldiers not only need to acquire good manual and soldierly skills, they also require an extensive education in various disciplines: law (international and national), politics, history, intercultural communication and ethics. On top of this, soldiers often find it difficult to relate experiences from their deployments to family and friends at home or, more widely, to civil society.

Ethical issues, meanwhile, are rarely black or white. Dealing with shades of gray is a skill frequently required when it comes to taking decisions in extreme situations and answering to one's conscience.

Ethical education in the German armed forces (*Bundeswehr*) has long been a fixture of soldiers' education and training. The challenge in ethical education for soldiers is to combine theory with practice, or rather to make abstract theory accessible and applicable to soldiers. This requires a translation of values and principles into actions and decisions.

Can an online teaching portal, an e-journal and events assist and perhaps even encourage ethical learning by soldiers? Can e-learning even be used in the complex field of ethical education? This article aims to answer these questions based on our experiences.

 | DOI 10.1163/9789004312135_007

ZEBIS

ZEBIS[1] is a center for ethical education in the armed forces which assists military chaplains by providing theoretical and practical knowledge for their teaching activities, as well as creating awareness and fostering dialog among and between soldiers (especially officers), civilian members of the armed forces and a broader public by organizing and documenting training events. ZEBIS was instituted on behalf of the Catholic Military Bishop for the German *Bundeswehr* at the Institute for Theology and Peace,[2] the research facility of the Catholic military pastoral care service (*katholische Militärseelsorge*) for peace ethics. The legal entity is Katholische Soldatenseelsorge, a public-law institution.

The ZEBIS teaching portal is intended for military chaplains who discuss issues in general ethics, peace ethics and military ethics with German soldiers in character guidance training (CGT)[3] classes. Current topics and background information about military ethics are available online anytime in the e-journal 'Ethics and Armed Forces – Controversies in Military Ethics & Security Policy'.[4]

Through increased use of digital media and the online presence, the aim is to add variety to ethical education in the armed forces beyond classroom teaching and training events. The guiding idea is always 'from theory for practice and in practice'.

Requirements of Ethical Education

What requirements do an online teaching portal for ethical education, an e-journal and events in the field of ethical education need to fulfill?

"Ethical competence means empowering soldiers to self-determinedly adhere to the values and standards of the Basic Law and resulting values and standards of military conduct, and adopt these as a guiding principle for everything they do as 'citizens in uniform'."[5]

To live up to this high standard, in addition to the requirements for good teaching[6] it is also important to take the specific features of ethical education

1 The acronym 'ZEBIS' stands for '*Zentrum für ethische Bildung in den Streitkräften*', Center for Ethics Education in the Armed Forces.

2 *Institut für Theologie und Frieden*, ithf.

3 *Lebenskundlicher Unterricht*, LKU.

4 http://www.ethikundmilitaer.de/.

5 Joint Service Regulation (Zentrale Dienstvorschrift, ZDv) 10/4, no. 103.

6 Problem-oriented questions, prepared learning environment, varying social forms, clarity of content, individual support, a high proportion of real learning time, transparent achievement expectations, consistent target group orientation, clear lesson structure, variety of

(especially for adults) into account. Added to this are the challenges entailed by the soldier's profession and therefore also issues of military ethics.

But what do soldiers themselves expect from ethical education? – For one thing, ethical education should appeal to them on various levels, and be a stimulating and interesting classroom experience that gives them scope for open and extensive discussion. In addition, it should prepare soldiers in the best possible way for questions and demands in respect of military ethics that are associated with the soldier's profession and particularly with deployments.

The learners themselves should feel and perceive the ethical issues. To find oneself in and have experience of an ethical dilemma situation makes it easier to grasp and comprehend ethical issues, which in turn facilitates engagement in a learning process involving in-depth discussion of the content matter.

Of course this also requires the instructor to impart detailed specialist knowledge. However, this knowledge transfer should not be one-sided in taking the form only of teacher-centered teaching, but rather should always involve the learners and offer a varied selection of adult education methods and diverse teaching materials. Ethical education is not static or once-only but instead is a life-long process.

'Ethical competence comprises […] ethically relevant knowledge via which a moral problem can be identified in a given situation, and the ability, with the aid of reasoning processes, to form a moral judgment. Yet it is just as important to have the awareness to feel that one is challenged by a moral problem, and the motivation to act in accordance with this moral judgment. Ethical action has taken place when a moral problem can be dealt with better after the learning process than before owing to an increase in competence in at least one of these four dimensions, i.e. in the areas of extended knowledge, greater judgment competence, increased awareness and/or stronger motivation' (Kruip and Winkler 2010: 25–26).

The challenge in ethical education is to combine theory and practice, or rather to make abstract theory accessible and applicable to soldiers. This requires a translation of values and principles into actions and decisions. Soldiers on deployment have a particularly great desire for practical and practicable teaching content.

However, ethics or moral behavior cannot be learned like a mathematical formula. Rather it is necessary to apply theoretical learning time and again in practical situations (Elßner 2009: 94) until this accumulated practice provides a reliable framework for actions and decisions in similar situations. 'The capacity to perceive,

---

media, variety of methods, constructive atmosphere, anchored learning strategies and presentation techniques. – From: Meyer, Hilbert (2004): Praxisbuch: Was ist guter Unterricht? Mit didaktischer Landkarte, Cornelsen Verlag Scriptor Berlin.

think and act morally needs to be acquired over the course of a lifetime and constantly enhanced' (Bock 2013: 42; Kenngott 2011: 217; Ebeling 2006: 13).

'Ethical learning should ultimately be geared to moral verbal, action and decision-making competencies in the social context. Learners should be encouraged and enabled to get involved and under the given social conditions to develop an independent, reflected and responsible value system' (Kruip and Winkler 2010: 29).

Knowledge transfer in the field of ethics should start at an appropriate level for the course participants. So that they can appropriately implement moral verbal, action and decision-making competencies themselves later on, the issues addressed should be familiar from their own lives, professional experiences and other experiences.

Ethical education and hence CGT for *Bundeswehr* soldiers can only succeed if purely instructive teaching methods are avoided (Bendel and Suermann 2013: 343), and instead a course is offered which encourages dialog and discussion (Pfeifer 2003: 34, 35), with a variety of methods appropriate to the target group (such as exercises, seminars, discussion and role-play) and extensive teaching materials. The aim here is to enable participants to identify a moral problem in a situation and to form a judgment with the aid of reasoning processes. Acquisition of ethical competence also involves 'awareness, to understand that one is challenged by a moral problem, and the motivation to act according to the moral judgment' (Bock 2013: 42, 43; Wilke 2011: 97; Kruip and Winkler 2010: 26).

The multifaceted nature of this process can also be seen in the various objectives of ethical education. After all, it is not a purely cognitive process, in which ethically relevant knowledge is taught. At the same time, the emotive and motivational aspects of ethical conduct should be addressed (Schmid 2000: 54, 59). Ethical education should therefore develop people's cognitive skills so that they can make moral judgments, and in addition promote emotional skills to cultivate the motivation to act according to this moral judgment (Pfeifer 2003: 35–37).

Communication succeeds by considering the other person's range of experience.

Via the teaching portal, the various events and the e-journal, ZEBIS can help by providing a wide range of cognitive and motivational approaches to character guidance training (CGT) classes.

The portal's lesson plans and materials need to respect the proper 'pick-up points' (Bach 2012: 111) with regard to the target group specification. Especially in mixed groups, participants should not find the classes too easy or too demanding. This creates great challenges for CGT instructors.

To make CGT a varied, appealing and high-quality ethics course for adults requires a variety of materials and methods as well as qualified instructors. The portal assists in this process by offering a wide variety of all kinds of materials with different types of content, which also cover the requirements of course participants with different backgrounds and levels of education.

Teaching Portal: Idea and Intention

Can an online teaching portal, an e-journal and events assist and perhaps even encourage ethical learning by soldiers? Can e-learning even be used in the complex field of ethical education? This chapter answers these questions based on the experiences gained with the teaching portal for character guidance training (CGT) at ZEBIS. In addition to an extensive description of the teaching portal, the challenges and demands of ethical education are discussed with particular regard to military ethics.

The ZEBIS teaching portal – a password-protected internet platform for military chaplains and character guidance training instructors – has been online and usable since December 2011.

Based on the curriculum in Joint Service Regulation 10/4 'Character guidance training. Taking responsibility for your own life – being able to take responsibility for others',[7] the ZEBIS teaching portal provides lesson plans, which in addition to presenting the subject in an educational format also include a wealth of teaching materials (e.g. video and audio clips, essays, book excerpts, PowerPoint presentations and images) for which copyright permission has been obtained.

The available materials give instructors a wide and flexible range of options to choose from, according to their own priorities. The portal also offers users a collection of teaching methods for adult education.

To encourage dialog between instructors, the section 'From CGT for CGT' (*Aus dem LKU für den LKU*) contains lesson plans and materials produced and tested in practice by CGT instructors.

The aim of the portal is to assist CGT instructors in their work. Lessons are taught by Catholic and Protestant military chaplains. The portal is intended to offer them a wide selection of materials (e.g. video and audio files, essays, book excerpts, cartoons, images) for their own preparation and for actual use in the

7 (*Zentrale Dienstvorschrift 10/4 "Lebenskundlicher Unterricht. Selbstverantwortlich leben – Verantwortung für andere übernehmen können"*, German Federal Ministry of Defense 2011). Henceforth referred to as ZDv 10/4.

classroom. It also provides educational ideas and lesson planning tips as well as examples of how the material can be related to the subjects. It is designed to be modular, i.e. CGT instructors select the files they want to use according to their own lesson plans and subject focuses.

The portal's content and materials have to be geared to the curriculum set out in ZDv 10/4, and be appropriate for the soldiers as a target group with respect to their environment and experiences.

Curriculum content for attaining ethical competence (German Federal Ministry of Defense 2011, Annex 3):

1. The individual and society
1.1. Our conception of humanity in accordance with the German Basic Law (*Grundgesetz*) and other conceptions of humanity
1.3 Identity and tolerance
3. Freedom, conscience and responsibility
1.4 Religion in state and society in the Federal Republic of Germany
1.5 Religion in state and society in other countries
2. Personal lifestyle and military service
2.1 Personal/family life and duty
2.2 Taking responsibility
2.3 Life and death
3. Moral and psychological challenges of military service
3.1 Introduction to culture and religions/ethics in world religions
3.2 Approaches to ethics of peace and conflict resolution from the European canon of values
3.3 Operational stress: responsibility and guilt
3.4 Dealing with conflicts, stressful situations and extreme situations

Character guidance training (CGT) is a 'professional ethics qualification measure and therefore compulsory' for soldiers (German Federal Ministry of Defense 2011, no. 104). As a safe zone for free and stimulating discussion, CGT is intended to assist soldiers' personal development and enhance their powers of political and ethical judgment (Dörfler-Dierken 2010: 291; Griese 2009: 348).

Particularly the aspect of 'free and trustful discussion' (German Federal Ministry of Defense 2011, no. 104) is addressed by the fact that CGT is not relevant to appraisals (Griese 2009: 348). CGT instructors are not superiors of the soldiers, which allows a classroom atmosphere to be created in which concerns and fears as well as personal experiences can be voiced, analyzed and discussed.

CGT therefore goes beyond simply imparting knowledge. In addition to understanding theoretical ethical concepts, participants should be familiar with and be able to distinguish between their own and other value systems. CGT aims to empower soldiers to recognize and evaluate the ethical dimension of their actions, and to base their actions on ethical reasoning. In addition, soldiers should be able to identify the consequences of their actions (Bendel and Suermann 2013: 341; Elßner 2009: 93; Jermer 2010: 135).

In ZDv 10/4, the German Federal Ministry of Defense defines its understanding of the ethical competence of soldiers as follows.

'Ethical competence means empowering soldiers to self-determinedly adhere to the values and standards of the Basic Law and resulting values and standards of military conduct, and adopt these as a guiding principle for everything they do as "citizens in uniform". Character guidance training is an essential complement in the development of professional ethical competence. In this respect, it influences personal development in the areas of "The individual and society", "Personal lifestyle and military service", and "Moral and psychological challenges of military service"' (German Federal Ministry of Defense 2011, no. 103).

The goals of CGT are therefore clearly defined. Soldiers in the *Bundeswehr* have not only to accept the values and standards of the German Basic Law but also to internalize them as a 'guiding principle' for their behavior. Human dignity, freedom, peace, justice, equality, solidarity and democracy (German Federal Ministry of Defense 2011, no. 102) thus serve as the basis for all their actions.

However, this 'moral loyalty' (Bendel and Suermann 2013: 342; Bendel 2006: 127) can neither be ordered by the employer, nor simply learned as knowledge in the classroom, since it must be fulfilled through experience and the soldier's own decisions. However, the classroom can provide a setting for examining and elucidating the values and standards of human rights and constitutional law. Alongside this, ethical education in CGT aims to improve soldiers' ability to make moral judgments. As a result, soldiers should be able to apply ethical standards and principles in specific decision-making situations, and in this way determine the morally correct action (Bach 2012: 110; Jermer 2010: 129; Elßner 2009: 94; Bendel 2006: 124). 'Moral judgments are the result of applying general standards and universal principles in a specific situation.' (Bendel and Suermann 2013: 342).

This image of the soldier in the German *Bundeswehr* is essentially shaped by the concept of '*Innere Führung*' (leadership development and civic education):

> Through *Innere Führung*, the values and norms of the Basic Law are realized in the *Bundeswehr*. It embodies the principles of freedom, democracy and the rule of law in the armed forces. Its guiding principle is the

> "citizen in uniform". Respecting and protecting human dignity are an obligation of the German state and thus the *Bundeswehr*. This obligation is at once the ethical justification and the limitation of military service. Values based on human dignity are also the foundation for the principles of *Innere Führung* and thus for legal norms within the *Bundeswehr* as well as the structure of its internal order.
>
> GERMAN FEDERAL MINISTRY OF DEFENSE ZDV 10/1 2008: NOS. 301, 305

Through *Innere Führung*, soldiers of the *Bundeswehr* are at all times and in all places bound by the fundamental rights of the Basic Law. At the same time, the concept of the 'citizen in uniform' yields an ideal of professional ethics in the responsible soldier. In all their actions, such soldiers are guided by the norms and standards of the Federal Republic of Germany, which are founded in human rights (Bock 2013: 36; Bendel 1999: 313–14). 'It binds soldiers to an ethos of respect for human rights, of fairness, tolerance, and loyalty to democratic decisions' (Bock 2013: 36).

For soldiers as 'citizens in uniform', responsibility for their own life is inseparable from their military responsibility. Ethical guidance as a framework for action is indispensable particularly in times of social change, and for armed forces on overseas deployments and missions. In the diversity of opinions and values, soldiers especially need clear life guidance empowering them to act responsibly. To this extent, CGT is all the more important in soldiers' development of professional ethical competence, and as a task delegated to the military chaplaincy. The concept of *Innere Führung* in the *Bundeswehr* lays out a binding set of values based on human dignity. It follows for the soldier as citizens in uniform that responsible military conduct must be guided by these values. Furthermore, *Innere Führung* binds military action directly to the rule of law (German Federal Ministry of Defense ZDv 10/1 2008: nos. 301, 304, 305; Bendel and Suermann 2013: 341).

'The main goal of ethical education processes is to improve soldiers' powers of moral judgment, i.e. their ability in specific decision-making situations to properly apply general standards according to the situation and so determine the morally correct action to take. Moral judgments are the result of applying general standards to specific situations. Moral judgment competence therefore requires not only sufficient normative knowledge, but also the ability to identify the relevant empirical features of a situation and connect the two together' (Bock 2013: 49).

Soldiers often have to act in dangerous and unclear situations, where they are under enormous time pressure and to some extent under stress. This makes it impossible to spend lots of time considering the morally best solution.

Soldiers must satisfy the challenging requirement of choosing and implementing the likely best solution in the time available to them (Bohrmann 2011: 19; Spreckelmeier 2010: 165; Bendel 2006: 128). Another difficulty may become apparent after the action: Once a decision has been taken and acted upon, that person has to live with the consequences and results. Soldiers are therefore under pressure to meet potentially conflicting demands (Dörfler-Dierken 2010: 288; Schreiner 2005: 69).

The task and purpose of CGT is to address these difficulties as well, to reflect on them, and to develop alternative options for the respective situation. As a place for open and free discussion, CGT classes aim to give soldiers the opportunity to share their experiences in the classroom, but moreover to name their concerns and fears with regard to taking the morally right action under operational pressure.

Yet the ZEBIS teaching portal has to meet the challenge of satisfying two target groups: CGT instructors, who are the portal's direct users, and the soldiers who are the 'end users' of the lesson plans and materials. Hence the reality of soldiers' lives, their specific problems and requests (Jermer 2005: 144) should find expression in the portal's materials.

'Old Portal'

The aim of the teaching portal was and is to provide instructors with extensive material, in an educational format for teaching purposes, for enhancing professional ethical competence in character guidance training (CGT) according to the curriculum of ZDv 10/4. It went online at the end of 2011. After two years of working on, experience with and feedback from instructors and soldiers about the portal, the decision was taken to review the concept, structure and content of the portal.

The result is that ZEBIS currently works with two portals. The new portal has been completely redesigned and its content is currently being successively revised.

This section first describes the structure of the old portal, before discussing constructive comments from users and their consequences.

Previously, the teaching portal's structure was based on distinctions of rank, and divided into lesson plans, materials for lesson plans, and extra material.

In the old portal, lesson plans are organized according to rank groups: lower ranks, sergeants and officers. They are also subdivided chronologically into course durations of 2 hours, 1 day and 1.5 days.

The lesson plans are available in table form, and as detailed versions. The lesson plan in table form gives the instructor a quick overview of the topics, goals and learning content of the individual units along with the envisaged materials and teaching method. The detailed versions of the lesson plans contain a full description of the individual course units and use of the envisaged materials.

The structure of the teaching portal is divided into 'Materials for teaching modules' and 'Additional materials'.[8] Materials (PowerPoint presentations, images, texts, cartoons, figures, audio and video clips) stored under 'Materials for teaching modules' are used directly in the lesson plans and integrated into classroom activities via the teaching methods.

'Additional materials' contains further materials that can be used by instructors for preparation, or for consolidation, or as alternative material for character guidance training.

The portal provides users with an extensive choice of adult education teaching methods, in an interactive format, for diverse seminar structures and activities. The individual methods are presented with a short description, and range from activity-based tasks, to methods involving the emotions, to thematically oriented approaches, which cover the various phases of teaching (introduction/ motivation, group work and working on problems, discussion, presentation and evaluation). Following the description, the respective potential applications in lessons are listed along with the necessary materials.

In the section 'From CGT for CGT',[9] instructors are able to upload their own lesson plans onto the portal, where they are available to all users. 'From CGT for CGT' was created with the aim of encouraging dialog between instructors and steadily expanding the range of lesson plans.

Copyright permission has been obtained for all materials used and cited on the portal, so instructors can safely use the materials in class. The licenses are of two types: either free or purchased. With the free licenses – mainly concerning images – the rights holders have approved use of the materials provided the source is accurately quoted. For all other materials in the portal, licenses had to be purchased.

What has been our experience of the portal, at ZEBIS? What feedback have we received from users, and what has our response been?

The teaching portal is a living medium. It is updated and new topics and materials are added on an ongoing basis. There is a danger, however, that the large choice of materials – and hence the sheer number of files – could cause confusion, making the portal difficult to use. User-friendliness is particularly relevant for an online portal, and it suffers the larger the portal becomes. To counteract this, special attention was paid when redesigning the portal to

8 *Materialien der Unterrichtsmodule* and *Zusatzmaterial.*

9 *Aus dem LKU für den LKU.*

ensuring that users can find what they are looking for – i.e. the materials they are planning to use in class – within a small number of clicks.

Grouping the lesson plans according to the three rank groups of lower ranks, sergeants and officers (also as files) proved to be impractical in terms of the portal's usability. CGT instructors reported that it was virtually impossible to give classes differentiated by rank owing to the tight schedule operating at *Bundeswehr* sites. Often it was the case that all rank groups were represented among CGT participants, which led to requests for differentiation in the classroom, i.e. notes within the lesson plans which would facilitate adaptation to the group's learning needs.[10]

Another factor is that the reform of the German armed forces has changed the composition of the ranks. The individual rank groups have become more permeable and much more heterogeneous, with the result that this should also be taken into account in a reworking of teaching material for specific target groups. It can no longer be assumed that tuition can be given 'separately for lower ranks, sergeants and officers' (German Federal Ministry of Defense 2011: no. 202).

Open discussion during classes and the sharing of own experiences are particularly important in the context of ethical education in the *Bundeswehr*. The materials available in the portal need to reflect this. Feedback from portal users indicated that the lesson plans are too compact. Realistically, the lesson plans as they stand would require at least twice as much time. This finding is a key element in the revision of the portal's content. The new lesson plans and materials provide more space for discussion and focus work on specific problems, not least to satisfy the requirement of ethical education through practice.

Military relevance, particularly the inclusion of aspects of deployment preparation (Bach 2012: 113) is an important element of CGT. The *Bundeswehr* is regularly deployed overseas. Consequently, soldiers increasingly have to grapple with ethical issues during their deployment, and moreover possess intercultural skills, requiring knowledge of other cultures and their values and standards (Illauer 2011: 61). In the revision of the portal, this military relevance is given more prominence than previously.

'New Portal'

An online teaching portal needs to fulfill various requirements, relating to its content and of a technical nature. It needs to be designed for specific target groups. The materials and content should be tailored to the respective target group.

10 For example with references to more detailed texts on the topic.

The portal should be simple and quick to use. It should be user-friendly and clearly structured. Its technical elements should function reliably so that users can always use the portal. The redesigned teaching portal offers many advantages, both technical and content-related, for the benefit of both target groups – CGT instructors and soldiers.

- **Clear structure of the portal:** Users can find out in one click what the portal has to offer on the topic they are searching for.
- **Uncluttered layout:** Allows users to take in relevant information more quickly, and they like using the portal. A user-friendly interface makes the portal simpler to use.
- **Icons:** Icons make it easier for users to find their way around the portal, helping them get their work done quicker. The redesigned portal now features icons for movies, audio clips, PowerPoint presentations, working papers, texts and the 'From CGT for CGT' lesson plans. Users can see immediately what types of material are available.
- Integrated **media library:** In the new portal, the video material is also accessible in a media library. The media library is tailored to CGT instructors' needs in terms of content and themes, and is also a collection of materials for this field for which copyright licenses have been secured. In the media library, the video material is systematically arranged according to the ZDv 10/4 curriculum. A thematic search in the media library, together with references to further video material relevant to the topic, produces an extensive pool of materials. This reduces the amount of time the instructor needs to spend doing research, enriches soldiers' ethical education and allows more diverse CGT course offerings. A particular feature of the media library in the teaching portal is that copyright permission has been obtained for all the available material, and therefore all material can be safely used in character guidance training classes.

  In ad eaching portal and hence also the media library is accessible and available for use at any time via the internet. Instructors can either play videos directly from the media library or download a copy onto their own storage device.
- **Software for video formats:** External software runs in the background to automatically detect the media player, hardware and operating system (Mac, Linux, Windows) used on the terminal device so that the video plays in the correct format. Users don't need to worry about installing a special video player or choosing the right video formats.

Alongside these extensive new technical features, the content of the portal is also being successively revised.

New lesson plans are being produced for sergeants, and will each contain notes for officers and lower ranks to facilitate differentiation in the classroom. Consequently, the individual units of the lesson plan offer alternative problems/tasks with the corresponding materials, which are respectively more academic or more activity-based.

At the beginning of each lesson plan, there is an introduction of 1–2 pages giving portal users a quick overview of the plan. The introduction includes the following points:

- Description/explanation of the topic covered
- Reasons for selecting/singling out this topic
- Description of the scope in which the topic is covered
- Explanation of the structure and goals of the lesson plan
- Explanation of the educational methods used to implement the goals and content of the lesson plan

All materials (working materials, texts, PowerPoint presentations, video and audio descriptions, and images) are also provided with usage notes stating the subject area and the module in the ZDv 10/4 curriculum that the material applies to. Possible uses for additional topics are also stated. Following a brief description of the content of the respective material, points for further discussion/questions/tasks/instructions for use in the classroom are listed for the instructor. The final point in the usage notes consists of examples of educational uses for the respective material. Here users are offered suggestions of appropriate teaching methods for using the material in class.

E-Journal

The second element of the military ethics education formats at ZEBIS is the e-journal 'Ethics and Armed Forces – Controversies in Military Ethics & Security Policy'.[11]

With regard to content, the e-journal sets out to analyze and discuss current and controversial topics in military ethics. The e-journal pursues a multi-perspective and interdisciplinary approach. Topics are considered by experts in various specialist disciplines (e.g. ethics, medicine, educational science, political science, psychology, theology and international law). The e-journal is not only an interdisciplinary periodical for an academic readership. Above all, it

11 http://www.ethikundmilitaer.de/.

provides background and information material for soldiers and military chaplains who act as multipliers in ethical education in the German armed forces.

The e-journal is published twice a year in a German and an English version, and is provided free-of-charge to users on the ZEBIS website. The articles are also available in the German National Library[12] via their International Standard Serial Number[13] record.

So how does the e-journal fit into the military ethics education formats at ZEBIS?

As mentioned above, ethical education is not an isolated field or detached from other disciplines. Particularly for soldiers, ethical issues are a challenging aspect in their work and everyday lives. Not only the specific military ethics issues, such as responsibility and guilt or dealing with death, killing and wounding, but also personal issues such as the 'personal/family life and duty' topic play a role.

A good example to illustrate this is the debate surrounding fully autonomous weapons systems and unmanned weapons delivery systems: issues in military ethics, far from existing in isolation, instead arise directly from the lives and experiences of soldiers. Here military ethics refers to the challenges which accompany asymmetric conflicts and wars or technological advancements in warfare, for example.

The e-journal pursues various objectives:

- Scholarly standards: With qualified and internationally renowned authors, the e-journal offers thematic articles that either help instructors to prepare lessons or can be used directly as teaching material in the classroom.
- Interdisciplinarity: The topics covered in the e-journal are discussed from multiple perspectives in keeping with the principle that military ethics should be an interdisciplinary subject. Military expertise, the international law perspective, the moral philosophical or even theological point of view, as well as current findings in the empirical sciences – such as psychology and political science – should be sought and examined so as to enable an appropriate response to current issues and avoid taking a too narrow view. Via the combination of different disciplines, users are offered wide-ranging specialist knowledge concerning the respective topics. Ethical issues can therefore be considered from different perspectives and points of view.
- Internationalness: Publication in two languages and contributions by international authors ensure that the journal has international relevance. Since

12 Deutsche Nationalbibliothek.

13 (ISSN).

armed forces today are involved in international and multicultural missions increasingly often, this should be reflected in the soldiers' training.

The three aspects mentioned – scholarly standards, interdisciplinarity, and internationalness – are also incorporated into the design and documentation of ZEBIS events.

Events and Documentation

'Communication enables people to learn their whole life long.' This is how the Catholic military bishop for the German armed forces, Dr. Franz-Josef Overbeck, describes the importance of communication.

With the aid of training events such as panel discussions and study days for soldiers, CGT instructors and an interested public, ZEBIS promotes dialog and discussion concerning current topics in military ethics. The emphasis is on practical relevance and usefulness as well as the aspects mentioned above of scholarly standards, interdisciplinarity and internationalness, for the full spectrum of the human sciences plays a major role in ethical guidance for soldiers.

The creation of opportunities for talks and discussion involving experts in a wide variety of disciplines and the persons directly affected allows soldiers to contribute their own experiences to the dialog. Since events are documented on the ZEBIS website, the content is subsequently available to instructors for teaching purposes, or can be used by soldiers for their own continuing education.

Training events are themed on current security policy challenges and military ethics debates in the Bundeswehr. For ethical education to be exciting and interesting, it has to be relevant to soldiers' lives and experiences. Purely academic examinations of abstract issues without any practical relevance to soldiers' lives do not constitute an appropriate framework for motivating soldiers to participate in ethical education.

One example of this is the current debate over whether the Bundeswehr should acquire armed drones. In the discussion it is said that in future the Bundeswehr too should be equipped with armed drones so that in the context of justifiable operations, the risk to the Bundeswehr's own soldiers is kept to a minimum. In Germany, unmanned weapons delivery systems have met with great moral skepticism. Some people believe that armed drones are the first step towards automated or even autonomously acting weapons systems. Modern technologies are intended to relieve soldiers from particularly dangerous missions. But unmanned weapons delivery systems raise a series of issues concerning international law and ethics: What new challenges do automated systems create for international law? Are reconnaissance drones a kind of 'starter drone' marking the first step towards 'remote-controlled killing'? Do drones reduce soldiers' sympathy? What does it mean when attacks no longer put any of your own soldiers in danger? Are algorithm-equipped autonomous weapons systems actually capable of taking over highly complex decision processes in all kinds of deployment scenarios? Doesn't responsible decision-making require a conscience? Do unmanned weapons systems aggravate or defuse conflicts? How much scope for decision-making should be left to humans? These questions have been hotly debated from military, security policy and ethical perspectives at various ZEBIS training events.

All of these questions lead directly into ethical discussion that reflects soldiers' worlds of experience. They are directly affected by this debate and the associated issues, and they themselves want either to be given or to develop answers to these questions. They do not want to wait until they find themselves in a dilemma situation before they attempt to answer or learn how to answer these questions. They expect ethical education in the armed forces to prepare them as well as possible for such situations, and also to provide a form of assurance with regard to the appropriate course of action.

'Soldiers are placed in decision-making situations which are uncertain in respect of the consequences and effects of actions, and are therefore risky. Decisions can often be taken only on the basis of probabilities and with a degree of uncertainty. Especially in conflict situations under such conditions of insecurity and uncertainty, soldiers must act in a morally responsible way. Soldiers often operate in danger situations and in addition under time pressure, making it morally indefensible to spend too much time trying to find the morally best solution. Within the available time, the probably best solution must be sought.' (Bendel 2006: 128)

Conclusion

So how can the initial questions be answered? Can an online teaching portal, an e-journal and events assist and perhaps even encourage ethical learning by soldiers?

Yes – but it is a constantly evolving process.

'Ethical learning should ultimately be geared to moral verbal, action and decision-making competence in the social context. Learners should be encouraged and enabled to get involved and under the given social conditions to develop an independent, reflected and responsible value system. The teaching of ethical competence becomes a communicative process in which the foundations of the individual's values are taken seriously and the development of their capacity for ethical judgment is specifically stimulated' (Kruip & Winkler 2010: 29).

Apart from in-depth specialist knowledge in a wide range of disciplines, ethical education for soldiers also requires practice and experience. The ability to make moral judgments cannot be learned by rote, like a mathematical formula. It is acquired through a combination of taught normative and specialist knowledge, own practice and experience, and ethical reflection.

Work on an e-learning portal is not static. User behavior on the online portal needs to be taken into account, and technical requirements implemented. It needs regular updating and new content provision, yet must not become overloaded. The requirements of teaching ethics need to be satisfied, and translated into lesson plans for specific topics and target groups.

An online teaching portal can serve as a valuable aid for CGT instructors by offering material, which is thematically tailored to character guidance training and presented in an educational format.

Tying in an online teaching portal with an e-journal and events with corresponding event documentation creates synergy effects and combination possibilities in the field of ethical education for soldiers. All three areas promote ethical education for soldiers: These three areas generate a variety of cognitive and motivational approaches to issues in military ethics which can be used by soldiers directly or incorporated by CGT instructors into ethical teaching in the armed forces.

Bibliography

Bach, Alois 2012, Ethische Bildung in der Bundeswehr und das Zentrum Innere Führung, in: Thomas Schirmacher, Edwin R. Micewski (ed), Ethik im Kontext individueller Verantwortung und militärischer Führung, Berlin 2012, 109–15.

Bendel, Lothar 1999, Menschenwürde und militärisches Handeln. Überlegungen zu einem Curriculum für die Laufbahnlehrgänge der Offiziere und Unteroffiziere der Bundeswehr, in: Jürgen Nabbefeld (ed), Meinen Frieden gebe ich Euch: Festschrift für den Katholischen Militärbischof für die Deutsche Bundeswehr Erzbischof Dr. Dr. Johannes Dyba, Bischof von Fulda, Köln 1999, 308–14.

Bendel, Lothar 2006, Ethische Bildung in der Bundeswehr – Chancen und Risiken, in: Militärseelsorge 44. (2006): 115–28.

Bendel, Lothar/*Suermann,* Manfred 2013, Der Lebenskundliche Unterricht als Lernort ethischer Reflexion, in: Thomas Bohrmann, Karl-Heinz Lather, Friedrich Lohmann (ed), Handbuch Militärische Berufsethik. Band 1 Grundlagen, Wiesbaden 2013, 333–54.

Bock, Veronika 2013, Der Soldat als moralischer Akteur, in: Thomas Bohrmann, Karl-Heinz Lather, Friedrich Lohmann (ed), Handbuch Militärische Berufsethik. Band 1 Grundlagen, Wiesbaden 2013, 35–52.

Bohrmann, Thomas 2011, Person, Staatsbürger, Soldat. Sozialethische Herausforderungen für die Innere Führung, in: Jochen Bohn/Thomas Bohrmann (ed), Die Bundeswehr heute: Berufsethische Perspektiven für eine Armee im Einsatz, Stuttgart 2011, 11–26.

Bundesministerium der Verteidigung (ed) 2006. Weißbuch Bundesministerium der Verteidigung, 2011 zur Sicherheitspolitik Deutschlands und zur Zukunft der Bundeswehr, Berlin 2006.

Bundesministerium der Verteidigung (ed) 2008. ZDv 10/1. Innere Führung, Berlin 2008.

Bundesministerium der Verteidigung (ed) 2011. ZDv 10/4. Lebenskundlicher Unterricht. Selbstverantwortlich leben – Verantwortung für andere übernehmen können, Berlin 2011.

Dörfler-Dierken, Angelika 2010, Militärseelsorge und Friedensethik, in: Evangelische Theologie 65 (2010) 278–92.

Ebeling, Klaus 2006, Militär und Ethik. Moral- und militärkritische Reflexionen zum Selbstverständnis der Bundeswehr, Stuttgart 2006.

Elßner, Thomas R. 2009, Stärkung ethischer Grundlagen in der Bundeswehr, in: Militärseelsorge 47 (2009) 93–98.

Griese, Sabine 2009, Didaktische Überlegungen zum Lebenskundlichen Unterricht, in: Evangelisches Kirchenamt für die Bundeswehr (ed), Friedensethik im Einsatz: ein Handbuch der Evangelischen Seelsorge in der Bundeswehr, Gütersloh 2009, 348–57.

Illauer, Ralf 2011, Quo vadis, Staatsbürger in Uniform, in: Hans-Christian Beck, Christian Singer (ed), Entscheiden Führen Verantworten. Soldatsein im 21. Jahrhundert, Berlin 2011, 57–62.

Jermer, Helmut 2005, Die Katholische Militärseelsorge in der Bundeswehr – ein Überblick Kirche und Staat – konstitutiv, kooperativ, konstruktiv, in: Militärseelsorge 43 (2005) 127–56.

Jermer, Helmut 2010, Ethische Bildung für Soldaten, in: Militärseelsorge 48 (2010) 129–38.

Kenngott, Eva-Maria 2011, Ethik im Unterricht, in: Ralf Stoecker, Christian Neuhäuser, Marie-Luise Raters (ed), Handbuch Angewandte Ethik, Stuttgart; Weimar 2011, 215–18.

Kruip, Gerhard/*Winkler*, Katja 2010, Moraltheologische, entwicklungspsychologische und andragogisch-konzeptionelle Grundlagen ethischen Lernens, in: Helge

Gisbertz, Gerhard Kruip, Markus Tolksdorf (ed), Ethisches Lernen in der allgemeinen Erwachsenenbildung, Bielefeld 2010, 15–55.

Meyer, Hilbert, Was ist guter Unterricht, Berlin 2004.

Pfeifer, Volker 2003, Didaktik des Ethikunterrichts. Wie lässt sich Moral lehren und lernen?, Stuttgart 2003.

Schmid, Bruno 2000, Ethisches Lernen im Unterricht, in: Johann-Baptist Metz, Lothar Kuld, Adolf Weisbrod (ed), Compassion. Weltprogramm des Christentums. Soziale Verantwortung lernen, Freiburg i. Br. 2000, 53–74.

Schreiner, Karl H. 2005, Welchen Soldaten/welche Soldatin braucht die Deutsche Bundeswehr, in: Militärseelsorge 43 (2005): 59–72.

Spreckelmeier, Klaus 2010, Kernkompetenz Verantwortung. Zur Vermittlung einer wertebezogenen Verantwortungsethik im Lebenskundlichen Unterricht mit Soldatinnen und Soldaten der Bundeswehr. Ein Werkstattbericht auf der Grundlage zentraler Dienstvorschriften, in: Paul Chummar Chittilappilly (ed), Ethik der Lebensfelder. Festschrift für Philipp Schmitz SJ, Freiburg i.Br. 2010, 155–79.

Wilke, Carl Mathias 2011, Überlegungen zur Gewinnung ethischer Handlungssicherheit, in: Hans-Christian Beck, Christian Singer (ed), Entscheiden Führen Verantworten. Soldatsein im 21. Jahrhundert, Berlin 2011, 95–99.

CHAPTER 7

Menschengerechte Soldaten – Soldatengerechte Ethikausbildung: Am Beispiel der Unteroffiziersausbildung im Österreichischen Bundesheer

Stefan Gugerel

Die Aufgabe der berufsethischen Bildung für Soldaten liegt darin, den Soldaten die Reflexion ihres eigenen Verhaltens zu erleichtern und sie dadurch auf das Fällen von Entscheidungen vorzubereiten; Entscheidungen, durch die sie nicht nur das Ansehen ihres Staates verändern, sondern auch eigenes und fremdes Leben gefährden.

Wird dem Soldaten Ethik allerdings ausschließlich in Form spezieller Unterlagen, Faltkarten oder Unterrichtseinheiten präsentiert, muss in ihm der Gedanke aufkeimen, dass Ethik ein Fach *neben* anderen, eine Denkmöglichkeit neben anderen ist. Anzustreben ist hingegen, dass der Soldat Ethik als allen anderen Fächern vorausliegende und innewohnende Disziplin erkennt, auf der Ebene der Vernunft wie auf der Ebene der Beobachtung des Verhaltens der Lehrenden: 'Als soziale Konstrukte kommt den Werten, Normen, Beurteilungskriterien und Prinzipien keine "Faktizität", d.h. faktische Existenz zu wie den raumzeitlichen Dingen in der Welt. Vielmehr haben sie "Geltung", wenn und solange sie von rationalen Wesen entwickelt, begründet und eingesehen werden.'[1] Diese Einsicht und Akzeptanz zu fördern, ist Aufgabe des Ethikunterrichts.

Die folgenden Ausführungen setzten daher nicht zuerst bei Regeln und deren Begründung in Gesetz und kultureller Tradition an, sondern bei der Grundsatzfrage nach dem Soldaten. Ist dessen Aufgabe bestimmt, so kann daraus ein Gerüst an Orientierungspunkten abgeleitet werden (*agere sequitur esse*).

Der menschengerechte Soldat

Der Soldat ist zuerst und vor jedem Auftrag Mensch. Was immer er daher tut, geschieht in der grundsätzlichen Solidarität mit allen anderen Menschen.

1 Fenner, Dagmar, Ethik, Wie soll ich handeln? (UTB Basics, 2008), 67.

 | DOI 10.1163/9789004312135_008

Maßstab seines Handelns kann daher nichts anderes als der Schutz der Menschenrechte sein, dem jedes Sekundärziel (Verteidigung der territorialen Einheit des Heimastlandes, Schutz der politischen Einrichtungen und der öffentlichen Ordnung…) untergeordnet ist. Wie wird nun in allgemeinster Form der Mensch umschrieben?

Gemäß der Allgemeinen Erklärung der Menschenrechte der Vereinten Nationen von 1948 ist der Mensch 'frei und gleich an Würde und Rechten geboren.'[2]

Aus dieser Freiheit ergibt sich, dass der Mensch sich entscheiden muss; wählen muss, wie er sich verhält. Anders als das Tier kann er sich nicht auf Instinkte, ererbte oder erlernte genormte Verhaltensweisen, die unwillkürlich als Reaktion auf bestimmte Schlüsselreize erfolgen, berufen. Es 'gilt, daß wir Menschen nur als Kulturmenschen kennen, also als tätig in unbeschreiblich vielseitigen, sozial vermittelten Handlungen, d.h. solchen, die ohne andere Handlungen anderer Menschen gar nicht zu verstehen sind, und die man gelernt hat.'[3] Gelingt es, dem Soldaten am Beginn die Bedingtheit seines Verhaltens im erhalten anderer und in seiner eigenen Erfahrung aufzuzeigen, verschafft man ihm damit die nötige Distanz zu Entscheidungsabläufen. Er sieht, wie er grundsätzlich in ähnlichen Situationen entschieden hat, er ersteht, warum er das auch in ähnlichen Situationen in der Zukunft wahrscheinlich so tun wird, aber er lernt auch, dass diese Verhaltensgewohnheiten kein Zwang sind. Er *kann* sich auch in Zukunft anders erhalten und dieses neue erhalten zur Gewohnheit machen.

Die Gleichheit an Würde und daraus erfließenden Rechten stellt vor das nächste Interpretationsproblem: 'Die große Bedeutung, die dem Gedanken der Menschenwürde zugemessen wird, kann freilich nicht darüber hinwegtäuschen, dass es schwierig ist anzugeben, was er genau beinhaltet. Was ist mit dem Wort 'Würde' gemeint? Inwiefern haben Menschen eine Würde, die andere Wesen nicht haben? All diese Fragen sind in der Debatte über die Menschenwürde strittig. Sie bedürfen nicht zuletzt deshalb einer sorgfältigen ethischen Klärung, weil durch einen teilweise inflationären Gebrauch dieses Begriffs die Gefahr besteht, dass er zu einer Leerformel verkommt.'[4] Der Ausdruck 'Würde' klingt in den Ohren vieler Auszubildender antiquiert und unverständlich. Viele versuchen eine Annäherung über das Wort 'Wert', der die Gefahr beinhaltet, immer zuerst finanziell gedacht zu werden. Es ist dann auf

2 AEM 1.

3 Gehlen, A, Der Mensch, Seine Natur und Stellung in der Welt, Wiebelsheim, Hunsrück 2009, 329.

4 Fischer, J, Gruden, S, Imhof, E, Strub, D, Grundkurs Ethik, Grundbegriffe philosophischer und theologischer Ethik, Stuttgart 2008, 390.

jeden Fall darauf zu verweisen, dass dieser Wert unabhängig von erbrachten 'Leistungen' des Menschen gegeben ist. Gerade in Zeiten, in denen der Arbeit höchste Bedeutung zugemessen wird, liegt die Versuchung nahe, noch nicht, nicht mehr oder gar nicht arbeiten Könnende für weniger wertvoll und deshalb weniger schützenswert zu erachten. Der deutsche Philosoph Hans Dieter Bahr hat das so zusammengefasst:

> Abgesehen davon, daß man so Arbeit mit Handlung gleichzusetzen suchte, konnte nun alles zur "Arbeit" (im Sinne von *ponos, molestia, labor*) werden, was einen Aufwand und eine erfolgversprechende Verausgabung erforderte, ob solche Arbeit bezahlt wurde oder nicht. Und man kam zur Auffassung selbst sportliche oder kriegerische Leistungen und sogar wissenschaftliche und philosophische Tätigkeiten sowie jede psychische Bewältigung von Krisen und Konflikten dadurch zu "würdigen" oder zumindest ihren Aufwand an Kräften sozial legitimieren zu können, daß man sie "Arbeit" nannte; so wie sogar das Massenmorden noch von seinen Agenten als "notwendige Drecksarbeit" bezeichnet wurde.[5]

In den Untiefen von Friedensarbeit und Trauerarbeit bzw. der Aufarbeitung von traumatisierenden Erlebnissen in Krisenräumen oder nach Einsätzen werden Menschen, mit denen Soldaten täglich zu tun haben sowohl als Subjekte, als Arbeitende, dargestellt, wie auch als Objekte, Bearbeitete, Personen, für die etwas getan wird oder werden muss.

Liest man den ersten Artikel der Menschenrechtskonvention weiter, so folgt dort: 'Sie [Die Menschen] sind mit Vernunft und Gewissen begabt.'[6]

Die Vernunftbegabtheit, die hier nicht als auszubildendes Ziel einer wie auch immer gestalteten Erziehung vorgestellt, sondern als von Anfang an gegeben festgehalten wird, ist grundlegend für einen vernunftgemäßen Zugang zur Entscheidungsfindung. Die Reflexion über das eigene Handeln, im Besonderen über das Erteilen und Befolgen von Befehlen, scheint der vernünftig begründeten Effizienz hierarchischer Systeme zu widersprechen: wer zu viel fragt, lähmt das System, das seine Wirksamkeit nur in der Geschwindigkeit der Entscheidungsumsetzung hat. Jeder Mensch ist in unserem kulturellen Kontext in Hierarchien eingebunden, die sein Alltagsleben regeln und erleichtern. Der italienische Philosoph Giorgio Agamben sieht sogar eine der größten Kulturleistungen Europas in der Depotenzierung charismatischer Einzelanführer

5 Bahr, H D, Zeit der Muße – Zeit der Musen, Tübingen 2008, 71.

6 AEM 1.

durch ministerielle Apparate. Er macht dies an Beobachtungen zur politischen Verwirklichung theologischer Spekulationen über die Engel fest:

> Hat sich erst einmal die Hierarchie als zentraler Begriff herausgebildet, sind Engel und Bürokraten, genau wie in Kafkas Universums, nicht mehr voneinander zu unterscheiden…Entscheidend ist jedoch, daß lange bevor damit begonnen wurde, die Terminologie der zivilen Verwaltung und Regierung auszuarbeiten und festzulegen, sie auf dem Gebiet der Angelologie bereits feste Konturen angenommen hatte. Nicht nur der Begriff der Hierarchie, sondern auch der des Ministeriums und der Mission finden, wie wir sagen, ihre erste und feingliedrigste Systematisierung auf dem Gebiet der Engel und ihrer Tätigkeiten.[7]

Es ist die menschliche Vernunft, die Menschen in Systemen Funktionen zuweist und ihnen damit zugleich ihre Selbstverwirklichung ermöglicht und beschneidet. Ermöglicht, weil sie dem einzelnen (in Berufsarmeen und nach Verfügbarkeit der Plätze) die Wahl lässt, für welche Waffengattung er sich qualifiziert; beschneidet, weil es kaum Funktionen gibt, in denen der einzelnen völlig frei nach eigenem Gutdünken entscheiden und handeln kann.

Kann dem auszubildenden Soldaten vermittelt werden, dass die Frage der Loyalität und des Gehorsams schon weit vor dem Kasernentor und dem militärischen Einsatz beginnt, eröffnet das auch neue Perspektiven jenseits von Befehlsverweigerung und Kadavergehorsam. Dazu kommt die europäische Geistesgeschichte zu Hilfe, die auf der Basis der christlich – islamischen Entmachtung gottgleicher Herrscher den Samen des kritischen Gehorsams seit Jahrhunderten in jede Generation einsäen. Als ein Beispiel soll die Infragestellung monarchischer Herrschaft durch das Christentum herangezogen werden:

> Auch der König, das verlangt die Kirche zunächst ohne jede Chance, es auch durchsetzen zu können, soll dem Recht unterworfen sein. Auch königlich angeordneter Mord bleibt Mord. Darin folgt die apostolische Kirche der prophetischen Lehre des Alten Testaments, dass man Gott mehr Gehorsam schulde als den Menschen, und seien sie auch noch so mächtig. Durch seine Verbindung mit dem biblischen Gottesgehorsam wird das römische Naturrecht zu einer potentiell kritischen Instanz.[8]

---

7 Agamben, G, Herrschaft und Herrlichkeit, Zur theologischen Genealogie von Ökonomie und Regierung, Homo sacer II.2, Berlin 2010, 189.

8 Brunkhorst, H, Einführung in die Geschichte politischer Ideen, München 2000, 127.

Der Soldat als Mensch und die Menschen, für die er Soldat ist (zum Schutz wie zur Abwehr), stehen also auf dem Fundament derselben Vernunft. Daraus ergibt sich von selbst, dass jedes Handeln vernünftig begründbar sein muss, auch wenn diese Begründung nicht jedes Mal ausdrücklich ausgesprochen wird. Deshalb kann man mit der Vorbereitung dieser Erklärungen auch nicht bis zum Ernstfall warten, in dem Emotionen und Ängste die Wahrnehmungsfähigkeit trüben. Theoretischer Unterricht und ethische Praxis in taktischen Übungsverläufen sind daher eine Selbstverständlichkeit.

Den Abschluss des ersten Artikels der Menschenrechtserklärung macht nicht wie bei den Punkten der Freiheit, der gleichen Würde oder der Vernünftigkeit eine Feststellung, sondern eine Aufforderung: 'Sie [die Menschen] sollen einander im Geist der Brüderlichkeit begegnen.'[9] Neben die allgemeine Aufforderung zur Begegnung wird auch die Art der Begegnung näher definiert 'im Geist der Brüderlichkeit', der heute natürlich zum 'Geist der Geschwisterlichkeit' umformuliert werden müsste. Während Freiheit, Würde und Vernunft ungefragt vorausgesetzt werden, muss dieser Umgang angesichts der zahllosen Grausamkeiten auf individueller, institutioneller und internationaler Ebene eingemahnt werden.

Der menschengerechte Soldat basiert nun sein Entscheiden und Handeln auf die Freiheit (er entscheidet und er ermöglicht den ihm Anvertrauten die Freiheit), auf die Würde (die er in seiner Person und der Personen jedes anderen, Verbündeten, Anvertrauten und Feindes, schützt) und die Vernunft (worunter auch alle militärischen Überlegungen zur Legitimität des Gewalteinsatzes, der Verhältnismäßigkeit, der Einhaltung der Bestimmungen des Völkerrechts, der Einsatzbestimmungen etc. zu zählen sind). Insofern unterscheidet er sich dem Fundament nach in nichts von den übrigen Menschen, den Zivilisten. Erst bei der Aufforderung zur geschwisterlichen Begegnung erhält er in seiner Funktion als Repräsentant staatlicher wie internationaler Ordnung eine Aufgabe, die über den Auftrag der Zivilisten hinausgeht: Er wird – theologisch gesprochen zum Sakrament – Personifikation dieses Umgangs: Wie der Soldat mit seinen Kameraden im Inland (Dienstbetrieb) und Ausland (Einsatz) umgeht ist für die übrigen Soldaten und für die Zivilisten erste Schule der Brüderlichkeit. Wo der Soldat in Erfüllung seiner Aufträge auf eigene oder fremde Zivilbevölkerung trifft, setzt sich dieser am Kameraden eingeübte Umgang fort. Der Soldat kann ja nicht durch unverhältnismäßige Gewaltanwendung, Überheblichkeit oder unachtsames Auftreten denen Recht geben, zu deren Eindämmung er eingesetzt wird. In äußerster Zuspitzung muss sich der geschwisterliche Umgang im scharfen Einsatz zeigen, dort, wo

9 AEM 1.

ohne Gewaltanwendung das Ziel des Schutzes der Anvertrauten nicht mehr erreicht werden kann. Auch dort ist der Feind dann nicht depersonifiziertes 'Ziel', das beliebig 'ausgeschaltet' werden kann. Der Angreifer bleibt, auch wenn er verletzt oder getötet werden muss, Mensch und muss dementsprechend behandelt werden. Da auch der Angreifer über Vernunft verfügt, wird er vorgewarnt und auf die möglichen Konsequenzen seines Handelns hingewiesen. Wenn er diese Konsequenzen in Kauf nehmen will, weil ihm sein Ziel wichtiger als seine physische Unversehrtheit oder sein Leben ist, dann wird auch in seiner Bekämpfung seine Würde gewahrt.

Die soldatengerechte Ethikausbildung

Dieser kurze Überblick über zentrale Ausbildungsinhalte soll nun eingeordnet werden in die konkrete Unteroffiziersausbildung des Österreichischen Bundesheeres. Typisch dafür ist die enge Vernetzung der Inhalte mit Politischer Bildung und Rechtskunde, um einen möglichst umfassenden Blick auf bestimmte Themenbereiche zu geben (Gehorsam, Legitimität der Gewaltanwendung, Menschenrechtsschutz). Die Einbindung militärethischer Überlegungen in die konkrete Planung von Übungen wird weiter ausgebaut.

Besonders bewährt hat sich die Eröffnung militärethischer Diskussionen anhand historischer Beispiele, bei denen oft weit verbreitete Vorurteile aufgebrochen werden können. Zudem macht der zeitliche Abstand es auch möglich, ohne unmittelbare Emotionen und Parteinahme (unsere Verbündeten/unsere Feinde) auf die Fragestellung einzugehen. Die historische Betrachtungsweise hat auch den Vorteil, keine virtuellen oder fiktiven Beispiele zu bringen, die manchmal als unrealistisch oder realitätsfern kritisiert werden: Niemand von uns muss das Schienendilemma in Wirklichkeit lösen, aber Menschen standen auf Revolutionsplätzen oder an Fronten aller Art mit ihrem Leben für Veränderung oder Verteidigung politischer Systeme, territorialer Grenzen oder religiöser Überzeugungen ein. Bei der Betrachtung historischer

Entscheidungen geht es nicht um die moralische Entrüstung über mögliches oder tatsächliches Fehlverhalten, es geht vielmehr um das Aufspüren der Entscheidungsmotive, die zu den Handlungen geführt haben; und zur Extrapolation auf den heutigen Soldaten, der, auch wenn er das nicht immer mitbedenkt, ebenfalls mit seinem Leben für seine Ideale und den von ihm gewählten Beruf einsteht:

> Erstens kann das Leben nicht simuliert werden. Alle Fiktionen und Simulationen fallen zuletzt auf das Sosein meines Daseins zurück und

> weisen den Menschen in die Prämissen ein, die seinem Leben Grund und Gewissheit geben. An der "Grenze" des Lebens und seiner Sinnstiftung, die der Tod ist (Foucault), kommt der Mensch zur Wahrheit seines Lebens, ist er zu letzter Selbstbestimmung 'verurteilt' (Sartre)...Drittens ist es eine selbstwidersprüchliche Wahrheitsbezeugung und Wirklichkeitsgestaltung (performativer Widerspruch), wenn ein Kreuzritter im Namen Jesu Christi und des in ihm zugesagten Heiles für alle Sünder, für Juden und Heiden, das Schwert zückte, um einen Nichtchristen zu töten. Entsprechendes gilt für japanische Auftragskiller, die sich als Buddhisten des reinen Landes und der reinen Gnade verstanden.[10]

Neben der Frage der Sklaverei und ihrer schrittweisen Ächtung und Abschaffung (entgegen allen Beteuerungen, dass ohne sie die gesamte Weltwirtschaft zusammenbrechen würde), ist besonders die Zeit des Kolonialismus interessant, erscheinen doch manchen heutige Auslandseinsätze abgesehen von persönlichen Motiven (Geldverdienen, fixe Anstellung oder Beförderung beim Militär) oft als kaum verhohlene neokolonialistische Besatzungspolitik. Gerade die Analyse frühneuzeitlicher Herrschaftsformen über fremde Territorien kann hier auf nach außen bekannte und wahre Motive erhellen:

> Die Vizekönige hatten eigentlich nur Repräsentationsfunktionen, sie sollten in den Kolonien die souveräne Gewalt des Monarchen mit entsprechenden äußerlichen königlichen Attributen stellvertretend repäsentieren. Erst dadurch, dass sie zugleich die Ämter des Gouverneurs und des Generalkapitäns in ihrem *Gobierno* und des Präsidenten der an ihrem Sitz residierenden *Audiencia* innehatten, nahmen die Vizekönige neben ihrer politischen auch administrative Funktionen in einem engeren territorialen Rahmen wahr und erhielten dadurch ihr besonderes Gewicht, während sie in dem riesigen Gebiet des jeweiligen Vizekönigreichs lediglich eine allgemeine politische Autorität besaßen.[11]

Für das in den Medien seit dem Ende des Kapitalismus-Kommunismus-Konflikts neu aufgebaute Feindbild einer Erbfehde zwischen 'westlicher Welt'

---

10 Nitsche, B, "Viele Welten – eine Wahrheit? Transzendentallogische Forderungen nach Wittgenstein," in: Hafner, J E, Valentin, J (Hg.), Parallelwelten, Christliche Religion und die Vervielfachung von Wirklichkeit, Stuttgart 2009, 51–79, 78.

11 11 König, J, Riekenberg, M,Rinke, S, Die Eroberung einer neuen Welt, Präkolumbianische Kulturen, europäische Eroberung, Kolonialherrschaft in Amerika, Schwalbach/Taunus 2008, 171.

und ‘islamischer Welt’ kann durch differenzierte historische Analyse und Darstellung der inneren Differenziertheiten beider Welten (selbst in früheren Jahrhunderten trat ‘der’ Islam in Form dreier parallel existierender und zu Europa in unterschiedlicher Weise stehenden Weltreiche – Osmanen, Perser, Inder – auf); exemplarisch etwa am zeitgleich zur Französischen Revolution ablaufenden Umstrukturierungsprozess des Osmanischen Reiches:

> Die Diplomatie im Kontext dieses Krieges [Russisch-osmanischer Krieg 1787–1792] bewirkte, dass der Osmanische Hof nun erstmals ständige Gesandtschaften in den wichtigsten europäischen Residenzstädten einrichtete. Zugleich lieferte der Krieg dem neuen osmanischen Sultan Selim III. (1789–1807) genügend Argumente für eine Neuformierung des Osmanischen Reiches. Da er die bestehenden Einheiten nicht ohne weiteres umbauen lassen konnte, befürwortete er die Einrichtung einer komplementären militärischen Einheit. Um diese abzusichern, forderte er eine “Neue Ordnung” (*nizam-i jedid*) im Bereich der Truppenaushebung, Steuern, Rechtsnormen und einer territorialstaatlichen Verwaltung. Da mit Hilfe europäischer Militärberater faktisch nur die Errichtung einer neuen Armee gelang, wurde die Bezeichnung “neue Ordnung” bald schon zum Begriff für dieses neue, stehende Heer. Das Osmanische Reich erschien manchen nun wie ein Reformmarkt.[12]

Auch die Kooperation mit der Ausbildung in Gender Mainstreaming kann auf diese historische Zugangsweise gegründet werden, wenn neuer Geschichte und krampfhafte Versuche einer Definition des Männlichen uralten Erfahrungen weiblicher Selbstbestimmung gegenübergestellt werden (um das doppelte Vorurteil von Feminismus als neuem Phänomen und ungebrochener männlicher Dominanz als kontinuierlicher Tradition zu zertrümmern):

> Aus diesem Grund genügten nach Ansicht Roosevelts die viktorianischen Tugenden nicht für eine Abwehr rassebedingter Dekadenz, die für ihn gleichbedeutend mit dem Verlust von Männlichkeit war. Im Auf- und Ausbau der amerikanischen Nation war es die Zukunftsvision Roosevelts, einer überzivilisierten Rassedekadenz den Kampf anzusagen, und der

12 Schulze, B, “Das Warten auf die Moderne. Die Islamische Welt”; in: Hausberger, B, Lehners, J-P (Hg.), Die Welt im 18. Jahrhundert. Globalgeschichte. Die Welt 1000–2000, Wien 2011, 243–273, 268.

sportlich sich betätigende Kerl nach dem Vorbild der rauen, maskulären *frontier*-Männlichkeit sollte als Muster hierfür gelten.[13]

Roosevelts 'Zurück zum Naturburschen' kann man ohne Schwierigkeiten die biblische Figur der Judit gegenüberstellen, die entgegen der ihr zugeordneten 'natürlichen' Stellung als Witwe zur Heldin wird:

> Die alexandrinische Judittradition betont den Mut gerade einer Frau im Angesicht der tödlichen Bedrohung durch den Feind des Glaubens. Das griechische Wort für "Mut", ἀνδρεία, ist vom Wort "Mann" abgeleitet. Dementsprechend wird die Frau Judit, der diese Eigenschaft 'von Natur aus' nicht zukommt, eigens für ihre Tat – immer als Rettung des Volkes verstanden – gepriesen.[14]

So interessant wie die Betrachtung historischer Entscheidungssituationen ist auch die Analyse früherer und heutiger Mechanismen zur Bestrafung devianten Verhaltens, das aoft mehr über den Bestrafer als über die Tat aussagt, wie ein Blick in das tendenziell furchtsame 19. Jahrhundert zeigt:

> Tatsächlich wurde diese Frage [Feststellung der Identität] angesichts des Auftauchens und der zunehmenden Verbreitung des "Gewohnheitsverbrechers", einer Gestalt, von der die Bourgeoise des 19. Jahrhunderts nachgerade besessen war, jenen zum drängenden Problem, die sich als "Verteidiger der Gesellschaft" verstanden. Sowohl in Frankreich als auch in England wurden Gesetze erlassen, die fein säuberlich zwischen Ersttat, auf die eine Gefängnisstrafe stand, und Wiederholungstat, die mit der Deportation in die Kolonien geahndet wurde, unterschieden.[15]

Die Konkretheit der genannten Beispiele, die historische Nachvollziehbarkeit und die Erweiterung des Bildungshorizonts tragen hier gemeinsam zum Training der Reflexion eigener Entscheidungsfindung bei: Keine der genannten historischen Persönlichkeiten konnte den Ausgang ihrer der Entscheidung

13 Poole, R J, "Männer im Pelz: Entblößungen und Verhüllungen des natürlichen Körpers um 1900,"; in: ders.: Gefährliche Maskulinitäten, Männlichkeit und Subversion am Rande der Kulturen, Bielefeld 2012, 93–121, 99.

14 Siquans, A, "Die Macht der Rezeption, Eckpunkte der patristischen Juditinterpretation,", in: Fischer, I (Hg.), Macht – Gewalt – Krieg im Alten Testament. Gesellschaftliche Problematik und das Problem ihrer Repräsentation (QD 254), (Freiburg i. Br. 2013) 171–197, 191.

15 Agamben, G, Nacktheiten, Frankfurt/Main 2010, 85.

folgenden Handlungen bzw. der Handlungen, die andere aufgrund ihrer Entscheidungen setzten, kennen. Trotzdem haben sie Mut bewiesen. Und sind, das ist eine wichtige Erkenntnis, nicht automatisch zu Siegern und Helden geworden.

Welche weiteren Beispiele herangezogen werden (Kubakrise, Kindersoldaten seit den 1980er Jahren, Arabischer Frühling…), liegt dann zu einem Großteil bei den Lehrenden. Dabei liegt der Schwerpunkt auf der Darstellung der Fakten anhand möglichst ungefärbter Information. Deutung und Interpretation ist Aufgabe der Auszubildenden, denn 'wenn Lernende keine Möglichkeit haben, die Deutungen als Deutungen zu erkennen und zu überprüfen, ist ein Deutungskanon kontraproduktiv zur Schulung der Kritikfähigkeit, die in demokratischen Gesellschaften von basaler Qualität ist.'[16]

Eine zweite Quelle der Anschauung sind Kunstwerke und Filme, die allgemein bekannt sind und nun aus ethischer Perspektive analysiert werden. Dem Verständnis des Richtigen kommt dort die Angenehmheit der Unterhaltung zu Hilfe, wie auch der bekannte italienische Philosoph Umberto Eco in seiner Analyse von Texten des Thomas von Aquin ausführt:

> Schönes und Gutes im selben Gegenstand sind ein und dieselbe Realität, weil beide auf der Form beruhen…; während aber das Gute bewirkt, daß die Form Gegenstand des Begehrens, des Strebens nach Verwirklichung oder nach Besitz der als positiv beurteilten Form wird, setzt das Schöne die Form in Bezug zum reinen Erkennen. Schön sind die Dinge, die *visa placent. Visa* bedeutet hier nicht nur "gesehen", sondern "wahrgenommen", also in vollem Bewußtsein "perzipiert". Die *visio* ist eine *apprehensio*, ein Erkennen: Das Schöne ist *id cuius apprehensio placet*, das, dessen Erkennen Freude bereitet.[17]

Einzelne Gemälde und Statuen, die Soldaten als Helden oder als Verlierer darstellen, können für diesen Zweck genauso herangezogen werden wie Filmausschnitte oder Filme. Ein interessanter Zugang bietet sich zum Beispiel über einzelne Folgen der 6 Serien, die in Gene Roddenberrys Star Trek-Universum spielen. Dort wird sogar von den Protagnisten selbst oft das Wort ‚Ethik' gebraucht, um eine dramaturgische zugespitzte Entscheidungssituation zu beschreiben. Auch wenn die Handlung in eine hochtechnisierte und von

16 Albus, V., "Kanonbildungsprozesse im Philosophieunterricht – deskriptive, evaluative und präskiptive Betrachtungen"; in: Albus Vanessa (Hg.): Kanon II, Zeitschrift für Didaktik der Philosophie und Ethik, (2013) Jg. 35, 3–14, 8.

17 Eco, U., Kunst und Schönheit im Mittelalter, München 2011, 8. Auflage, 124.

Rohstoffknappheit befreite Zukunft verlegt ist, tragen doch alle dargestellten Konflikte mehr oder weniger deutlich die Züge ihrer irdischen Vorbilder, die von der Gegenwart der jeweiligen Produktion (seit 1962) bis zur – gewiss für Europäer gewöhnungsbedürftigen – Antikenrezeption geht.[18]

Abschluss

Der Weg berufsethischer Bildung an der österreichischen Heeresunteroffiziersakademie versucht vom Konkreten zum Theoretischen, von der Analyse (historischer oder fiktiver) Praxis zur Anregung der Reflexion eigenen Verhaltens zu gehen. Sie fragt daher zuerst nach dem Menschen, dann nach dem diesem Menschenbild gerechten Soldaten und zuletzt nach der optimalen Form, Menschen zu solchen Soldaten auszubilden. Dabei ist auch dieser Ausbildungsprozess regelmäßiger Reflexion und Anpassung unterworfen. Es gibt kein unveränderliches "Erfolgsmodell", sondern von Kurs zu Kurs werden Anregungen der Lernenden für die nächsten Teilnehmenden fruchtbar gemacht. Ziel sind verantwortungsvolle Kommandanten auf Gruppen- und Zugsebene, die nicht nur Entscheidungen treffen, sondern sie auch vor sich selbst und vor anderen nachvollziehbar begründen können.

18 Vgl. Wenskus, O., Umwege in die Vergangenheit. Star Trek und die griechisch-römische Antike, (Comparanda Literaturwissenschaftliche Studien zu Antike und Moderne Bd. 13), Innsbruck; Wien; Bozen 2009.

CHAPTER 8

Moral Judgement in War and Peacekeeping Operations: An Empirical Review

Miriam C. de Graaff

The mission of the Netherlands Armed Forces in Afghanistan included training the Afghan police and renovating their police stations by installing some basic safety measures. One of these measures included installing a munitions locker in the police station so that firearms, mines and explosives found in the police district could be stored securely. Imagine a situation in which Dutch personnel are carrying out a regular patrol mission, making contact with the local population and checking in on several of these police stations. Upon arrival at one of the police stations, the soldiers discover a woman who had been arrested earlier that day locked up in the munitions locker. The Afghan policemen inform the Dutch soldiers that, according to Afghan principles, the woman's honour is compromised if she is in a room with men other than her husband or other male relative. So, while waiting for her husband to arrive, her honour is protected by allowing her to wait in the munitions locker. For the Dutch personnel on site, this situation creates a dilemma: should safety concerns or sensitivity to cultural norms prevail?

This real-life example was described by a Dutch non-commissioned officer (NCO) in an interview session with the authors (2013) discussing dilemma situations during deployment. The NCO's narrative reflects the day-to-day challenges of servicemen during military operations. The scientific field that addresses such dilemmas in work contexts is that of business ethics, leaving ethics to a variety of scientists such as psychologists, sociologists, theologists and philosophers addressing ethical issues in work-contexts from their own perspectives. The domain of business ethics is commonly divided into two realms: that of normative ethics on the one side and that of empirical ethics on the other.[1] The normative realm focuses on organizational ethics, whereas the empirical realm addresses morality at a personal and individual level (also see the distinction made by Paine[2]). Within organizations and societies, organizational ethics

1 M.J. O'Fallon, & K.D. Butterfield, 'A review of the empirical ethical decision-making literature: 1996–2003' (2005) 59 *Journal of Business Ethics* 375.

2 L.S. Paine, 'Managing for organizational integrity' (1994) 72 *Harvard Business Review* 106/L.S. Paine, 'Moral thinking in management: An essential capability' (1996) 6 *Business Ethics Quarterly* 477.

 | DOI 10.1163/9789004312135_009

largely result in behavioural codes that guide individual actions. This field also addresses conceptual and contextual issues regarding putting ethics into practice. Research in this area deals with issues such as moral character building and training programs[3] and business ethos[4] and considers the legitimacy of the use of force.[5] Only a few scholarly papers addressed the effects of these training programs and behavioural codes on the soldiers' moral judgement. Studies that address such 'transfer' have their place in the empirical realm.[6] Research in the empirical realm – regarding individual personal morality – addresses individual behaviour by studying and explaining events in the past and by predicting individual behaviour in the future.[7] Research in this area focuses on issues such as individual ethical decision-making behaviour,[8] moral reasoning,[9] and moral disengagement or abusive behaviour.[10]

---

3 D.P. Baker, 'Making good better: A proposal for teaching ethics at the service academies' (2012) 11 (3) JME 208/E.H. Offstein, & R.L. Dufresne, 'Building strong ethics and promoting positive character development: The influence of HRM at the United States Military Academy at West Point' (2007) 46 *Human Resource Management* 95/S. Seiler, A. Fischer, & S.A. Voegtli, 'Developing moral decision-making competence: A quasi-experimental intervention study in the Swiss Armed Forces' (2011) 21 *Ethics & Behavior* 452/E. Wortel, & J. Bosch, 'Strengthening moral competence: A 'train the trainer' course on military ethics' (2011) 10 JME 17.

4 M.S. Frankel, (1989), 'Professional codes: Why, how, and with what impact?' (1989) 8 *Journal of business ethics* 109/P. Tripodi, (2006), 'Peacekeepers, moral autonomy and the use of force' (2006) 5 JME 214.

5 G. Reichberg, & H. Syse, 'Humanitarian Intervention: A Case of Offensive Force?' (2002) 33 (3) *Security Dialogue* 309.

6 For example: C.H. Warner, G.N. Appenzeller, A. Mobbs, J.R. Parker, C.M. Warner, T. Grieger, & C.W. Hoge, 'Effectiveness of battlefield-ethics training during combat deployment: A program assessment' (2011) 378 *Lancet* 915.

7 O'Fallon and Butterfield 2005, n3.

8 R.P. Bagozzi, L.E. Sekerka, V. Hill, & F. Sguera, 'The Role of Moral Values in Instigating Morally Responsible Decisions' (2013) 49 *The Journal of Applied Behavioral Science* 69/A.R. Blais, & M.M. Thompson, 'What Would I Do? Civilians' Ethical Decision Making in Response to Military Dilemmas' (2013) 23 *Ethics & Behavior* 237/C.A. Simmons, & J.R. Rycraft, 'Ethical challenges of military social workers serving in a combat zone' (2010) 55 *Social work* 9.

9 R. Linn, 'Hypothetical and actual moral reasoning of Israeli selective conscientious objectors during the war in Lebanon' (1989) 10 *Journal of Applied Developmental Psychology* 19.

10 K. Aquino, A. Reed, S. Thau, & D. Freeman, 'A grotesque and dark beauty: How moral identity and mechanisms of moral disengagement influence cognitive and emotional reactions to war' (2007) 43 *Journal of Experimental Social Psychology* 385/A. Bandura, 'Moral disengagement in the perpetration of inhumanities' (1999) 3 *Personality and Social Psychology Review* 193/A. Bandura, C. Barbaranelli, G.V. Caprara, & C. Pastorelli, C., 'Mechanisms of

Thus far, research within the military has focused largely on organizational ethical issues such as policy, education and behavioural codes.[11] Much less attention has been devoted to the role of intra-individual processes in moral judgement.[12] This is unfortunate, because soldiers are regularly confronted with conflicting values such as in the dilemma described in the opening example of this article. Although the military has traditionally dealt with problem solving on the basis of rules and hierarchy, morally challenging situations are difficult to deal with on the basis of rules, codes and principles due to their indeterminate nature.[13] We define morally challenging situations as situations in which an individual is confronted with an intrapersonal "clash" of values caused by interaction with others. Olsthoorn, Meijer and Verweij[14] argue that current military operations tend to focus on humanitarian goals, such as winning over the local population and establishing a stable environment. These specific goals restrict the use of force to a minimum, but can cause a dilemma-rich situation. "Civilian casualties are usually considered an unintended side effect of legitimate attacks on military goals".[15] Another dilemma is created by societies' contemporary viewpoint that military losses are unacceptable. In current military operations, military and civilian losses are unavoidable due to the risks present in the mission area. The question arises as to whether the commanders should focus on the safety of their personnel, or on achieving the military goals.[16] Those (societal) restrictions and the familiarity with their comrades is most likely the reason that soldiers value the lives of their comrades

moral disengagement in the exercise of moral agency' (1996) 71 *Journal of Personality and Social Psychology* 364/S.T. Hannah, J.M. Schaubroeck, A.C. Peng, R.G. Lord, L.K. Trevino, S.W.J. Kozlowski, B.J. Avolio, N. Dimotakis, & J. Doty, 'Joint Influences of Individual and Work Unit Abusive Supervision on Ethical Intentions and Behaviors: A Moderated Mediation Model' (2013) 98 *Journal of Applied Psychology* 579.

11 P.T. Bartone, 'Preventing prisoner abuse: Leadership lessons of Abu Ghraib' (2010) 20 *Ethics & Behavior* 161/R. Richardson, D. Verweij, & D. Winslow, 'Moral fitness for peace operations' (2004) 32 *Journal of Political and Military Sociology* 99/Seiler, Fischer & Voegtli 2011, n5/Tripodi 2006, n6/Wortel & Bosch 2011, n5.

12 For example: S. Nilsson, M. Sjöberg, K. Kallenberg, & G. Larsson, 'Moral stress in international humanitarian aid and rescue operations: A grounded theory study' (2011) 21 *Ethics & Behavior* 49.

13 E.H. Kramer, *Organizing doubt: grounded theory, army units and dealing with dynamic complexity* (Copenhagen: Business School Press 2007).

14 P. Olsthoorn, M. Meijer, & D. Verweij, 'Managing moral professionalism in military operations' in J. Soeters, P.C.V. Fenema & R. Beeres (Eds.), *Managing Military Organizations: Theory and Practice* (New York: Routledge 2010) 138.

15 Olsthoorn et al., 2010 p. 141; n16.

16 Olsthoorn et al., 2010; n16.

above those of the local population, even though this runs counter to the basic premise of most modern military interventions.[17] In military operations, the individual serviceman's competence in moral judgement is addressed, and this should be considered vital for today's military operations.[18] It therefore seems important to gain insight into the intra-individual processes surrounding moral judgement in a military context. The current study aims to provide a systematic overview of empirical studies conducted on moral judgement, focusing on the specific context of the military. Before discussing the methodology and outcomes of this search, we first define moral judgement conceptually and introduce three broad frameworks for how moral judgement can be approached.

Theoretical Background

Moral judgement has been defined in various ways by different authors. Occasionally, the term moral judgement is used interchangeably with the terms 'ethical decision-making' or 'moral reasoning'.[19] Some define moral judgement as the ability to recognize and assess the values, norms and interests that are at stake in a given situation.[20] Others define moral judgement as the evaluation of the rightness or wrongness of either the actions or the character of an individual.[21] As such, the individual is judged on the basis of a set of virtues held to be essential within a culture or subculture.[22] In this article, moral judgement refers to all intra-individual processes that contribute to the assessment of the cognitive, affective and behavioural reactions towards morally challenging situations.[23] This definition is the most comprehensive, since it includes both conscious and deliberate reasoning (e.g., information processing)

17 Olsthoorn et al., 2010; n216.

18 cf. Richardson et al., 2004; n13.

19 J.R. Detert, L.K. Treviño, & V.L. Sweitzer, 'Moral disengagement in ethical decision making: a study of antecedents and outcomes' (2008) 93 *Journal of Applied Psychology* 374/A. O'Kane, D. Fawcett, & R. Blackburn, 'Psychopathy and moral reasoning: Comparison of two classifications' (1996) 20 Personality and Individual Differences 505.

20 e.g., D. Verweij, K. Hofhuis, & J. Soeters, 'Moral judgement within the armed forces' (2007) 6 JME 19.

21 J. Haidt, 'The emotional dog and its rational tail: a social intuitionist approach to moral judgment' (2001) 108 *Psychological Review* 814.

22 Haidt, 2001; n23/D. Pizarro,'Nothing more than feelings? The role of emotions in moral judgment' (2000) 30 *Journal for the Theory of Social Behaviour* 355.

23 Kahneman & Sunstein 2005; n2.

as well as unconscious and unintentional processes (e.g., intuition and emotions). This is important to note, because moral judgement research is often outlined in fragments, focusing on a specific element in the judgement process such as cognitive processes. The fragmented elements in moral judgement research can be categorized in three main approaches: (1) the cognitive approach (also referred to in literature as the *'rationalist approach'*[24]), (2) the affective approach, or (3) the integrative approach, combining cognitive and affective elements into automatic or effortless sense-making processes.[25]

The cognitive approach claims that individuals use deliberate and extensive moral reasoning in order to respond to morally challenging situations. This approach revolves around an individual's cognitive sophistication. Within the cognitive approach, three streams stand out. The first explains individual responses to morally challenging situations by using normative theories from traditional philosophical ethics, meaning the individual's considerations are classified as explanations drawn from the major schools of philosophy: utilitarianism, deontology and virtue ethics.[26] The second stream proposes that it is not the philosophical theory that underpins the responses in moral reasoning, but the (1) individual's personal cognitive abilities (cf. Kohlberg's[27] stages of moral development), (2) individual difference moderators (such as moral identity, ego-strength, locus of control), and (3) situational moderators (such as organizational culture).[28] The third stream of the cognitive approach is based on the *'issue-contingency model'*, which calls attention to the specific characteristics (often referred to as 'moral intensity') of the ethical issue itself'[29]). Not all psychologists have accepted the premise that emotions should be banned from the field of moral judgement.[30] For example, Sigmund Freud

24 cf. S. Sonenshein, 'The role of construction, intuition, and justification in responding to ethical issues at work: The sensemaking-intuition model' (2007) 32 *Academy of Management Review* 1022.

25 J. Greene, & J. Haidt, 'How (and where) does moral judgment work?' (2002) 6 *TRENDS in Cognitive Sciences* 517/Kahneman & Sunstein 2005; n2/Sonenshein 2007; n26.

26 Sonenshein 2007; n26.

27 L. Kohlberg, *Essays on moral development. Vol. 1, The philosophy of moral development: moral stages and the idea of justice* (San Fransisco, CA: Harper & Row 1981).

28 Sonenshein 2007; n26.

29 S.A. Morris, & R.A. McDonald, 'The role of moral intensity in moral judgments: An empirical investigation' (1995) 14 *Journal of Business Ethics* 715/J.G. Paolillo, & S.J. Vitell, 'An empirical investigation of the influence of selected personal, organizational and moral intensity factors on ethical decision making' (2002) 35 Journal of Business Ethics 65.

30 Greene, & Haidt 2002; n27/C.E. Thiel, Z. Bagdasarov, L. Harkrider, J.F. Johnson, & M.D. Mumford, 'Leader ethical decision-making in organizations: Strategies for sensemaking' (2012) 107 *Journal of Business Ethics* 1.

(1856–1939) exploited emotions and intuition in his construction of the human psyche. According to Freud, the human psyche includes unconscious instincts and desires (Id), incorporation of societal values in personal moral judgement (Super-Ego), and a mediator between Id and Super-Ego (Ego). Intuition[31] and emotions[32] are quite prominent in today's moral psychological research on decision-making. This approach is referred to as the affective approach. Researchers in this work field believe that many of the decisions made in daily life are rapid, effortless and unconscious.[33] In contrast to (complex) deliberation, emotions are considered to be an intuitive and biologically based reaction that influences an individual's response to important events.[34] These feelings are referred to as affect-laden intuitions[35] or moral emotions.[36] Moral emotions are distinguished from general basic human emotions in terms of the 'third-party' aspect they enclose: they suddenly appear and immediately have an affective valence regarding good or bad in interpersonal interactions.[37]

When studying the decision-making process, using only the cognitive approach, the problem that individuals all make a unique construction of the situation at hand comes to the fore. Even though a situation is objectively the same, the solutions are different. On the other hand, when using the affective approach alone, only the emotional/intuitive reactions are addressed, although research shows that certain emotions promote cognitive operations such as information processing.[38] The debate concerning whether to use a cognitive or an affective approach seems to resolve itself in uniting the two perspectives into an integrative approach.[39] This approach is based on the assumption that – in case of a disruption of the 'expected state of the world', or when there is no obvious way to engage the world – it is not a matter of deciding what to do, but a

31 J. Haidt, 'The moral emotions' in R.J. Davidson, K.R. Scherer & H.H. Goldsmith (Eds.), *Handbook of affective sciences* (Oxford: Oxford University Press, 2003) 852.

32 J.J. Gross, & R.W. Levenson, 'Emotional suppression: physiology, self-report, and expressive behaviour' (1993) 64 *Journal of Personality and Social Psychology* 970/C.A. Hutcherson, & J.J. Gross, (2011), 'The moral emotions: A social – functionalist account of anger, disgust, and contempt' (2011) 100 *Journal of personality and social psychology* 719.

33 e.g., Greene & Haidt 2002; n32/Haidt 2003; n33.

34 Gross & Levenson 1993; n34.

35 cf. Greene & Haidt 2002; n32.

36 cf. Haidt 2003; n33/Hutcherson & Gross 2011; n34.

37 Greene & Haidt 2002; n32.

38 J.S. Lerner, & D. Keltner, 'Fear, anger, and risk' (2001) 81 *Journal of Personality and Social Psychology* 146/Thiel et al., 2012; n32.

39 Lerner & Keltner 2001; n40/Thiel et al., 2012; n32.

matter of interpretation.[40] A framework that offers a solution to the interpretation of challenging situations such as moral dilemmas is that of 'sense making'. Sense making is the retrospective activity an individual engages in in order to develop plausible explanations of what is happening in the current situation, so that the individual will be able to resume interrupted activity and stay in action.[41] This is related to the perspective that is referred to as *'affectual intuitionism'*, which considers ethical intuitions as cognitive moral emotions.[42] According to this theoretical context, emotions originate from a cognitive foundation. For example, cognitions regarding humaneness or equality experienced in a specific situation form a foundation for emotions such as sympathy or anger. In this perspective, emotions are necessary for making practical and rational decisions: emotions present a normative guide in moral judgements.[43]

In this review, we place an emphasis on revealing trends in moral judgement research in the military by using these approaches as a manner for categorization. Previous systematic reviews on moral judgement in other or more general contexts did not primarily focus on the different conceptual approaches in this field.[44] As such, this review complements existing insights in this field. Table 8.1 presents the operationalization of moral judgement according these categories.

Method

Search Strategy

For the purpose of this review, we applied a sensitive search strategy in order to identify relevant studies regarding moral judgement in the military context. We searched three electronic databases: Scopus, Web of Science and PsycINFO for relevant articles published between January 1985 and December 2013. The decision for using this time period was based on a broader review study by O'Fallon and Butterfield into ethical decision-making.[45] They signalled a significant increase in empirical studies starting in the mid-nineties following

40 Sonenshein 2007, n26/K.E. Weick, K.M. Sutcliffe, & D. Obstfeld, 'Organizing and the process of sensemaking' (2005) 16 *Organization Science* 409.

41 Weick et al., 2005; n42.

42 cf. Greene & Haidt 2002; n32/cf. S. Roeser, (2010), 'Intuitions, emotions and gut reactions in directions about risks: toward a different interpretation of neuroethics' (2010) 13 *Journal of Risk Research* 175.

43 Roeser 2010; n44.

44 e.g., O'Fallon & Butterfield 2005; n3.

45 O'Fallon & Butterfield 2005; n3.

TABLE 8.1 *Operationalization of moral judgement in research*

Framework for Moral Judgement		Operationalization
Approach	**Stream**	
Cognitive approach	Normative ethics & philosophy	Studies addressing, *inter alia:* values; virtues or utilitarianism
	Individual's personal cognitive abilities Individual difference moderators Situational moderators	Studies addressing, *inter alia*: moral development; moral identity; moral reasoning; leadership and training effects; organizational culture; coping strategies (disobedience)
	Issue contingency model	Studies addressing, *inter alia*: moral intensity appraisal
Affective approach	–	Studies addressing, *inter alia*: moral emotions; moral stress/ distress; intuition
Integrative approach	–	Studies addressing, *inter alia*: sense-making/interpretation; experience-based intuitions; integration of emotions and cognitions

the development of theoretical ethical models in the 1980s.[46] To ensure that all relevant studies regarding moral judgement in the military would be included in this review, we chose the time period from 1985 onwards.

We used the following search strategy: ('moral judgement' OR 'ethical decision making' OR 'moral dilemma' OR 'ethics' OR 'morality') AND ('military'). Limits were: 'peer reviewed journal', 'publication not older than 1985' 'language: English'. We also examined the reference lists of the identified publications.

46 e.g., T.M. Jones, 'Ethical decision making by individuals in organizations: An issue-contingent model' (1991) 16 *Acadamy of Management Review* 366/e.g., J.R. Rest, & R. Barnett, *Moral development: Advances in theory and research* (New York: Praeger 1986)/L.K. Trevino, 'Ethical decision making in organizations: A person-situation interactionist model' (1986) 11 *Academy of management Review* 601/O'Fallon & Butterfield 2005; n3.

Our search strategy generated in total 820 publications in Scopus, 362 in Web of Science and 469 in PsycINFO.

Selection of Studies

The articles identified by the search were critically assessed based on the following inclusion criteria: first, the publication had to describe the empirical measurement of (elements of) moral judgement. Thus, non-empirical publications were excluded. Second, the publication's measurement of moral judgement had to be conducted in a military sample. Using these restrictions, the first author evaluated the titles and abstracts of the publications, which limited our search further to 72 publications. Thereafter, the first two authors evaluated the full content of the articles for inclusion in this review, leaving 33 publications for further in-depth analysis. Reasons for not including the remaining publications were that they did not contain any empirical data was collected or the sample used was not military. The first author reviewed all 33 studies for further analysis, while a second reviewer selected 50% of the publications at random and appraised them independently. There were no disagreements on whether to include or exclude any of these 33 publications.

Results

Thirty-three references were classified as relevant with respect to moral judgement in a military context. Table 8.3 provides a summary of these studies in terms of the conceptual framework chosen, the methodology and the main findings of the study.

Conceptual Issues

Of the three approaches, the majority of the studies (N = 28) used the cognitive approach to address moral judgement. Within this subsample, six studies placed the respondents' reasoning central when they were asked to describe the type of moral dilemmas they encountered[47] or the values that were at stake.[48] These studies correspond with the first stream in the cognitive

47 e.g., Simmons & Rycraft 2010; n10.

48 Bagozzi et al., 2013; n10.

approach, focusing on traditional schools of philosophy (N = 6). These studies show, for example, that social workers encounter specific moral dilemmas during deployment due to conflicting clinical and military values.[49] Other studies focused on personal values that are challenged during deployment[50] and addressed the organisation's responsibility in order to guide and assist individual servicemen in their dilemmas.[51] In addition, mechanisms for reflection upon and evaluating personal deployment experiences showed that a sense of 'duty' (e.g., patriotic or professional duty) is most central and salient as a motive for servicemen.[52]

The second stream within the cognitive approach contains three subcategories. Four studies were labelled in the first category since they focused on individual's personal cognitive abilities, mostly by testing (Kohlberg's) stages of moral development[53] (N = 4). The higher the serviceman's moral development, the more consistent the serviceman is in actual moral behaviour.[54] Nevertheless, some scholars claim that testing an individual's morality with such scales is arguable when it comes to predicting future behaviour by means of the scores.[55] Four studies fitted the second subcategory and addressed individual difference moderators such as moral identity and moral courage[56] (N = 4). These studies show that ethical training improves the willingness to report

---

49 T.B. Jeffrey, R.J. Rankin, & L.K. Jeffrey, 'In service of two masters: The ethical-legal dilemma faced by military psychologists' (1992) 23 *Professional Psychology: Research and Practice* 91/Simmons & Rycraft 2010; n10.

50 Bagozzi et al., 2013; n10/J. Benham Rennick, 'Canadian values and military operations in the twenty-first century' (2012) 39 *Armed Forces & Society* 511.

51 Benham Rennick 2012; n52.

52 R.P. Bagozzi, L.E. Sekerka, & V. Hill, 'Hierarchical motive structures and their role in moral choices' (2009) 90 *Journal of Business Ethics* 461./K.J. Burnell, N. Boyce, & N. Hunt, 'A good war? Exploring British veterans' moral evaluation of deployment' (2011) 25 *Journal of Anxiety Disorders* 36.

53 Linn 1989; n11/R. Linn, 'Moral judgment in extreme social contexts: Soldiers who refuse to fight and physicians who strike?' (1988) 18 *Journal of Applied Social Psychology* 1149/ Verweij et al., 2007; n22/R.D. White, 'Are women more ethical? Recent findings on the effects of gender upon moral development' (1999) 9 *Journal of Public Administration Research and Theory* 459.

54 Linn 1988; Linn 1989; n55; n11.

55 e.g., Verweij et al., 2007; n22.

56 W.A. Gouveia, 'An analysis of moral dissent: An army officer's public protest of the Vietnam war' (2004) 3 JME 53/L.E. Sekerka, R.P. Bagozzi, & R. Charnigo, 'Facing ethical challenges in the workplace: Conceptualizing and measuring professional moral courage' (2009) 89 *Journal of Business Ethics* 565.

misconduct[57] and that moral disobedience and moral dissent are influenced by a sense of loyalty towards society.[58] Furthermore, servicemen tend to cope with moral dilemmas by using rational or cognitive strategies.[59] Eight studies focused on situational moderators such as organisational culture[60] and leadership[61] and were labelled as the third subcategory (N = 8). Two of these studies focused on both situational as well as individual difference moderators,[62] and another study combined situational moderators with individual's personal cognitive abilities.[63] These studies suggest leadership (i.e. role models and examples) and hierarchy have a great influence on individual moral behaviour.[64] For example, Hannah et al., (2013)[65] showed that there is a relationship between the presence of abusive supervision and higher rates of unethical acts towards the local population.

The third stream of the cognitive approach focuses on moral intensity; it considers the characteristics of the situation as direct influencers of moral judgement. Only two studies addressed this issue.[66] Seiler et al., (2011)[67] indicate that high moral ability is used in high moral intensity. Therefore, they argue, it is not only individual competencies, but also the context that is

57 Warner et al., 2011; n8.

58 Gouveia 2004; n57/R. Linn, 'Soldiers with conscience never die – They are just ignored by their society. Moral disobedience in the Israel defense forces' (2002) 1 JME 57.

59 T. Liebes, & S. Blum-Kulka, 'Managing a moral dilemma: Isreali soldiers in the intifada' (1994) 21 *Armed Forces & Society* 45.

60 e.g., M.A. Reger, J.R. Etherage, G.M. Reger, & G.A. Gahm, 'Civilian psychologists in an army culture: The ethical challenge of cultural competence' (2008) 20 *Military Psychology* 21.

61 Bartone 2010; n13/Hannah et al., 2013; n12.

62 O.K. Olsen, J. Eid, & B.H. Johnsen, 'Moral behaviour and transformational leadership in Norwegian naval cadets' (2006) 18 *Military Psychology* 37/Y.M. Yu, 'Between an Example and a Precept, which has Greater Importance? A Comparison of the Channels of Socialization in Military Ethics' (2013) 23 *Ethics & Behavior* 341.

63 K.R. Williams, (2010), 'An assessment of moral and character education in initial entry training (IET)' (2010) 9 JME 41.

64 Bartone 2010; n13/S.T. Hannah, B.J. Avolio, & F.O. Walumbwa, F.O. 'Relationships between authentic leadership, moral courage, and ethical and pro-social behaviors' (2011) 21 *Business Ethics Quarterly* 555/Yu 2013; n63/Williams 2010; n64/Olsen et al., 2006; 63/ Hannah et al., 2013; n12/J.M. Schaubroeck, S.T. Hannah, B.J. Avolio, S.W.J. Kozlowski, R.G. Lord, L.K. Treviño, N. Dimotakis, & A.C. Peng, 'Embedding ethical leadership within and across organization levels' (2012) 55 *Academy of Management Journal* 1053.

65 Hannah et al., 2013; n12.

66 S.H. Lincoln, & E.K. Holmes, 'The psychology of making ethical decisions: What affects the decision?' (2010) 7 *Psychological Services* 57/Seiler et al., 2011; n5.

67 Seiler et al., 2011; n5.

important in ethical decision-making.[68] Lincoln and Holmes[69] highlighted that moral intensity is an important moderator in moral judgement as well. Furthermore, the magnitude of the consequences and social consensus are considered key features in this process.[70]

Two studies used the affective approach.[71] Nilson et al.[72] focussed on feelings of stress and frustration in ethical decision-making and found four instigators of moral stress: insufficiency, powerlessness, meaninglessness and frustration. Fry et al.[73] also focused on feelings of stress, showing there are several dimensions to be distinguished in relation with military moral challenges (i.e. initial moral distress and reactive moral stress).

Three studies used the integrative approach.[74] Moral potency (i.e. moral ownership, moral courage and moral efficacy) is shown to increase after exposure to incidents; it influences moral behaviour by means of intentions,[75] while experience-based intuitions translate moral judgement into intuitive coping.[76] Furthermore, results show that sleep-deprivation impairs the ability to integrate emotion and cognition in moral judgement, causing an increase in response time in solving moral dilemmas.[77]

Methodological Issues

Research design and instrumental issues. Both qualitative (N = 16) and quantitative (N = 17) research methods were used in the studies of moral judgement. Of the qualitative studies, six were conducted as case studies and focused on a

68 Seiler et al., 2011; n5.

69 Lincoln & Holmes 2010; n68.

70 Lincoln & Holmes 2010; n68.

71 S.T. Fry, R.M. Harvey, A.C. Hurley, & B.J. Foley, 'Development of a model of moral distress in military nursing' (2002) 9 *Nursing Ethics* 373/Nilsson et al., 2011; n14.

72 Nilsson et al., 2011; n14.

73 Fry et al., 2002; n73.

74 J.W. Eriksen, 'Should soldiers think before they shoot?' (2010) 9 JME 195/S.T. Hannah, & B.J. Avolio, 'Moral potency: Building the capacity for character-based leadership' (2010) 62 *Consulting Psychology Journal: Practice and Research* 291/W.D.S. Killgore, D.B. Killgore, L.M. Day, C. Li, G.H. Kamimori & T.J. Balkin, 'The effects of 53 hours of sleep deprivation on moral judgment' (2007) 30 *SLEEP* 345.

75 Hannah & Avolio 2010; n76.

76 Erikson 2010; n76.

77 Killgore et al., 2007; n76.

single event or incident.[78] The majority of qualitative studies (N = 8) used interviews to examine moral judgement. The majority of the quantitative studies (N = 12) used surveys (*self-reports*). Five studies used an experimental design, such as peer-ratings[79] or a pre-post test design (N = 4). In these pre-post test design studies, respondents were asked to fill out surveys before and after training in ethical decision-making.[80] Other pre-post test design studies tested moral judgement before and after sleep deprivation.[81] In one study, qualitative and quantitative research methods were combined, using a survey and focus groups for matched-pairs.[82] This study showed that servicemen are inclined to rule-based judgement, but when no rules are available, their decisions are based on personal benefit.[83]

Population. See Table 8.3 for a complete overview of the number of studies conducted in different countries around the world and the professional background of the respondents. Table 8.2 shows that the samples of the studies were diverse: a first subsample (N = 9) consisted entirely of military leaders, i.e. officers, or officer-cadets. Others focused solely on military personnel with specific tasks in social, psychological or medical combat support, i.e. military psychologists/military social workers/military chaplains (N = 5), military reserve personnel (N = 3), troops (N = 1), or veterans (N = 1). In eight studies, all ranks participated (i.e. officers, as well as NCOs and troops). In six studies, the ranks and professional background of the participants were not specified. Most of the studies were conducted within the U.S. armed forces (N = 20) or within European armed forces (N = 7).

Contextual Issues

Fifteen studies addressed moral judgement in relation to military deployment or combat situations (N = 15). The remaining studies (N = 18) addressed moral judgement processes in non-combat situations, such as in educational or training settings. The case studies in particular addressed moral judgement in the 'battlefield theatre', because they concentrated on incidents (e.g., Abu Ghraib

78 e.g., Bartone 2010; n13/e.g., Gouveia 2004; n58.

79 e.g., Hannah et al., 2011; n65.

80 Seiler et al., 2011; n5/Warner et al., 2011; n8.

81 Killgore et al., 2007; n75/O.K. Olsen, S. Pallesen, & J. Eid, 'The impact of partial sleep deprivation on moral reasoning in military officers' (2010) 33 *SLEEP* 1086.

82 Williams 2010; n65.

83 Williams 2010; n65.

TABLE 8.2 *Background of the respondents in studies of moral judgement conducted around the world*

Cultural background	United States	Canada	United Kingdom
Professional Background			
Military officers/officer cadets	4		
Military social workers/nurses/psychologists/chaplains	5		
Reserve soldiers			
Troops	3		
Infantry	1[b]		
Coast Guard	1[b]		
Military personnel background unspecified	3[c]	1	
All ranks	3		
Veterans			1
Total	20	1	1

[a] In one of these studies both unspecified active servicemen as well as reserve soldiers participated.
[b] In these studies all ranks of the specific Arms of Service participated.
[c] Of these studies, two used a case-study design.

The Netherlands	Norway	Switzerland	Sweden	Israel	Taiwan
1	2	1	1		1
				3[a]	
				1	
	1				
1	3	1	1	4	1

prison abuse[84]). Moreover, some studies asked the servicemen to reflect upon and evaluate their deployment experiences.[85] Two studies were conducted during military deployment.[86] These studies focused on the display of moral courage and the occurrence of unethical acts during military operations and deployment.

Discussion

Despite the fact that ethics have received growing attention in military handbooks, training and practice, there seems to be a paucity of empirically based research in the military regarding servicemen's moral judgement. This first systematic review revealed that a total of 31 papers between 1985 and 2013 addressed intra-individual processes concerning moral judgement in the military. A factor that might contribute to this limited number of relevant papers is that research into this population is usually considered difficult. The military is an in-group oriented society[87] and it is difficult for researchers to gain access to the military population or to get them to speak freely about themselves and their actions, also because of a feeling that civilians would not understand their experiences anyway. In addition, military personnel may be reluctant to share their experiences with outsiders, not just because they are outsiders, but also because they are taught not to share information with others. Therefore, it is possible there are more, maybe classified, studies conducted.

With respect to peer-reviewed papers, our search reveals that, by far, most studies departed from the cognitive approach. This is understandable; historically, that approach has been used most frequently since the 1950s.[88] In line with developments within the broader psychological literature, which only recently began to address the link between emotions and moral judgement, both the affective approach and the integrative approach are less highlighted. An increase in empirical research in this field can be discerned[89] since the

84 Bartone 2010; n13.

85 e.g., Burnell et al., 2011; n54.

86 Hannah et al., 2013; n12/Hannah & Avolio 2010; n76.

87 cf. J. Soeters, *Geweld en conflict, het ontstaan en verloop van burgeroorlogen, etnische strijd en terrorisme* (Amsterdam: Boom 2004).

88 cf. Greene & Haidt 2002; n27.

89 cf. Haidt 2003; n33/P. Rozin, L. Lowery, S. Imada, & J. Haidt, 'The CAD triad hypothesis: a mapping between three moral emotions (contempt, anger, disgust) and three moral codes (community, autonomy, divinity)' (1999) 76 *Journal of Personality and Social Psychology* 574.

1990s. Although these trends are in line with developments in the broader field, it is also well acknowledged that the military is an organisation that usually pays much attention to risk analyses, facts and checklists.[90] Problems are tackled using "[…] true and fixed structure[s] that can be revealed by analysis".[91] Therefore, emotions and intuitions traditionally receive less attention. At the same time, we observe a welcome increase in attention for emotion in the broader military research literature.[92] This is also important because of the high levels of stress as well as the intensity of the operational context in which servicemen operate during deployment, arguably evoking strong emotions.[93] A first direction for future research is therefore to further intensify the attention for the role of emotions in moral judgement notions. Due to the masculine organisational culture in military organisations, however, – in which emotions are considered unprofessional – it may be challenging to study emotions among active military personnel. Therefore, we suggest providing room for emotions in operational tasks (such as in debriefing-procedures) and in training programs for all servicemen, to ensure that emotions not remain unspoken.

A second observation is that the majority of the studies address moral judgement processes in non-combat settings. It can be argued that moral judgement is most crucial in the theatre of war, however.[94] Granted, some studies address moral judgement in the 'war zone' by means of the servicemen's personal reflection and evaluation of their deployment experiences.[95] Others focus on specific incidents (e.g., Abu Ghraib prison abuse[96]). A limitation of these

90 M.C. De Graaff, & M.J. Van Gils, 'Military Professionalism, an organizational challenge by itself' in J. Stouffer & D. Lindsay (Eds.), *Threats to military professionalism, international perspectives* (Kingston: Canadian Defence Academy Press 2012) 57.

91 Kramer 2007, p. 19; n15.

92 e.g., M. Andres, & N. Rietveld, 'It's not over till it's over' in R. Beeres, J. van der Meulen, J. Soeters, A. Vogelaar (Eds), *Mission Uruzgan Collaborating in multiple coalitions for Afghanistan* (Amsterdam: Pallas Publications 2012) 295/I.M. Engelhard, B.O. Olatunji, & P.J. de Jong, 'Disgust and the development of posttraumatic stress among soldiers deployed to Afghanistan' (2011) 25 *Journal of anxiety disorders* 58/L. Weibull, *Emotion matters. Emotion management in Swedish Peace Support Operations* (Doctoral Dissertation, Karlstad: University Studies 2012).

93 cf. B.T. Litz, W.E. Schlenger, F.W. Weathers, J.M. Caddell, J.A. Fairbank, & L.M. LaVange, 'Predictors of emotional numbing in posttraumatic stress disorder' (1997) 10 *Journal of Traumatic Stress* 607.

94 cf. Richardson et al., 2004; n13.

95 e.g., Burnell et al., 2011; n54.

96 see: Bartone 2010, n13.

studies is that they are susceptible to hindsight bias and framing,[97] since the events have taken place in the past. Therefore, the question is whether these studies can give reliable insights in the servicemen's moral judgement in daily life during deployment. Furthermore, most studies used self-reports as a research methodology (i.e. by means of surveys). In self-reports, researchers rely on the respondents' willingness and ability to communicate about their feelings, thoughts etc.[98] However, self-reports have certain limitations.[99] Specifically, research suggests that the use of self-reports and commonly used Likert scales for assessing responses in relation to ethical issues may be problematic for a number of reasons.[100] This relates to the way these items are usually framed, with social desirability issues, and with the impact of social presence, suggesting that people are more lenient in judging their own behaviour, thoughts and wrongdoings than those of others.[101] Also, the question arises of whether 'conventional' methods, such as self-reports and surveys, are appropriate when the conceptual framework shifts from the cognitive approach towards the affective or integrative approach. Therefore, a second focus point of attention for future research is to develop alternative research paradigms, most notably focusing on real-time psychological processes and behaviours in actual incidents.

A third observation is related to the research populations. The studies focus on different categories of servicemen, such as leaders or social workers. Groups of respondents were rather homogenous, in both cultural and professional background. Due to differences in training, responsibility or professional objectives (such as the difference between an infantryman and a medic), there may be group-based differences in moral judgement. We suggest that research should be conducted in a diversity of branches of service (i.e., air force, marine corps, army, military police and navy) and rank (e.g., officers, non-commissioned officers and troops).

Moreover, the studies that have been conducted until now focus mainly on Western cultures (i.e. Western Europe, U.S. and Canada), with other cultures receiving less attention. Within these Western cultures, studies conducted

---

97 P.M. Podsakoff, & D.W. Organ, 'Self-reports in organizational research: Problems and prospects' (1986) 12 *Journal of Management* 531.

98 cf. N. Schwarz, 'Self-reports: how the questions shape the answers' (1999) 54 *American Psychologist* 93.

99 see Podsakoff & Organ 1986, for an overview; n99.

100 cf. K. Janhunen, 'A comparison of Likert-type rating and visually-aided rating in a simple moral judgment experiment' (2012) 46 *Quality & Quantity* 1471.

101 Janhunen 2012; n102.

in the U.S. tend to dominate the field. Nevertheless, extrapolating results from U.S. military personnel onto other Western countries such as France, Norway or the Netherlands, for example, would be difficult due to the cultural differences between these countries.[102] We suggest that research should be conducted in a variety of cultures, including both Western and non-Western cultures, in order to gain insights that are relevant in a larger context. Cross-cultural studies would also give insights into moral judgement in relation to cultural background. After all, an individual's cultural background is of great influence in what individuals consider moral and immoral, and in forming their moral identity and moral foundations.[103]

In terms of research content, this systematic review shows that moral judgement research has addressed themes such as moral reasoning, moral courage and moral development of military personnel, and these are well documented and studied. Also, certain dilemma types are distinguished, particularly confidentiality vs. loyalty issues and duty vs. personal sense of justice issues. Furthermore, the collection of works shows that leadership, sleep-deprivation and ethical-decision making training are shown to influence moral judgement in individual servicemen. However, there seems to be a dearth of work focusing on how servicemen make sense of their personal moral dilemmas as well as their behavioural reactions in the mission area. Issues such as moral intensity of the situation and individual (moral) emotions do receive attention, but to a very limited degree. Also, as far as we know, no empirical studies into the effect of military deployment on moral identity or moral disengagement have been conducted.

Practical Considerations

In addition to the scientific considerations described in the sections above, we believe it to be relevant to note some practical considerations that may be drawn from this overview regarding the studies conducted. After all, military ethics were developed to be of service for the military professionals who are supposed to carry out tasks in challenging and high-stake situations.[104] The importance of moral judgement in the military is undisputed. Nevertheless, it

102 G.H. Hofstede, *Culture's consequences: Comparing values, behaviors, institutions and organizations across nations* (Thousand Oaks: Sage 2001).

103 J. Haidt, J. Graham, & C. Joseph, 'Above and below left-right: Ideological narratives and moral foundations' (2009) 20 *Psychological Inquiry* 110.

104 cf. M.L. Cook, & H. Syse, 'What Should We Mean by 'Military Ethics'?' (2010) 9 (2) JME 119.

is not uncommon for servicemen to question whether ethics is a field worth considering in the military arguing that it is something for the armchair philosopher, but not at all useful for the 'boots on the ground'.[105] This may be caused by the fact that indeed few answers are available for the servicemen with practical questions. Where organisations like financial banking institutions, universities and medical centres have 'ethical committees' that help individuals with their doubts and dilemmas regarding their profession, such committees seem unavailable in the military. After all, different organisations are available to assist servicemen to cope with difficult situations (such as mental health departments and chaplains services). There is also a legal department available (even during military operations). Practical ethical guidance for 'small questions' is unavailable, however. The ethical committees that do exist concentrate primarily on resolution of incidents.

Many defence organisations rely on the use of Codes of Conduct and (legal) rules instead. Although servicemen tend to use rule-based judgement[106] the effects of having a Code of Conduct remain vague.[107] After all, Verweij et al.[108] showed that agreement with the content of the Code of Conduct influences moral judgement, whereas simply knowing its content does not. Also, moral reasoning (knowing what the right thing to do might be) and actual moral behaviour is not necessarily consistent under different circumstances.[109] Therefore, it seems insufficient for the organisation to trust that when a Code of Conduct is published all employees will respond with morally responsible behaviour. Or, as Verweij[110] states: "For it is obvious that a definition of responsibility is by no means a guarantee for actual morally responsible behaviour [...]". Thus, transference from the Code of Conduct to for example ethical (dilemma) training and moral character building seems advisable. Focusing solely on strengthening the moral character of the individual serviceman is not enough to ensure morally responsible behaviour, however. After all, the organisational culture, group dynamical processes and leadership behaviours

105 cf. M.C. De Graaff, & C.E.M. Van den Berg, 'Moral Professionalism within the Royal Netherlands Armed Forces' in J. Stouffer & S. Seiler (Eds.), *Military ethics, international perspectives* (Kingston: Canadian Defence Academy Press 2010) 1.

106 cf. Williams 2010; n65.

107 cf. De Graaff & Van den Berg 2010; n107.

108 Verweij et al., 2007; n22.

109 cf. J.T. Gire, & T.D. Williams, 'Dissonance and the honor system: Extending the severity of threat phenomenon' (2007) 147 *The Journal of Social Psychology* 501.

110 Verweij 2013, p. 26; D.E.M. Verweij, 'Responsibility as the 'Ability to Respond' Adequately' in H. Amersfoort, R. Moelker, & J. Soeters (Eds.), *Moral Responsibility & Military Effectiveness* (Den Haag: Asser Press 2013) 11.

are shown to influence the individual's behaviour as well.[111] Moreover, situational factors such as the intensity of the situation at hand should not be overlooked.[112] In adequate moral judgement, a balance is found between the perspective of the individual, the context and the organisation.[113] Notably, teaching morally responsible behaviour in an adequate way, within the military, will have to start by acknowledging that 'bad apples' may not be intrinsically bad; they may come to be because of 'bad barrels'. Zimbardo[114] used the metaphor of 'bad apple – bad barrel' in relation with the Abu Ghraib Prison incident in Iraq in which U.S. soldiers violated prisoners' human rights and abused Iraqi prisoners. Zimbardo[115] suggests that organisational and situational circumstances contributed to individuals behaving in this way. According to this presumption, the circumstances were crucial factors in this incident.

To conclude, in current military operations abroad, interactions with local populations and allied forces are more common than ever.[116] Consequently, morally challenging situations are inevitable due to new ways of operating.[117] It is our hope that this review will stimulate additional research in this discipline, as well as inspire others to conduct similar research in a wide range of high-stakes situations such as, for example, situations faced by law enforcement and humanitarian aid workers.

111 cf. M.P. Cunha, A. Rego, & S.R. Clegg, 'Obedience and evil: From Milgram and Kampuchea to normal organizations' (2010) 97 *Journal of Business Ethics* 291.

112 cf. P. Zimbardo, *The Lucifer effect: Understanding how good people turn evil* (New York: ME Sharpe 2007).

113 cf. Verweij 2013; n 112.

114 Zimbardo 2007; n114.

115 Zimbardo 2007; n114.

116 R. Moelker, 'The Genesis of the "Dutch Approach" to Asymmetric Conflicts Operations in Uruzgan and the "Softly, Softly" Manner of Approaching the Taleban' (2013) 40 *Armed Forces & Society* 96.

117 cf. Richardson et al., 2004; n13.

TABLE 8.3 *Moral judgment research conducted in military organizations*

Cognitive approach: Stream one – foundation in normative ethics and philosophy				
Authors	**Journal; year**	**Operationalization of moral judgement**	**Sample (N)**	**Rank; cultural background**
Bagozzi, Sekerka, Hill & Sguera	The Journal of Applied Behavioural Science; 2013	Moral values in ethical decision-making (EDM)	N = 289	Military officers; United States
Benham Rennick	Armed Forces and Society; 2013	Values	N = 32	Military Personnel; Canada
Burnell, Boyce & Hunt	Journal of Anxiety Disorders; 2011	Moral evaluation of deployment experiences	N = 30	Veterans of all ranks; United Kingdom
Simmons & Rycraft	Social Work; 2010	Ethical challenges and EDM in a combat zone	N = 24	Military social workers; United States
Bagozzi, Sekerka & Hill	Journal of Business Ethics; 2009	Moral motives in Ethical Decision Making (EDM)	N = 101	Military officers; United States

Research design	Findings regarding moral judgement
Qualitative (laddering procedure)	In this study, values that are prominent in EDM are addressed. The results show that 'retribution' was mentioned most; least mentioned was 'perspective-taking'. The value 'retribution' was also found to be the most central. Either directly or indirectly, it was linked to all other values. The authors state that this value might function as an organizing principle and serve to activate or resonate with other values in an emotive network.
Qualitative (interviews and informal discussions)	This study focuses on the soldiers' values that are frustrated during deployment. The author argues that religious resources (such as chaplains) can help any soldier – regardless of his background – to cope with these shattered beliefs. The author states that moral anomie will develop in the absence of such guidance. That leads to mental stress and potential harm doing. Moreover, due to increasingly religiously heterogeneous social structures, organizational values must be clearly named, defined and enforced.
Qualitative (interviews)	This study shows that the majority of servicemen use three mechanisms to evaluate the morality of their deployment experience: a. patriotic justification, b. altruistic justification and c. professional justification.
Qualitative (open-ended questions in survey)	The results show that military social workers make more use of clinical judgement than moral reasoning. Four clusters were distinguished in types of dilemmas that were encountered by social workers during deployment: (1) confidentiality and privacy issues, (2) conflicts with commanders, (3) relationships and boundary issues, (4) diagnosis and treatment issues. Respondents with no ethical dilemmas also took part.
Qualitative (interviews)	This study shows that an important motive for acting upon a work-related ethical dilemma was 'self-interest'. 'The golden rule' and 'family' were the motives mentioned least. Research into the linkages

TABLE 8.3 *Moral judgment research conducted in military organizations* (cont.)

Cognitive approach: Stream one – foundation in normative ethics and philosophy				
Authors	**Journal; year**	**Operationalization of moral judgement**	**Sample (N)**	**Rank; cultural background**
Jeffrey, Rankin & Jeffrey	Professional Psychology: Research and Practice; 1992	Ethical-legal dilemmas	N = 2	Military psychologists; United States

Cognitive Approach: Stream two – individual personal cognitive abilities				
Authors	**Journal; year**	**Operationalization of moral judgement**	**Sample (N)**	**Rank; cultural background**
Verweij, Hofhuis & Soeters	Journal of Military Ethics; 2007	Moral reasoning, ethical awareness	N = 400	Officer cadets and officers in academy training (N = 322) compared with university students (N = 78); The Netherlands
White	Journal of Public Administration Research and Theory; 1999	Moral development of U.S. Coast Guard members	N = 299	Coast Guard all ranks; United States

Research design	Findings regarding moral judgement
	between motives showed that the hierarchy of motives goes from concrete (e.g.: 'empathy') to abstract (e.g.: 'justice'). 'Duty' was found to be the most central and salient motive of all.
Qualitative (Case study)	This study addresses the dilemma of patient-confidentiality that military psychologists may face. In addition, the consequences of their decisions in terms of accountability and legal issues from both the organization as well as from the psychological professional association are discussed. Guidelines for working-procedures/protocols are proposed.

Research design	Findings regarding moral judgement
Quantitative (survey)	This study shows that civilian dilemmas are solved using arguments from Kohlberg's moral development stages phase 5 and 6. Civilian students and first-year officer cadets scored lower in solving military problems due to unfamiliarity with the tasks and context presented. Knowledge of the Code of Conduct does not influence moral judgement, however agreement with the Code of Conduct does. When servicemen agree with the Code of Conduct they are more likely to stick to any given rules even if people die, than to bend them in order to save lives.
Quantitative (survey)	The results of this study show that female U.S. coast guard members score significantly higher in moral development than their male colleagues. Male coastguard members score significantly lower than average adults in the general population. No significant effect of age and education was found.

TABLE 8.3 *Moral judgment research conducted in military organizations* (cont.)

Cognitive approach: Stream two – individual personal cognitive abilities

Authors	Journal; year	Operationalization of moral judgement	Sample (N)	Rank; cultural background
Linn	Journal of Applied Developmental Psychology; 1989	Consistency between hypothetical and actual moral reasoning	N = 36	Reserve soldiers all ranks; Israel
Linn	Journal of Applied Social Psychology; 1988	Moral reasoning in extreme contexts	N = 86	Reserve soldiers all ranks (N = 36) compared with physicians (N = 50); Israel

Cognitive Approach: Stream two – individual difference moderators

Authors	Journal; year	Operationalization of moral judgement	Sample (N)	Rank; cultural background
Warner, Appenzeller, Mobbs, Parker, Warner, Grieger & Hoge	The Lancet; 2011	Ethical attitudes in relation to training in battlefield ethics	N = 397	Infantry, combat unit[c] United States
Sekerka, Bagozzi & Charnigo	Journal of Business Ethics; 2009	Moral courage	N = 199	Military officers; United States

Research design	Findings regarding moral judgement
Qualitative (interviews)	The consistency between the hypothetical and the actual moral reasoning of Israeli reserve soldiers who refused to perform their military services in Lebanon during the war, claiming that this service would violate their moral convictions, turned out to be significant across Kohlberg's stages of moral development.
Qualitative (interviews)	The results of this study show that soldiers who refuse to serve show consistency between their moral competence (reasoning) and their actual moral behaviour in real life situations. Also, a significant difference between the soldiers and physicians on strike was found: military personnel proved higher in moral development and more consistent in their behaviour. Important factors that positively influenced the soldier's objection to serve were: (a) the courage to act alone, (b) detachment – since, being reservists, it was not their profession they were refusing to carry out, (c) movement – knowing that, although alone in their unit, more soldiers were refusing to serve.

Research design	Findings regarding moral judgement
Quasi experimental (pre-post design in surveys)	The results show that training in battlefield ethics improves the willingness to report misconduct and lowers the rate of unethical conduct by the individual servicemen.
Quantitative (survey)	This study used a military sample to validate their five-dimensional scale for moral courage. The five dimensions are moral agency, multiple values, endurance of threats, going beyond compliance and moral goals. This study provides supporting evidence for the existence of the five dimensions of moral courage.

TABLE 8.3 *Moral judgment research conducted in military organizations* (cont.)

Cognitive approach: Stream two – individual difference moderators

Authors	Journal; year	Operationalization of moral judgement	Sample (N)	Rank; cultural background
Gouveia	Journal of Military Ethics; 2004	Moral judgement in case of moral dissent	N = 1	Military officer; United States
Linn	Journal of Military Ethics; 2002	Moral disobedience	N = 170	Reserve soldiers, all ranks; Israel
Liebes & Blum-Kulka	Armed Forces & Society; 1994	Coping with moral dilemmas	N = 36	Active military personnel (N = 23), military reservists (N = 13)[c]; Israel

Cognitive Approach: Stream two – situational moderators

Authors	Journal; year	Operationalization of moral judgement	Sample (N)	Rank; cultural background
Hannah et al.	Journal of Applied Psychology; 2013	Ethical intentions and behaviours in relation with abusive supervision (leadership)	N = 2572	Military personnel all ranks; United States

Research design	Findings regarding moral judgement
Qualitative (Case study)	The case of David Hackworth, a former military officer who publicly condemned the Vietnam war, is used to address the issue of how a military officer should act when moral dilemmas arise from conflicting obligations to his/her conscience and to his/her duty. It was concluded that there are three options: (1) to serve as ably as possible, (2) to resign, (3) or to speak out publicly. Deciding which option is the best depends on whom military officers feel they owe their loyalty to.
Qualitative (case study)	This article studied reserve soldiers who disobeyed the order to serve in the war zone because of moral concerns. Arguments for refusal were mostly motivated by a sense of patriotism. Because of the soldiers' sense of belonging to a society, they feel more obliged to care about the moral value of the war and its overall goal. Therefore, the author argues, these forms of moral disobedience should be seen as signs of attachment to society.
Qualitative (interviews)	This study shows that the coping strategy of 'negotiation' is the most preferred choice for minimizing the dilemma (51.9%), followed by the strategy of 'redefinition' (35.8%). The least used strategy is that of 'radical action' (12.2%).

Research design	Findings regarding moral judgement
Quantitative (survey)	The results show there is a relationship between the presence of abusive supervision and higher rates of unethical acts. Mediating factors are lower levels of moral courage and lower identification with organizational values

TABLE 8.3 *Moral judgment research conducted in military organizations* (cont.)

Cognitive approach: Stream two – situational moderators				
Authors	**Journal; year**	**Operationalization of moral judgement**	**Sample (N)**	**Rank; cultural background**
Yu[b]	Ethics & Behavior; 2013	Moral behaviour in relation with education	N = 399	Officer cadets; Taiwan
Schaubroeck et al.	Academy of Management Journal; 2012	Moral behaviour and cognition in relation with moral culture and leadership	N = 2572	Military personnel all ranks; United States
Hannah, Avolio, Walumba	Business Ethics Quarterly; 2011	Moral courage in relation with leadership	N1 = 162 N2 = 162	Army school, troops; United States
Bartone	Ethics & Behavior; 2010	The role of leadership in preventing moral degradation	N = 1	Incident; United States
Cunha, Rego & Clegg	Journal of Business Ethics; 2010	The process through which unquestioned obedience can be created	N = 2	Incident; United States

Research design	Findings regarding moral judgement
Quantitative (survey)	The results show that gender and religious background have no effect on an individual's values towards justice and care. Teaching by example has the greatest influence on moral behaviour.
Quantitative (survey)	The results of this study show that ethical leadership influences moral behaviour and cognition of troops indirectly, meaning next-higher level leaders need to support their subordinate leaders to intensify the effect of ethical leadership on the troops. Moreover, ethical culture in units proved to mediate the effect of ethical leadership.
(field study) (Surveys, peer-ratings)	The results of this study show that authentic leadership is positively related to followers' displays of moral courage. Also, leadership influence on followers' pro-social behaviours is mediated by the display of moral courage. Social Cognitive Theory is used as a framework, suggesting individuals are not only products of their environment, but also produce their own environment (reciprocity). To promote moral courage in their followers, leaders should demonstrate moral perspective, self-awareness and transparency/openness towards their followers.
Qualitative (Case study)	This article examines contextual- and individual factors that explain the abuse at Abu Ghraib. The contextual factors are: leadership ambiguity, laissez-faire leadership, lack of training, poor discipline, psychological stressors and ambiguous rules of engagement. The individual factors that were found are: psychological fitness, personality traits and a lack of psychological hardiness.
Qualitative (Case study)	The results show that a culture of obedience, a gradual increase in demands, control of access to information and collective responsibility are factors that contributed to the existence of unquestioned obedience in Milgram's laboratory experiment as well as in the Khmer Rouge regime of Pol Pot.

TABLE 8.3 *Moral judgment research conducted in military organizations* (cont.)

Cognitive approach: Stream two – situational moderators

Authors	Journal; year	Operationalization of moral judgement	Sample (N)	Rank; cultural background
Olsen, Pallesen & Eid	Sleep; 2010	Moral reasoning in relation with sleep deprivation	N = 72	Naval officer cadets; Norway
Williams[a]	Journal of Military Ethics; 2010	Moral character development	N1 = 120 (matched pairs) N2 = 40 4 groups	Military, all ranks; United States
Reger, Etherage, Reger & Gahm	Military Psychology; 2008	Ethical challenges for psychologists in the military	N = 1	Military psychologists; United States
Gire & Williams	The Journal of Social Psychology; 2007	Moral dissonance in an honour system	N = 80	Military students (N = 40) non-military (N = 40) students; United States
Olsen, Eid & Johnson[b]	Military Psychology; 2006	Moral behaviour in relation with leadership	N = 190	Naval officer cadets; Norway

Research design	Findings regarding moral judgement
Quantitative (pre-post design survey)	The results show that sleep deprivation has a negative influence on moral reasoning, resulting in more rule-oriented and self-oriented decisions than when not sleep-deprived.
Quantitative (survey) Qualitative (Focus groups)	The quantitative study shows that servicemen are inclined to rule-based judgement. When rules (drills) are not available they consider their personal benefit as most important in judgement. The qualitative study shows conflicting changes in moral character development (decision making and values). The study shows that leaders play a key-role in moral behaviour.
Qualitative (Case study)	According to the authors, this case examines ethical challenges psychologists face when working in a military context. Challenges arise due to specific army culture issues (such as rank and language, manner and norms). The authors argue psychologists are in need for specific skills and knowledge to balance between organizational interests and culture on the one hand and APA norms on the other.
Quantitative (Field experiment)	This study showed that students from a military school with a strong honour code were less likely to pick up money from the street that did not belong to them then students from a non-military school. It also showed that military students were far more likely to take the money in a private setting than in a public setting. This finding is explained by the fact that the action of not picking up the money in a public setting was not internalized because they had enough external justification for not taking the money (the high risk of being caught and the severe punishment they would receive).
Quantitative (survey)	The results show that there is a strong relationship between transformational leadership and high self-importance of moral identity and high moral reasoning.

TABLE 8.3 *Moral judgment research conducted in military organizations* (cont.)

Cognitive approach: Stream three – foundation in issue contingency model				
Authors	**Journal; year**	**Operationalization of moral judgement**	**Sample (N)**	**Rank; cultural background**
Seiler, Fischer & Voegtli	Ethics & Behavior; 2011	EDM and moral intensity	N = 130	Military officers; Switzerland
Lincoln & Holmes	Psychological Services; 2010	Ethical Decision Making (EDM)	N = 352	Navy Chaplains; United States

Affective approach				
Authors	**Journal; year**	**Operationalization of moral judgement**	**Sample (N)**	**Rank; cultural background**
Nilson, Sjöberg, Kallenberg & Larson	Ethics & Behavior; 2011	Moral stress in EDM	N = 16	Military personnel[c], Sweden
Fry, Harvey, Hurley & Foley	Nursing Ethics; 2002	Moral distress	N = 13	Military nurses; United States

Research design	Findings regarding moral judgement
Quasi experimental (pre-post design survey with control group)	The study explores the relationship between moral intensity and decision-making in relation to training effects. Results show that high mental ability is addressed in high moral intensity situations. This study suggests that individual competencies as well as the situation are important in EDM, especially when moral intensity increases.
Quantitative (survey)	This study shows that the dimensions of moral intensity have predictive value in explaining the individual ethical decision-making process. Moral awareness, moral judgement and moral intention can be explained in part by the moral intensity factors of an ethical dilemma. In addition to this, social consensus, magnitude of consequences and probability of effect were found to be strong predictors of moral judgement.

Research design	Findings regarding moral judgement
Qualitative (interviews)	In EDM, two decision-making strategies were found: (1) common sense guiding initial coping (i.e. gut feeling & intuition), (2) appraisal of leader support (i.e. in sanctions and support). Four types of moral stress were found in EDM: (a) insufficiency, (b) powerlessness, (c) meaninglessness, (d) frustration
Qualitative (Interviews)	This study shows that military nurses experience moral distress in several dimensions. The results show that both initial moral distress, i.e. (a) psychological disequilibrium experienced when intentions and actual behaviour are not in line, (b) negative feelings that accompany this disequilibrium and reactive moral stress (i.e. continuing moral stress when barriers to behave according to one's own intentions are not overcome, (b) (clinical) effects and consequences of this second dimension such as nightmares; headaches; loss of sleep etc.) are reported.

TABLE 8.3 *Moral judgment research conducted in military organizations* (cont.)

Integrative approach

Authors	**Journal; year**	**Operationalization of moral judgement**	**Sample (N)**	**Rank; cultural background**
Eriksen	Journal of Military Ethics; 2010	The role of experience-based intuition in moral judgement	N = (not specified)	Military personnel, all ranks; Norway
Hannah & Avolio	Consulting psychology journal: practice and research; 2010	Moral potency	N = 309 (study 1) N = 2572 (study 2)	Military personnel all ranks; United States
Killgore, Killgore, Day, Li, Kamimori & Balkin	Sleep; 2007	Influence of sleep deprivation on moral judgement	N = 26	Military personnel, all ranks; United States

[a] This study can be categorized in both stream two 'individual personal cognitive ability' as well as in stream two 'situational moderators'.
[b] This study can be categorized in both stream two individual difference moderators' as well as in stream two 'situational moderators'.
[c] Ranks unspecified

Research design	Findings regarding moral judgement
Qualitative (interviews and informal conversations)	Moral behaviour is formed by experience from our everyday, on-going ethical coping. Based on this experience-based knowledge, we cope intuitively with moral challenges in our normal daily life. The author concludes that this model should be transferable to the domain of military operations when the prerequisites for relevant experiences can be fulfilled.
Quantitative (survey)	The authors argue that there is a process between cognitive judgement and actual action that they refer to as moral potency, which influences intentions and, consequently, as such behaviour. The three elements of moral potency (moral ownership; moral courage and moral efficacy) were positively related to the servicemen's intention to report unethical behaviour. The results also show that individuals who are exposed more frequently to incidents (or unethical behaviour) score higher on moral potency.
Quantitative (pre-post design survey)	53 hours of sleep deprivation only showed to have a significant effect on the response time when it came to judging Moral Personal dilemmas as opposed to impersonal and non-dilemma situations. Also, people with high emotional intelligence were less susceptible to agree with solutions that violate personally held moral beliefs. This finding suggests that sleep deprivation impairs the ability of integrating emotion and cognition to guide moral judgements. Emotional intelligence moderated the influence of sleep loss on moral judgement.

CHAPTER 9

Explaining Military Ethics to Young People: Role and Teaching Methods of Youth Information Officers

Moritz Brake

West-German re-armament, the establishment of the Bundeswehr in 1955, was highly controversial at the time. Under the impression of the horrors of two World Wars, strong political currents in the German public rejected the idea to re-establish German armed forces. Three years after that, in 1958, while large parts of Germany were still in ruins, the first Federal German Chief of the Defence Staff, *Generalinspekteur* Heusinger instated the first Youth Information Officers (German: *Jugendoffiziere*), young officers that had the mission to inform the public about the purpose of the newly established Bundeswehr.[1] A key element of their mission in interacting with the public was – and is – to provide a transparent living link between the armed forces and society. Concerning the Bundeswehr, the most salient question troubling politicians, intellectuals and the public in general was this:

> How would the newly established Bundeswehr prevent following the example of the Wehrmacht and become once more a willing instrument of militarism and expansionism, a 'state within the state'?

This question was made that much more pressing by the fact that the newly formed military establishment consisted to a large extent of personnel taken over from the old Wehrmacht. Among several other ingenious institutional devices created to counter the danger of a continuation of un-democratic Wehrmacht traditions and a potential separation of Germany's armed forces from its increasingly liberal democratic society, the most revolutionary for the Bundeswehr itself was – and still is – Count Wolf Baudissin's concept of the 'citizen in uniform'.

Baudissin's ideas for modern, liberal democratic military ethics and traditions are summarized under his general category '*Innere Führung*' (translated

1 'Geschichte der Jugendoffiziere' (history of Youth Information Officers), http://www.jugendoffizier.eu (last accessed on 14.05.2014).

 | DOI 10.1163/9789004312135_010

by Baudissin as 'inner structure').[2] The German term coined by Baudissin actually describes the ethos, the ideology motivating *any* armed force's leadership's and personnel's behaviour. However, in its present use in the Bundeswehr, '*Innere Führung*' has effectively acquired the meaning of the ideal of the 'citizen in uniform' **exclusively** motivated and governed by the liberal democratic values of the German '*Grundgesetz*', the German constitution. Therefore, the principles of the Bundeswehr explicitly forbid the cultivation of a separate 'caste of warriors', a military driven by its own 'code of honour and conduct', a Praetorian's ethic unattached to the political system it is serving.

In order to facilitate a public understanding of the Bundeswehr, promote a wide debate about the military, its missions and structure and Germany's security and defence policy in general, Youth Information Officers have been a valuable contribution to public citizenship education ever since their establishment in 1958. Accordingly, discussing military ethics and the Bundeswehr's concept of the 'citizen in uniform' is an integral part of the Youth Information Officers' interaction with the public.

To explain the role and teaching methods of Youth Information Officers with regard to military ethics, it is the aim of this contribution to briefly outline the ideal of the 'citizen in uniform', Baudissin's '*Innere Führung*' governing the Bundeswehr's military ethics, before presenting the concept of Youth Information Officers, its historical roots and contemporary practice in the German Bundeswehr. Finally, raising three relevant examples from the author's experience in public debate, it is the aim of this presentation to promote an inspiring and mutually beneficial intellectual intercourse on the institution of Youth Information Officers and the ethical consequences of the ideal of the 'citizen in uniform'.

The Democratic 'Citizen in Uniform' – Baudissin's 'Innere Führung'

Firmly rejecting any notion that 'democracy' and 'military' might be irreconcilable concepts with fundamentally different ideals, Count Wolf Baudissin sums up the essence of his 'inner structure' for the armed forces of a democracy in 'simply three things: organic integration of the army [military] into the democratic state; devotion of its leaders to the state and its constitution; identity of values in the army [military] and in the democratic state.'[3]

2 Wolf Baudissin, 'The New German Army' (1955) vol. 34, no. 1, *Foreign Affairs*, 1–13.

3 *Ibid*, p. 3.

While the first two might not inspire much debate among international or German intellectuals, politicians, armed forces personnel and in the general public, the *third point is severely contested to this day*. The idea that civil society's democratic values can – even must – be identical with those of its military is radical, indeed revolutionary – even today. However, it might seem less so, if Baudissin's own distinction between democracy misunderstood as merely an organisational form, devoid of values, reduced to the expression of public will through voting,[4] and democracy's governing ideals of liberalism – chiefly the concept of *human dignity* – is recognised.[5]

It was neither Baudissin's nor is it the contemporary Bundeswehr's intention to apply parliamentary procedures to military command structures. However, the principles dictated by the ideal of human dignity are applied throughout. Furthermore, their application demands that members of the armed forces are not expected to blindly follow orders. Indeed, in this point, the Prussian-German military tradition of 'mission command' (*Auftragstaktik*) forms a perfect union with democracy's focus on the individual's conscience: 'conscientious obedience' is the term commonly applied in the Bundeswehr.[6]

The individual soldier is not only required to 'live' and 'affirm' the liberal democratic values of our society,[7] he is called upon to critically inquire into the nature of his mission and question the legality and morality of each order. While at a cursory glance this frequently provokes outcries predicting 'virtual anarchy' in the execution of orders and the maintenance of military discipline, this suspected contradiction between individual conscience and responsibility on the one hand and military hierarchy on the other is solved by *trust*. Split-second-decisions in emergencies, orders given in moments of crisis certainly do not lend themselves to lengthy debate or intensive contemplation on the part of those which are supposed to carry them out. However, the superiors giving them and those that are supposed to obey them have to rely on mutual trust. Only if those receiving orders *trust* their superiors to make decisions responsibly, *to the best of their knowledge and belief*, can they be expected to follow them. The requirement of trust in individual superiors extends to the political system. Thereby, the requirement to trust in our democracy and its

4 For the opinion of democracy as an empty shell, an organisational form devoid of values, see for example Carl Schmitt, '*Die geistesgeschichtliche Lage des heutigen Parlamentarismus*' (1923, 9th German Edition 2010, Duncker & Humblot, Berlin), 32–33.

5 Baudissin, *supra*, footnote 232, p. 3.

6 §12 Soldatengesetz (federal German law concerning the armed forces).

7 §8 Soldatengesetz (federal German law concerning the armed forces).

values and its decision-making-processes essentially extends in relevance all the way down to the individual tactical level.

Eventually, those of our citizens wearing uniforms, bearing arms, are called upon by law to take democratic citizenship that much more serious. While democracy challenges all of its citizens to continually engage in a process of critical self-reflection, self-education and assuming responsibility for the common good, it does so with particular emphasis with regard to all those that hold authority – armed or unarmed.

Youth Information Officers

Youth Information Officers, as mentioned above, are a long-standing feature of the German armed force's efforts to promote a popular public security policy debate in Germany. Indeed, all branches of government are called upon to further the individual citizen's ability to form a critical opinion of decisive matters of politics and policy. Ministries are to provide the public with information about their policies, actions and plans and pressing future questions.[8] Youth Information Officers are part of this over-all effort of the Federal German Government.

However, as objectivity and neutrality is required of government efforts in public citizenship information and education, Youth Information Officers – despite being members of the armed forces – are not restricted to representing official government positions along 'communication guidelines'. Furthermore, while candidates for the job are comparatively young (aged 25 to 35), the title-term 'Youth' should not be misleading with regard to the general audience these officers are addressing. In practice, the majority of their audience is made up of young people – secondary-school students and university students (upwards of 70%). Still, in working with political parties, various public associations, trade unions and the general public, the age-range of their audience extends from teenagers upwards to citizens of any age.

In promoting the discussion of topics as diverse as out-of-area missions of the Bundeswehr, current global security policy 'hot-spots' and challenges, to the individual experience of serving abroad, democratic values and military ethics or the armed forces structure in general, Youth Information Officers rely on their individual discretion in choosing the methodological and didactic

8 Bundesverfassungsgerichtsurteil 02.03.1977, Az. 2 BvE 1/76 'Öffentlichkeitsarbeit' (German constitutional court ruling concerning governmental public relations efforts).

approach to their audience. Adhering to neutrality in public citizenship education, various opinions in their field of expertise and current political debate are represented and juxtaposed by them. Personal opinion is not only frequently expected from them by their audiences, it forms an integral part of their work. This obvious academic liberty in the work of Youth Information Officers finds its inspirations – and has its limits – in the loyalty to the constitution and its institutions.

Furthermore, academic liberty is justified by the academic qualification and the individual motivation of the officers. Coming from the widest possible variety of backgrounds from the service, they all are volunteers for the position of Youth Information Officer. Uniting leadership experience, often combined with experience of service abroad, with expertise in matters of security politics and policy, they move on from carrying military responsibility for lives, material and mission to that of carrying public responsibility in promoting critical popular debate in a vital field of common concern.

Ensuring Youth Information Officer's objectivity, they are strictly separated from the armed force's efforts for recruitment. Indeed, the general requirements for public citizenship education prohibit any effort on the part of Youth Information Officers to advertise for the armed forces. Their value lies not in convincing anybody of a particular government position or official opinions, Youth Information Officers contribute to our society by *drawing attention to particular questions*, not in lobbying for particular attempts to address them.

The methods used for addressing particular topics and audiences are various and at the discretion of the individual Youth Information Officer. The most common are:

- Oral presentations and discussions
- Public debate (i.e with representatives of political parties, non-governmental-organisations, experts, practitioners and academics)
- Seminars and field-trips (i.e. up to several days under various topics, Berlin, Bonn, Bruxelles, Strasbourg, Vienna, to name a few of the more common destinations)
- Excursions to military formations and institutions, facilitating transparency of the armed forces and supporting the link with civil society.
- 'Politics and International Security' (Pol&iS), a simulation not unlike the 'Model United Nations'-simulation (students assume the roles of heads of state, various positions in government. Focus on debate and constructive compromise)

Explaining Military Ethics

In the case of military ethics, the topic might be approached by outlining the particular historic conditions under which the values of the Bundeswehr were established, the influences and personalities contributing to their formation. Furthermore, confronting the audience with the dilemma of the potential consequences of action and inaction in times of crisis – the inevitable ambiguity of prospective courses of action under incomplete knowledge of conditions – helps to develop an understanding of the strains and challenges military leadership faces. Issues of law and morality can be profitably debated when it comes to self-defence, rendering assistance and following orders. Drawing on realistic examples from recent experience, the situation of servicemen and – women in action becomes tangible. From hostage situations on merchant vessels pirated off the Horn of Africa, to the decision to authorise the bombing of an insurgent target in Afghanistan, the dilemma of action and inaction assumes a level allowing individual access.

Furthermore, as the ethics of the Bundeswehr are inseparable from our society, our democracy, an excursion into the value of individual liberty, tolerance and debate over meta-physical concepts of totalitarian ideologies might be profitable. Eventually, tracing the concept of 'human dignity' lays the foundation for the operational and tactical behaviour of our armed forces. Depending on the audience, even a Clausewitzean approach to the 'conditions of victory' and the 'political will' governing armed conflict promises valuable insight into ethical behaviour on the 'battlefield'.

A Selection of Relevant Questions Concerning Military Ethics

Eventually, beyond outlining an assessment of the current status quo, potential challenges and potential future developments, it is the focus of Youth Information Officers to spark debate – not to dominate or pre-determine it. Upon conclusion, three relevant questions are outlined which are frequently encountered by the author in discussing military ethics with various German audiences:

- Is racism, fascism or militarism a particularly common feature of character of members of the armed forces? Does military service attract people of an anti-democratic inclination?
- 'Soldiers are murderers!' – Killing is the primary feature of military service

- 'War is necessarily brutal!' – Implying that 'squeamish' or 'weak' democracies are unable to meet 'war's demands' in 'necessary brutality'. This relates to the thesis that Western democracies are inferior to insurgents in achieving victory in places like Afghanistan.

While not venturing to conclusively answer these questions, a few further aspects should be considered when debating them. First, while the make-up of the *Bundeswehr* ideally represents a broad average of society and its political currents, particular care is taken by all levels of leadership to counter anything even slightly implying un-democratic tendencies. A service that builds upon the ideals of our constitution, the principles inspired by human dignity, cannot tolerate those who reject this very foundation of our armed forces and democratic society. Furthermore, even in military cultures separate from humanistic values, 'killing' was rarely seen as the condition for victory – indeed, only genocide does. However, these 'traditional' borders blur, not only as area bombardments and especially the use of nuclear weapons target civilian populations. After all, 'mutually assured destruction' is certainly an extreme case – some might say even theologically extreme – for testing both international law and the ideals of human dignity. A case so far still relegated to political discretion in the case of extreme national emergency.[9]

Still, the contemporary Bundeswehr is motivated by the defence of our democracy, its laws and values, and dedicated to the ideal of contributing to the establishment of a peaceful international order. How this should be achieved by 'killing' as an end in itself seems highly dubious – to say the least. However, this does not negate the fact that the employment of armed forces is a decision to employ organised means of violence to achieve political ends. Still, trusting in the instruments and institutions of our democracy, violence is always the last resort and employed only after due and careful deliberation.

Finally, to all those who believe war to be necessarily brutal, and brutality the superior path to victory, a careful study of history is advised: even some of the systematically least morally inhibited armed forces in history, the German Wehrmacht and the Soviet Red Army failed to successfully handle insurgencies. Indeed, evidence suggests that Nazi Germany in the Balkans and the Soviet Union in Afghanistan perpetuated and increased resistance by their barbarity.[10]

---

9 International Court of Justice, (Advisory Opinion), ICJ Reports 1996, 'Legality of the Threat or Use of Nuclear Weapons': http://www.icj-cij.org/docket/index.php?sum=498&code=unan&p1=3&p2=4&case=95&k=e1&p3=5 (last accessed on 14.05.2014); paragraphs 88–89.

10 Yugoslavia and Nazi-Germany see: Ivan Arreguín-Toft 'The [F]utility of Barbarism: assessing the systemic harm of non-combatants in war' (2003) Belfer Center, Kennedy-School of

Conclusion

The above suggestions, examples and questions outline the unique position and liberties Youth Information Officers have in approaching their topics and audiences. In doing so, they fulfil three vital roles: expertise and experience in a field not easily accessible even to the interested public; forming a living link between the Bundeswehr and German civil society; offering first-hand experience of military service, oftentimes involving out-of-area mission experience.

Especially the second point, preserving and intensifying the link between society and its armed forces is of increasing relevance since the suspension of compulsory military service. While in former years Germany's citizens – at least its male half – had been compelled to engage with the Bundeswehr – either in serving or conscientiously refusing to serve, the tendency to reduce troop numbers and consolidate their dislocation across Germany increases the danger of society not noticing its military enough. This is of vital concern as the Bundeswehr – like all other institutions of society – needs the continuing, critical and informed attention of public debate. Furthermore, a close relationship between armed forces and society is a formidable safe-guard against tendencies to form a separate 'state within the state'. It is therefore suggested that the institution of Youth Information Officers receives continuing attention, even increasing support in inverse proportion to the decline of troop numbers.

Finally, this institution may not only be beneficial as a German but especially as a European model. After all, matters of security politics and policy have long since ceased to be of purely national concern. 94 Youth Information Officers serve a Germany of roughly 80.000.000. It would be a comparatively minor effort to muster a proportional amount in Europe for the whole of the union. Apart from the inspirational effect these officers have traditionally had on the armed forces themselves, we all benefit from debate conducted as wide and as public as possible. The European Union needs greater public tangibility and it is the European dimension which urgently needs more public attention – especially with regard to defence and security policy debate.

Government, Harvard University: http://belfercenter.ksg.harvard.edu/files/Arreguin_Toft_APSA_2003.pdf (last accessed on 14.05.2014); For Afghanistan and the Soviet Union see: Max Boot, *Invisible Armies: an epic history of guerrilla warfare from ancient times to the present*, (Norton & Company, 2013), 492–93.

CHAPTER 10

Ethics of War as a Part of Military Ethics

Jovan Babic

Military Ethics and Ethics of War

The Ethics of war are a part of military ethics, and military ethics are a part of political ethics. Although war has its own specific logic both in terms of its existence and its functioning the matter in the end is political: what is the political purpose of war, or what is the prerequisite of it. This prerequisite is the armed forces. It is true that armed forces have many different, often multifunctional, tasks and duties, but the main purpose of them is what makes the meaning and value of war, and that is the peace, the end state characterized by stability and predictability (the main job of an army is either to wage a war or to prepare for it). War is, by definition, a temporary state of affairs aimed to its end, which is a (new) peace. If this is so then the purpose of armed forces is not to be used but actually quite the opposite: not to be used, if possible. Its primary purpose is to avert a possible attack. That clearly establishes defence as the utmost and possibly only justification of war. The final mission of armed forces is to prevent war if possible, and only if necessary to engage if waging a war.

From this viewpoint military ethics covers a broader terrain than ethics of war. But what's 'ethical' there in the first place? On one side we have a belief that in war, like in business, 'everything is allowed'. This standpoint of *amorality* of war is very comfortable for warriors as it absolves them (and us, if we accept this standpoint) from the difficult analysing of complex issues that might seem hard to solve. This standpoint, however, is widespread as a kind of broadly accepted prejudice. It has a clear benefit of safeguarding all those engaged in a war from a too big burden of responsibility and often of the conflict of responsibilities. On the other side there is a strong attitude to assess war exclusively in terms of its badness as necessary something always and necessary "evil". If there is a possible justification for war it should be somewhere in between these opposite standpoints. This might produce the impression that justifying war is a hopeless task, or something utterly contradictory: impossible despite being necessary.

On the other side the *theoretical* justification seems to be at odds with what we find on the *phenomenological* level as the reality of war, as the real experience of many of those affected by it. There are many possibilities how this experience might be established and articulated. Those who make decisions,

© KONINKLIJKE BRILL NV, LEIDEN, 2016 | DOI 10.1163/9789004312135_011

and many of those who fight, may take their standpoint to express what they believe in and are ready to sacrifice for, by saying that the cause of the war is 'their own'. The readiness to fight for one's own cause is a paradigmatic form of defence. The conflict then is presumably a conflict of adverse political interests, where victory is being a substantive achievement (national freedom or even survival), and defeat is a significant loss. This is the standard *political approach* to war. However, there are other possibilities to interpret the case of having a 'cause of their own': it might be a deep belief of duty to defend what's perceived worth to be defended independently of whose interests are invested in that cause. In that case we are ready to fight for our ideals, which might incorporate more interests of others than of ourselves, implying our readiness to sacrifice for those ideals. Which ideals? They might be very different. Usually those are religious beliefs, or ideological schemes. Here we have an *eschatological approach* to war, frequently present not only in justifying the participation in wars but also in perceiving some wars as the fight for 'final' victory of 'good' over 'evil', as a 'war against the war itself'. There are still other possibilities on the level of phenomenology of experience. Many are going to war for reasons to experience pastime, or adventure, or to fight off boredom or the feeling of the absurdity of life. Some take war to be a kind of ceremony, something glorious. These borderline cases, exceptional or not, are of less interest to us in depicting the phenomenology of war.

However, there is one form of experiencing war that is, in my opinion, of special interest. For many a job is just another unfortunate accident, another limit and setback in their life, short and miserable as it can be. This, what I would like to call it, *third* approach to war (besides political and eschatological) we may call *cataclysmic*. According to this approach war is something that happens *to* us, as individuals or nations, and is catastrophic in its final meaning, similar to natural disasters. It seems to me that this aspect of war, although a grand theme in literature, is rather neglected in philosophical, and also ethical, elaboration of the phenomenology of war. The standard situation 'he or me', experienced by warriors in the middle of the battle belongs also here. However, some of the basic features of war, *unpredictability of* its outcome and irreversibility *of* its main course, corroborate this approach to war: war is a kind of disaster for many, or most, of those who participate in it. Jumping to the conclusion in a way, I would say that this approach indicates one of the most important features of war, a feature of the utmost ethical significance – *the lack of* any feasible, or even plausible, *control of future time* (at least for those inside the frame of it). This lack of control of our future is actually the absence of what makes life normal: predictability, existence of real and valid rules of life, the laws and customs which make our life plans realizable in the rather short time span of an individual life, and sometimes also within a viable span of collective life. In this sense the cataclysmic aspect of wars is a very basic feature of them.

Ethics of War and Ethics in War

Ethics of war traditionally encompasses two lines of argumentation in the course of its justification. First, what counts as a possible justification of war as such (*jus ad bellum*) – what could be a *legitimate basis* for going to war in the first place? Second, what are *the rules* of war (*jus in bello*), their purpose being to reduce the costs of war (as an action that is, by definition, a temporary state of affairs directed to its conclusion), and to make war more humane and less cruel (as it is an action in which, by definition, many civil laws are partially temporarily suspended, allowing killings and other serious immoral acts). Moreover, it seems absurd that both sides in a war can battle for a just cause.

This seeming absurdity, however, is a part of the definition of war and its constitutive rule: that *victory* gives right. The rule functions in a context of conflict characterized by two conditions: first, that there is no other way to resolve that conflict (the condition of last resort, meaning that all other possibilities had been exhausted), and, second, there is a mutual understanding not to allow the conflict to remain unsolved. This means that victory is a real constitutive rule not only of war but also of what its result is going to be. The winning is thus not only the defeat of the adversary but also the factor of legitimizing a new state of affairs, the one that should replace the old *status quo ante*.

Perhaps this legitimizing function of victory is the connecting line between *ius ad bellum* and *ius in bello*. The victory should be a legitimate victory. Victory has *the logical form of consent*, and consent is the acceptance of uncertainty contained in it. This implies that either side can win or lose; otherwise we would have a police action, which is characterized by lack of any normative reciprocity between sides in conflict. Both sides strive to win, and both sides should be ready to accept the defeat. This is the point where the concept of *capitulation* enters the field. If victory should serve as a *constitutive rule* of the war it has to have its counterpart in capitulation, which should contain the same form of consent as the victory.[1] Otherwise the defeated would not accept

---

1 Victory might also be a regulative rule, as an act of mere establishment of the state of affairs by which a war seems to end, without acceptance of the defeat by the vanquished. However, the outcome is more like a *ceasefire*, not a real peace (although it might start to look as a peace after relevantly long time, after some sort of acceptance of the new state of affairs has been established. But the feature of ceasefire might endure very long periods of time. For

the impression of the winning side that war had ended by their victory. This means that victory should be accompanied by a valid capitulation. What does this mean?

It means that capitulation is also a constitutive rule of the war. As a rule it has some distinct features, which make it to be such a rule. These are at least the following two features: (1) no annihilation of the defeated is allowed, and (2) capitulation must not imply humiliation of the defeated. (Kant would add a third condition: no formal punishment). This implies something that might has been forgotten in the contemporary inflated just war theorizing kind of justification of 'new wars': normative necessity of *honourable defeat*; or, in other words, the mutual, reciprocal, respect of warring sides. Put aside that this approach makes capitulation much easier (and the war less costly), it keeps safe the distinction between *ius ad bellum* and *ius in bello*,[2] corroborates the function of war as a (last but necessary) means of resolving of otherwise unresolvable conflicts (those for which neither side would allow to remain unresolved), preserves the distinction between being captured and being arrested, and so on. From the moral point of view this approach makes capitulation a matter of not only political but also moral responsibility: to capitulate can become a moral duty, and the last resort of defence. It cannot be thus if capitulation is not a constitutive rule with distinct conditions of validity, e.g. an 'unconditional capitulation'.

There are some further important features if capitulation is, along with the victory, another side of the same constitutive rule. First of all there is some accepted initial equality of warring sides in their assessment of a viable *prospect to success*. The absence of such prospect indicates radical irresponsibility, independently of the time frame (i.e. of how long they need to lose, if winning was absolutely hopeless). Then there is the *reciprocity* of warring sides, which is the base of their mutual respect. This respect implies that they are not treating each other as criminals: our enemies are not perceived by us as criminals (as we should not be perceived as criminals by our enemies). This is the famous Walzerian *prima facie* moral equality of combatants. Finally, there are many kinds of immunity, not only of non- combatants but also a fine graduation of responsibility depending of the situation, time, place, rank, etc.[3] Above all this approach

example, Corsica never sincerely accepted the fact that Republic of Genoa *sold* the Island and people living on it to the Kingdom of France (despite the fact that many generations have lived in this arguably politically undefined, and presumably uncomfortable, form of life).

2 Contrary to what we find as the main stream in contemporary just war theorizing, where the distinction is heavily attacked, for example by J. McMahan or D. Rodin (among others).

3 This resolve the famous case of the naked soldier (or the captured soldier, for that matter).

preserves the dignity of human beings as moral agents responsible for their decisions and actions (which forbids treating them without respect deserved by all, including those who are guilty of what they did). All this depends on the serious acceptance of the distinction between *ius ad bellum* and *ius in bello*.

New Approach

Perhaps these features are overcome and have become obsolete nowadays; perhaps a kind of inequality is what's needed for the maintenance of the world peace, or for some other goals, presumably political (e.g. democratization of the world). In this context we face several problems. First, the nature of victory and defeat change cardinally: the defeated side, having no equal moral standing (to set their own goals and try to achieve them by, *e.g.* defending those goals, or by defending themselves), become an unclear matter. What is victory today? What is its goal? And, especially, who are those who are doomed to lose? Should they remain what they were before (except of changing their constitutions as the result of capitulation, but without either annihilation or humiliation)? Or should they change more fundamentally by accepting what are the values the winners deem worthy enough to be defended, independently of whose values those are? If the goal is 'winning the hearts and minds' of those on the other side victory changes its very meaning, or become superfluous and not needed as a concept. Should 'others' become a part of what 'we' are for the process to end? Can this be a way to 'overcome' war, by making the world unique and uniform?

Why the Others Couldn't Just Capitulate, and Remained What They Were before?

There is one very strange question here: should winning the hearts and minds be the mutual goal of both sides in conflict? Or is it possible that it is goal of only one side, presumably the stronger one, and that the other side is not interested in winning the hearts and minds of their attackers (instead they might be only interested in defending themselves, and nothing else)? Finally, what would it mean if both sides were, mutually, interested, in winning the hearts and minds of the other side? Whichever the case is the victory, and for that matter also the defeat, seem to have become redundant. Is this the characteristic of contemporary *asymmetric wars*? What is the status of defence, or self-defence then? It seems that defence has become irrelevant. The main problem here is what is happening with freedom, the individual and the collective, if defence is either to become an unclear concept or entirely loses its meaning and relevance.

There are other complications: in contemporary asymmetric wars the condition of proportionality seems to imply a need to tailor the amount of force according to different kinds of adversaries: the weaker the other side the smaller amount of legitimate force is supposed to be proper to use; this might postpone the end of war, or preclude it.

Another issue is the so-called 'non-culpable ignorance' issue: the issue of responsibility in the context of the prospect of *possible* success. It is even metaethically interesting: how can we conclude from the *fact* that some were vanquished to the conclusion that they had no reason at all to sincerely and plausibly believe that they had a chance to win? If such a chance didn't exist in any possible world they would be irresponsibly in the sense that they do not deserve any respect as a warring side (as, e.g., terrorists). The role of their sincerity and the quality of their assessment seems to be in principle independent from the fact of defeat as such.

Finally, the on-going attempts to criminalize war imply reducing the war to a police action. This is a far-reaching process in which all the differences between war and police action collapse, replacing the war with a police action. But those differences seem to be significant: in police actions there is no equality, reciprocity and mutuality between two sides. There is also no normative unpredictability of the outcome: it is in advance determined who is having the right and who not. The normative (especially legal) control of the future in police actions, unlike in war, is entirely secured (and the result is *success*, rather than *victory* – the failure, if happens, must to be correctable). The distribution of rights and responsibilities is quite different. In police actions all rights are on the side of police, the "other side" has no rights at all: they have no right to counteract, to defend themselves, or even to run away. They have a *strictu senso* duty to surrender, and cooperate in that process. There is no victory or defeat there, only success or failure. However, in the absence of the world state what is the police action, which goes across national boarders? Reduced to the bottom line this implies that contemporary asymmetric warfare might be seen as the situation in which two police, or police-like, forces (one or both of which could be, regarding the modality of their representation, *ad hoc* self- defensive 'militias') fight, treating each other as criminals (as terrorists, usurpers, aggressors, crusaders, jihadists, etc.).

On the basis of all said my concluding questions are: does this new approach provide solutions for all important disputes and conflicts we are faced with, or rather normatively precludes many of them by making them illegitimate as such and therefore normatively impossible? What impact on freedom does, or could, it have? If the concept of defence is amputated from the inventory of concepts present in the world, which perhaps might maintain peace and prosperity in the world, how viable and stable can such a state be? The new approach might eliminate these questions of the main stream, and certainly they are hard to answer, but the duty of a philosopher is quite this: to raise questions which might be provocative, with the purpose to explore deeper issues contained in the essence of what we are thinking and doing. Especially when the theme is so practically important as the logic of solving conflicts, which will be with us as long as we are alive and free beings.

CHAPTER 11

Leadership for Mere Mortals

Timothy T. Lupfer

Introduction

Being social animals, we humans work with others to accomplish many of our most important tasks, in all varieties of endeavors: military, political, business, or social. But those interactions can become complex; energies are often misdirected, decision-making processes can be muddled, and success can be elusive. In many of these situations, especially those in an established organization with defined goals, the difference between success and failure is leadership, the ability to affect a group of people to achieve the organizational goal. As we confront increasingly complex and challenging goals in any type of endeavor, we often ask ourselves how we can become more effective in getting people to accomplish organizational tasks that lead to the achievement of the larger goals; that is, how we can be better leaders.

Approaches that Don't Help Mere Mortals

I will introduce a basic model for leadership, a framework both to help anyone in an organization accomplish goals through people, and to help organizations assess their own leadership development programs. But first I would like to survey popular approaches to leadership that, in my opinion, do not address the realities and complexities that leaders face. The first approach is the "Here's what *I've* done" genre, where someone who has achieved significant success in the military, business, politics, or sports describes his or her approach to leadership, and how it led to success in the given endeavor. I am not saying that some benefit cannot be derived from these works; in the best cases, these stories can inspire. But my biggest concern about this genre is that we should never lose sight of the specific context in which these people succeeded. If the context in which these people succeeded had changed, would they have been as successful? If they exercised their style of leadership in a different situation, would they have succeeded? In other words, how universal are their lessons? In the worst cases, a few of these authors come across as self-serving braggarts who may have simply been lucky in a specific set of circumstances.[1]

1 The one great exception to this genre that I will offer is Wooden on Leadership, by John Wooden, perhaps the greatest coach in American sports history. (He coached his college

© KONINKLIJKE BRILL NV, LEIDEN, 2016 | DOI 10.1163/9789004312135_012

The next problematic approach is the peddling of the secret elixir that will make anyone a successful leader. Countless studies show that our brains don't do well with complexity, and we instinctively seek quick solutions to problems. As a result, we are susceptible to confident assertions that something, especially something novel, is the "answer." We are often told, for example, that practices like communications or collaboration are the keys to success in leadership. What I intend to show with my leadership model is that each situation can be different, and these prescriptions of a magic elixir are simply not very helpful. One popular derivative of the magic potion approach is the aspirational solution. This approach identifies a single trait or tool that has great emotional appeal, such as consensus, as the key.

Unfortunately, too often the advocacy for these solutions is driven more by aspiration ("wouldn't it be better if we could just…") than by what actually exists. For example, it would indeed be wonderful if we all had the time to gain consensus for our decisions. But in the real world, gaining consensus requires a considerable amount of time, a luxury that we often don't possess. Also, in many cases our subordinates don't want to be bothered with something that they expect their superiors to decide. The reality is that often leaders must make quick decisions on their own, and then sell these decisions to their group as the decisions are being executed, using a set of tools ranging from direct authority to indirect influence. Therefore, advocating a secret ingredient, especially an aspirational one, as the key to successful leadership is unrealistic; our world is far more intricate than that.

Another approach is the diagnostic of individual style. There are several of these tools available, based either on theoretical constructs (such as the Myers-Briggs Type Indicator®) or on empirical studies with large databases for comparisons (such as the Leadership Potential Indicator). While any tool that generates more self-awareness certainly has some inherent value, I often wonder how effective these assessments can be for a leader in a specific, challenging situation, because we, as mere mortals, are prone to exaggerate our own abilities, rather than objectively applying facts. For example, when viewing an

---

team (UCLA) to ten national championships in the 1960s and 1970s.) Wooden, whose character was as legendary as his success on the basketball court, stated, "I know that 'one size fits all' doesn't apply when it comes to leadership… Nevertheless, I hope you've found something in my own experience and conclusions that will benefit you and your organization." If the other authors of the "here's what I've done" genre could be only half this straightforward and humble, we would all derive much more from their experiences. Regarding different contexts, however, it is sobering to consider if Wooden's approach would have worked in the NBA, or even in (US) collegiate athletics today.

assessment, rather than focusing on the deficiencies that the assessment suggests, we often wear the skills or inclinations that the assessment states we strongly possess as a badge of honor. Since numerous studies provide insights about our chronic lack of objectivity, such as over 30% of professionals placing themselves in the top 5% of their field, or that a leader's self evaluation is usually more generous than his or her subordinates' assessment of their leader, I fear that our tendency to distort and exaggerate our own abilities render these diagnostic tests less effective than if we were naturally more objective in applying the full range of what they reveal.

Management and Leadership

To make sense of any complex entity or interaction in our lives, we take mental shortcuts. We use heuristics, simple rules based on experience that give us reasonably good (but not perfect) solutions. Despite the academic world's insistence that we follow deliberate processes to capture and assess information and weigh options, most of us, most of the time, do not think that way; we use shortcuts. A large body of evidence from evolution strongly suggests that this is how the human brain has developed over time and even how we have survived – not by being perfect, but by being consistently "good enough." What I am going to offer is a framework, a model for quick assessments and decisions about leadership. It is based on the concept of heuristics – a way of addressing problems that does not get bogged down in too much detail within the model itself, but at the same time, it recognizes the challenging complexity of the situation.

My first step is to establish the basic terms, and in so doing, I also want to address what I believe is a false dichotomy. In much of writing about leadership today, one sees management contrasted with leadership, sometimes even as polar opposites. For example, one well-known writer has stated, "To survive in the 21st Century, we going to need a new generation of leaders – leaders [author's italics], not managers."[2] I beg to differ. I submit that a critical element of being an effective leader is being an effective manager. Leadership and management are not opposites. They are closely related; in fact, they overlap. In the most successful examples, they mutually reinforce each other. Please see the diagram in Figure 11.1.

A good working definition of management is: the employment of all resources to achieve the organizational goals. More specifically, it is the process

2 Bennis, Warren, Managing People is Like Herding Cats, 1997, Publishers Press, 63.

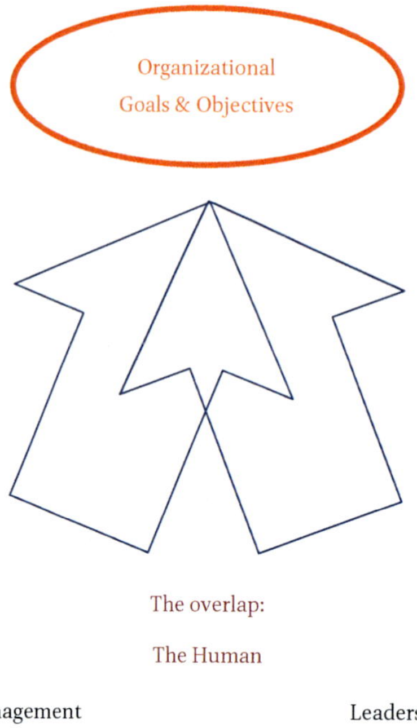

FIGURE 11.1 *Overlap between management and leadership*
COPYRIGHT TIMOTHY T. LUPFER, APRIL 2014

of planning, organizing, directing, coordinating, and controlling organizational resources to achieve the organizational goals. Among the most important resources to manage are: time, material, financial resources, processes/procedures, information, relationships/networks (including reputation), and human capital. Leadership is a concept more targeted than management. Leadership is the ability to affect a defined group of people to achieve the organizational goals, through both direct means (positional authority) and indirect means (influence). You manage several resources; you lead only people.

I believe it is crucial for a leader to utilize *both* his or her positional authority and the indirect influence to affect people. We are all very hierarchical, even though many are in denial about this well-established fact of human nature.[3] In established organizations, leaders receive their status as leaders from the organizational role they are given. In new organizations, the leader is

3 Numerous studies of humans and other primates show the importance of hierarchy in our social existence. For example, see the extract released by the (US) National Institutes of Health News, 23 April 2008, "Human Brain Appears to be 'Hard-Wired' for Hierarchy".

often the initiator, the founder of the enterprise. This positional authority can then either be reinforced or degraded by the subsequent behavior of the leader, that is, how the leader uses his or her indirect influence to affect the followers. (Indirect influence includes such attributes as appearance, communications skills, moral suasion, personality, and personal reputation.) While we often like to comfort ourselves by saying, "If a vote were held today, I'd still be in this position of authority," the reality is the organization bestows an initial advantage to us through our position within the hierarchy. Effective leaders know how to use both the formal position and the informal influences to achieve success.

As the diagram above shows, leadership and management intersect, and the crucial point of intersection is the human resource. This is one of the many resources we must *manage*, but it the *only* resource that we directly *lead*. [However, the competence of the leader in managing the other resources will have a significant impact on how followers assess a leader's capabilities, as I will discuss below.] The following scenario illustrates the overlap between leadership and management: a supervisor is responsible for a 24-hour operation. She establishes the process by which the workers will be selected to work during holidays. A big holiday is coming up, and she does not want the people on duty that day to call in sick. Her success will be a matter of both her management and leadership skills. How well she manages the selection process (who will work during the holiday) will impact how the workers perceive the fairness of the process. Here she is *managing* people. But when she meets, one-on-one, with the employee who will be working during that holiday to give him the news in advance and to emphasize how important this effort is for the entire team, she is *leading*. When she visits that worker on the job during that holiday to show her support for him or her, she is *really* leading.

A Leadership Model

To understand the situations in which we must lead, and to better identify the critical elements that can make us more effective, I offer the model in Figure 11.2 below as a framework (cf. next page):

The Broader Context:
Organizational · Competing Demands
Culture · Societal Norms
Higher Authority · Complexity/Change
Quality/Distribution of Resources

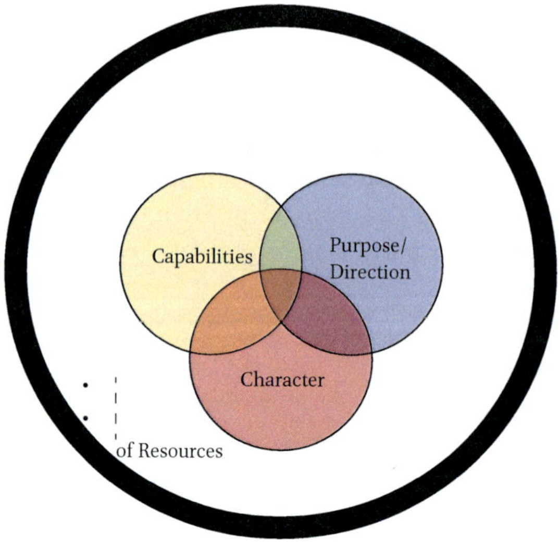

FIGURE 11.2 *The bounded triad of leadership*
COPYRIGHT TIMOTHY T. LUPFER, APRIL 2014

The model shows the triad of key leadership elements – Purpose/Direction, Capabilities, and Character – displayed here as intersecting circles, because these elements frequently overlap. But a ring of iron, shown in black, bounds these elements; this ring represents the specific context, the unique situation, in which the leader must attempt to affect others to achieve the organizational goal. It is the inevitable variation of contexts that renders glib leadership solutions ("it's all about collaboration") unhelpful, and makes unfiltered individual accounts ("Here's how I did it") impractical for any broader applications. For the mere mortals trying to lead, we must assess the context carefully and be constantly alert to changes in the context. In most situations, to be effective, the leader must adjust some of his or her elements to the context, rather than rigidly forcing a formula, a set of tools, or a specific style onto the context in the vain hope that the context will conform to the individual leader. As I will discuss under the heading of character, however, a challenge can arise when the set of values of the organization (the organizational culture, which is a key part of the context) differs significantly from the leader's own set of values. This can lead to incompatibility, intense friction, and leadership failure.

Because of the constant need to assess the context and adapt, this model shows the key leadership elements in very broad terms. The three intersecting circles represent all three elements as both individually critical and collectively complementary. The leader must constantly keep all three elements effectively in play. Ability in only one or two elements will not suffice in the long term, and failure in one element can often bring any leadership effort to a halt. The framework of these three intersecting elements mirrors similar, time-honored approaches that model similar complex challenges. For example, Purpose/Direction, Capabilities, and Character reflect the individual commitment of mind, strength, and heart found in biblical sources. The foundation of Western education, the liberal arts, has its first three disciplines (the trivium): logic, grammar, and rhetoric, which also mirror the three elements of leadership. These similarities do not make this leadership model a "perfect fit" for all situations, but they do suggest that such an approach can be an effective heuristic, or commonsense way of addressing a complex problem, reflecting other similar frameworks used in the past.

This model is also reinforced by one of the best surveys of successful leadership traits that I have seen. In the 1980s, the American Management Association sponsored a survey of thousands of participants, attempting to distill leadership success to basic traits. The consistent findings showed that honesty, being forward-looking, being inspiring, and possessing competence, in that order, were cited as the most important traits for a successful leader,[4] and this model reflects those insights.

The First Element: Purpose/Direction

To address the first of the three elements in my model, the element of Purpose/Direction means the leader must articulate the goals clearly and discern if the organizational goal is understood and adopted by the members of the group. To apply this approach to a specific situation, in the current (US) business environment of weak individual loyalty to institutions (due to, among other factors, much greater individual movement across different firms), the leader must recognize that an individual's (the follower's) goals may have a shorter time horizon than the broader organizational goals that the leader is communicating. By understanding that specific context, the leader can determine the mix of self-interest and aspiration that he or she must use to effectively frame the organizational goals for the members of the group to gain their commitment. For example, a member of the group may not intend to "stick around" for the results of a five-year expansion, but he or she will probably respond to the

4 I was introduced to the AMA survey on leadership by Barry Z. Posner at his presentation, "Lessons in Leading in Challenging Times," at a meeting of the New Jersey [US] Human Resource Planning Group on 12 October 1995. Dr. Posner, who has used the survey in his own co-authored works such as The Leadership Challenge, Jossey-Bass Publishers, San Francisco, was an academic researcher for the AMA survey.

more short-term benefits of gaining personal experience and development from the initial phase.

Relating the importance of purpose/direction even more directly to the success of the organization and the leader, the leader of a start-up must devote a significant effort to define and refine the purpose and direction of the endeavor. One of the recurring mistakes in the early stages of any enterprise is to try to be all things to all potential customers. The leader's clarity about what the enterprise is all about (and, equally important, what it is not about) is often the difference between success and failure for new endeavors.

The Second Element: Capabilities

Turning to the next element of the triad, the leader's *managerial* ability is the solid evidence of the leader's capabilities in the given role. In this model, *Capabilities* means the skills and knowledge, *appropriate for the leader's position in the organization that* the leader employs to achieve the organizational goals. The ability to apply these skills and knowledge in order to employ all the necessary resources effectively within the given organizational role is managerial ability. This is the overlap between management and leadership: followers expect their leader to be a capable manager in the position in which he or she is serving. I have observed that the importance of capabilities in leadership has often been diluted in recent years in many organizations by an over-emphasis on the emotional connections (which I will discuss, below, under character). Another dangerous form of eroding the importance of capabilities as a key element in leadership effectiveness is weakening the link between capabilities and purpose/direction, that is, the path from skills and knowledge to results. There are many potential detours on that path that can weaken this vital connection. A leader can become fixated on one of the intermediate activities, engaging in a short-term activity as an end-in-itself and not focusing on results. In a similar vein, leaders can become "enamored with the process," believing that simply "doing something" shows real accomplishment.

This dilution of the importance of raw ability can weaken the organization's duty to identify the skills and knowledge that matter – an increasingly challenging task, since globalization and technology often require both broader and deeper skill sets and knowledge. For that reason, organizations need to devote more effort to find the skills and knowledge that really count in critical leadership jobs – capabilities that get results.

Capabilities are also very vulnerable to sudden changes of context. Most organizations use the familiar heuristic that a person performing well in a subordinate position can assume the next higher position. That is a great example of an approach that is "good enough" in many cases, but this approach has also given us Parkinson's Law and the Peter Principle. To develop our leaders more effectively, we must address the unsettling risk that a promotion can place a person in a new context that demands different capabilities, which the newly promoted person may or may not possess. For this reason, "laundry lists" of competencies, separate from a specific organizational context, are of little use. What matters is: what skills and knowledge are necessary to achieve results in a specific role; whether the newly appointed occupant possesses them; if not, how quickly he or she can acquire them; and finally, who else may have those skills and knowledge.

The Third Element: Character

Finally, we have the character of the leader, the most complex element. In this model, character means the set of acquired individual values that consistently influence the leader's behavior. Of the three leadership elements, character is the most closely linked to the emotions of the followers. We are learning through neuroscience (especially through functional MRIs) and through Behavioral Economics that emotions are intertwined in our brains with our cognitive functions and that, therefore, the purely "rational person" is a myth. In other words, the ability to cleanly separate our reason from our emotions simply does not exist. This also means that followers, the people the leader is trying to affect to achieve the organizational goals, will always be touched emotionally by the leader.

Character is largely formed in each of us as we reach adulthood. The root word for "character" comes from the Greek expression "to engrave," so there is a sense of permanence regarding this leadership element. Also referring to the ancients, the importance of character in leadership in this model is a direct descendant of the classical emphasis on virtue, which celebrated the habits and practices that led to the right behavior. The element of character is also the most potentially challenging in terms of "fit" within the organization, of adjusting to the context. If the values of the organization (the organizational culture) and the values of the leader (his or her character) do not reasonably match, the long-term prognosis is not good, for neither is easy to change. Examining the concept of organizational culture in finer detail, the leader's values must also resonate reasonably (but in most instances, not perfectly) with his or her followers, the people whom the leader must affect.

Unrealistic Expectations: Everyone Will Get along

However, in the alignment of the leader's values with those of the followers (which can be a powerful emotional link), expectations can often become unrealistic. I have observed a recent tendency in many organizations in western culture, even including such organizations as the military, to aspire to achieve a complete reduction of tension among the participants in the given organization: a culture where everyone gets along "nicely" with no disagreement. In my opinion, a more realistic aspiration is to achieve *manageable tension* within the organization. This means basic agreement about the fundamental values, but recognizing that in the detailed applications, inevitable disagreements will emerge. Frequently it is the leader who must articulate the reasoning behind decisions that generate tensions. This is an important skill related to the leader's character, because the leader's character is not revealed in most cases by a saintly tendency to "do good," but by the more complex duty of explaining why difficult decisions were made.

A Difficult Challenge: Changing the Group's Values

There are also times that a leader must reset the values of the group, and this is one of the most difficult challenges a leader can face. Examples of this are when a leader is charged by the organization to improve the standards and performance of a group, to achieve a turnaround. In these roles the leader will almost certainly not be popular with the group initially. Especially in today's environment of individual sensitivity, few people like to be told that they are not performing well. If the leader's bosses have not anticipated the pushback from the followers and do not give the leader their full support, the needle can move very quickly from manageable tension to dysfunctional tension. Even with the full support of higher management, the leader with the mission of raising standards or improving performance will be faced by many challenges, and in these situations the importance of the leader's character emerges most vividly.

Trust is the Glue

But there is one emotional aspect in Character that should be top of mind in the leader as he or she assesses the challenges, and this aspect is more nuanced than the false ideal of "getting along" with everyone: trust. Based on numerous studies, trust is probably the most important attitude to foster in followers for the long-term success of a leader. The organizational status of the leader generates some initial trust among the followers through their basic acceptance of the leader's role through positional authority, but this capital can be built upon or squandered quickly through the subsequent behavior of the leader (his or her influence). Examining how trust can be built up or diluted through the leader's behavior is an example of using this leadership model is as a diagnostic tool for any organization. For example, a survey of subordinates that asks what behaviors of their leaders either foster or erode trust can yield very valuable insights or leaders at all levels. When this model was used in a consulting firm's preparation for new manager training, in interviews with potential followers of new managers, the followers were quick to point out that when a new manager assumed all the credit for the work of the team, trust in the new manager dropped precipitously. Therefore, this leadership model can be used as a tool to determine both the positive and negative behaviors in all three major elements (purpose/direction, capabilities, and character) so that new managers have concrete examples of what behaviors have worked for leaders, and what behaviors have hurt a leader's impact. Long term trust between a group and its leader is solidified when the leader's behavior shows all three leadership elements reinforcing each other: a clear purpose, demonstrated capabilities, and, most importantly, the values displayed through the leader's character.

The Limits of Character

But as important as character is, we must resist the temptation to make it a magic elixir for success. Irrespective of the leader's character, people don't "sign up" to fail. Character without a driving purpose and without the ability to succeed only wanders helplessly through the graveyard of good intentions. Followers must perceive that they are headed in the right direction and that the leader has the ability to help them get there, and a leader often reveals those two elements much earlier in the relationship with the subordinates than revealing his or her character. Ironically, the greatest challenge for the importance of character in any leadership model is that the siren song of success can initially obscure the importance of a leader's character, and thereby diminish its importance.

The greatest challenge in maintaining character as a key element of leadership is the issue of time. A leader can demonstrate both purpose/direction and capabilities fairly quickly. Character, in contrast, requires more time to be observed. The fundamental test of character is the test of commitment to values: does the behavior of the leader show that values are the primary driving force, as opposed to simply gaining personal advantage, that is, being opportunistic. This is not to say that values and self-interest are always in conflict; in the best (or luckiest) of situations they are both served. But the true test comes when a choice must be made between self-interest (personal advantage) and the more universal values that are shared across the organization. Does the leader default to only protecting his or her position, either in small ways (indulging in self-promotion by taking credit for a team effort) or in larger ones (guarding only his or her position/status in a time of reorganization)? When organizational values and the leader's self-interests collide, if the leader opts for the self-oriented, opportunistic choice, trust within the group erodes quickly. But such revealing situations may not occur frequently or immediately, so a leader's character may not be revealed at the outset of the relationship with the followers. Character is demonstrated over time, just as trust is built over time.

If followers require more time to discern the character of a leader, the ability of those *above* a leader in the hierarchy to assess his or her character is even more daunting. Very often character is simply assumed to exist already in the person, particularly in people in high-level positions. In my opinion, one of the most dangerous assumptions in any organization is a casual dismissal of the importance of character by assuming that character merely comes with the position or background. The lack of rigorously assessing the character of leaders at high levels has a long history, from false assumptions about Alcibiades of ancient Athens to mistakenly equating power with virtue in assessing the behavior of totalitarian tyrants of the twentieth century (and a few in the 21st century as well). In determining who should lead in a large organization, the top executives and boards should assess all three key elements in each candidate: Purpose/Direction, Capabilities, and Character. Character is the most difficult to assess, and it requires the most digging, especially drilling down to get feedback from subordinates. But neglect of this element can result in disastrous choices and bad outcomes for the organization.

Does Success Obviate the Need for Character?

The frequent time delay and the extra effort required to reveal a leader's character also suggest an even deeper dilemma: is character really that important in a leader? If the leader can just "get it done," isn't that enough to be successful? I want to suggest that just "getting it done" (which is focusing only on the first two elements, Purpose/Direction and Capabilities) can produce a successful leader *in the short term*. Sometimes specific circumstances evolve which favor this approach, a form of "leadership lite." For example, an organization can have a culture that neither values nor fosters long-term trust. The typical "leader" in this context is the self-absorbed but successful tyrant; he or she can often attract eager subordinates who want to get a piece of the action. Most often this results in a revolving door for personnel, where most of those who enter the wolf's lair eventually get chewed up and spit out. But many people are willing to take this risk for the benefit of gaining the "experience," so some organizations can certainly lumber along without inspiring leadership.

This leads to the depressing realization that, if the relationships between the leaders and subordinates are only transactional but are still successful by measured outcomes, the importance of the leader's character in that organizational context may be minimal. But in free societies where people exercise choice, I submit that this environment is the exception, rather than the rule. We are all very social animals; having no connection with one's leader other than performing as a worker bee would be difficult to tolerate for an extended period of time if one had any choice. Clearly, human history provides numerous examples of relationships enforced only by brute force and fear, from societies based on slavery to totalitarian states today, so "leaders" without character certainly exist. But a consistent theme in those societies is that the oppressed subordinates do only enough to "get by." The difference between an oppressed society and a free society is the giving of the extra effort, *the discretionary effort*, by the subordinates to the leader, and the element that delivers that discretionary effort is character.

Why Character Counts

Character remains, therefore, the most difficult leadership element to assess and the one that requires the most time to develop. Character alone cannot make an effective leader; the leader must also provide purpose and direction, and must display the capabilities to move the organization along the desired path. But character will sustain the effectiveness of the leader, especially through challenging times. *Character is the added factor that motivates followers to give their discretionary effort.* Character opens the emotional channel between the leader and the follower. When interviewing people and asking them to remember one incident where a leader did something that confirmed his or her status for them as an effective leader, I have been struck by the consistency in responses. Most often, the person I interviewed will remember an event where the leader intervened in a personal way, building a strong emotional connection. But when asked about the leader effectively demonstrating the complementary elements: capabilities and purpose/direction, the constant response is, "yes, of course." In other words, the emotional connections enabled by character are built on the existing foundation of effective purpose/direction and capability. Character is the element that opens the emotional channels that promote the discretionary effort in followers, but the other two elements must be in place for character to have its powerful influence. All three elements work in concert to promote trust, the most important component in any organizational culture. Trust is the glue that holds organizations together and promotes success, and character is the most important element in creating and sustaining trust.

Conclusion

The value of this model, this tool for us as mere mortals, is not that it provides the secret formula to make anyone a great leader, but that is suggests the key elements that an effective leader must employ. Leadership, with all three elements in play, is the difference between an organization that merely exists and an organization that grows and prospers. This model has neither long lists of competencies and skills, nor elaborate tools for self-diagnosis. But what it does offer is a framework for assessing the specific situation in which a leader finds him- or her- self, and for focusing on the three critical elements that must be constantly demonstrated by any leader: Purpose/Direction, Capabilities, and Character. The specifics of that effort will vary across different situations, and the leader must always be alert to changes in the context, but by using this model we can identify our leadership challenges, structure our leadership experiences to learn from them, and recognize the risks to our success in different situations. Most importantly, we can be especially mindful of the role of character in affecting our followers. Character is the element most difficult to measure and assess, but it is the "third element" that means the difference between just getting by and succeeding. By understanding our context and employing all three leadership elements, we can do a reasonably good job as imperfect leaders, leading imperfect people in our complex world.

Bibliography

Argyle, Michael, *The Social Psychology of Work*. Penguin Books; London, 1989.

Aristotle, *The Nicomachean Ethics*. Translated by J.A.K. Thomson. Penguin Classics; London, 2004.

Bennis, Warren, *Managing People is Like Herding Cats*. Publishers Press; Provo, UT USA, 1997.

Boyatzis, Richard, *The Competent Manager*. John Wiley & Sons; New York, 1982.

Conger, Jay A. *Learning to Lead*. Jossey-Bass; San Francisco, 1992.

Fukuyama, Francis, *Trust*. Simon & Schuster, Inc.; New York, 1995.

Kempf, James/Watkin, Malham/Wenker, Kenneth (eds.), *Military Ethics*. [US] National Defense University Press Publications, 1987.

Kouzes, James M./Posner, Barry Z., *The Leadership Challenge*. Jossey-Bass; San Francisco, 1995.

Wooden, John, *Wooden on Leadership*. McGraw-Hill; New York, 2005.

CHAPTER 12

Less Lethal Weapons in Military Operations

Patrice Mompeyssin

Introduction

As it is stated in the title, less lethal weapons will be considered in this presentation only in military operations. The other major framework is law enforcement within States. Two reasons for that. The first is that the subject would be too large including both aspects, the second is that I was an Army officer and I have no competence/skill at all in police tasks. However, there is some common ground when military forces do "police" tasks, or when units of Gendarmerie participate in external operations, mainly in peace keeping or stabilization operations, in crowd control missions (although there are differences between military and police (Gendarmerie) missions, between police law enforcement and military crowd control).[1]

However, even if I have participated in weapons development and experimentations (Ground Based Short Range Air Defence systems), I am not a technical expert of this particular area, and I have no practical experience on the Field of situations requiring less lethal weapons.

My starting point for this study is when I realized that there were very few discussions, articles, presentations, in circles non experts on less lethal weapons, on an issue which was very on the mood 10 years ago when I was in activity. Technical reviews for example do not present many articles on the subject,[2] as well as newspapers in general, like for example on armed drones or robots. So my question was: what are the reasons: technical difficulties, ethical or legal issues, lack of a major operational interest, fear of protestations by NGOs, media and public opinions? I will report the results of my studies on all these aspects and give my conclusion which is not enthusiastic.

1 The policeman/gendarme faces a citizen of his own country who demonstrates democratically, even if it is violent. The soldiers uses his force as the last resort to defend or apply the policy of his government, cf. Brice Houdet, review Inflexions No 4. 2006.

2 Nothing on Defence News, or in: Jane's International Defense Reviews 2012.

 | DOI 10.1163/9789004312135_013

General Considerations

The legal use of military force has to be the last resort, and respect the Just War theory, in both aspects of jus ad bellum and jus in bello. It must respect the Law Of Armed Conflicts, international law and Human Rights.

There has always been two approaches to war. The first is the direct approach where the aim is to destroy the enemy by the battle, even if it is sad and unfortunate, as a tragic necessity, even in self defence or for a just cause. The second is the indirect one, with minimum violence, the ideal being to win without fighting. In this regard we can find the dream of a war with zero dead. Non lethal weapons were one way to this aim. We know now that it is technically impossible.

Lastly, obviously, the best way to have zero death is to get peace by prevention, negotiation and deterrence. "Si vis pacem para bellum" (Cicero). Knowing however that non military measures and factors (blockades, finance, economy, poverty) can destroy lives and even may kill more than wars and conflicts. And it is strange that peace could rely on the threat of mutual destruction by nuclear weapons, at the extreme range of lethality.

Definitions

They are essential for the subject because they have consequences on the concepts, on operational legal and ethical issues.

Most experts underline firstly that defining what is a weapon is difficult. Basic day to day objects can be used as weapons and lethal weapons do not always kill. General Jean Yves Saffray (French Gendarmerie) declared during a conference; "a fist blow in the throat is more lethal than a bullet in the foot".[3] And a 30 g anti personnel mine do not kill always, if medical care arrives quickly, but nobody would declare that it is non lethal.[4]

Everybody agrees today that it is impossible to produce fully non lethal weapons, in terms of probability, scientifically speaking. Then, experience shows that there are always possible casualties, according to the range, the power of the weapons, their accuracy, the physical conditions of the targeted persons (children, pregnant women, ill or drunk people are more vulnerable), and mistakes by the user.

As an example among many, this is the NATO definition:

3 François Bernard Huyghe, les armes non létales, 14.

4 Cf. François Bernard Huyghe, les armes non létales, 22.

> Non-Lethal Weapons are weapons which are explicitly designed and developed to incapacitate or repel personnel, with a low probability of fatality or permanent injury, or to disable equipment with minimal undesired damage or impact on the environment.

The other definitions use terms such as reduced lethality (France), sub lethal, less lethal. There are mainly two difficulties raised regarding these definitions. Firstly, human beings can be dead or alive, they can't be in the middle. The second is to define the acceptable criteria of residual lethality, in terms of figures. The only one I found is given by Pierre Thys.[5]

> "The ideal kinetic projectile should neutralize 98% of the targeted population.
> 1% max of the population would not be sensitive to the effects.
> 1% max would support permanent lesions.
> Death rate should be max de 5% among the 1%, which means 0,02% population.
> Temporary effects should not last more than de 30 min".

Furthermore, in a 1986 US Department of Justice conference, it was observed that the "excessive use of non-lethal weapons may result in no net improvement in rates of fatal injury when compared to lethal weapons practice. If, for example, a less lethal weapon is one-tenth as lethal as a handgun but is used ten times more frequently, an identical number of subjects will be fatally injured."[6]

These kinds of calculations and considerations are however dangerous. For example, some argue on the fact that a lot of conventional munitions are required to kill an adversary, that we can obtain equivalent rates of lethality between lethal and less lethal weapons. The Federation of American scientists Working Group has thus developed a mathematical model showing that incapacitating anaesthetizing biochemical agents are likely to cause at least 10% fatalities. In comparison firearms lead generally to 35% deaths among casualties, shells to 20%, grenades to 10%. Chemical weapons lethality during 1st World war was estimated at 7%.[7]

It can lead also to the conclusion that the end (reducing casualties on a global scale) may justify very lethal means. Thus, at the extreme, the atomic

5 Pierre Thys, Les armes à létalité réduite, 228.

6 Stuart Casey-Maslen, Non-kinetic Energy weapons termed 'non-lethal', 9.

7 Neil Davison, 'Non-Lethal' Weapsons, 6.

bomb in Hiroshima is supposed to have saved many lives in shortening the war. Finally, it is impossible to calculate afterwards what would have been the exact amount of casualties in using lethal weapons instead of less lethal ones.

Some replace the word weapon by capability, device, system, or means. The US Long Range Acoustic Device LRAD for example is named "hailing and warning device". The French Gendarmerie names these weapons: "intermediate-middle force means".

Stuart Casey-Maslen uses the definition: non kinetic energy weapons termed non lethal, which is long and does not include thus the kinetic ones.

The best definition, avoiding all the traps is that chosen by Pierre Thys, which is : weapon of momentary neutralization. It remains a weapon which indicates that it is dangerous, but that there is no intent to kill, and that the effects are reversible. It is not perfect because lethal classic weapons intend firstly to obtain an effect, before killing. Killing is a likely issue but not an aim in itself, at least today for democratic forces. Armed forces today are no more in a position to "bleed" the enemy like in Verdun during the 1st World War. We speak about taking a position, holding it, or to separate belligerents, defend safe areas, protect populations, etc.

Technical Aspects

I would place the results in 3 categories:

In the first are the "exotic/utopic" systems, in which hopes had been put and the development of which have failed. There are for example slippery (black ice) or adhesive foams, glues, obscuring products, malodorants (ill smelling), 81 mm mortars rounds,[8] vortex rings, etc..... They do not work.

There are mixed information on Radio Frequency vehicle stoppers, High Power Micro waves and Electro-Magnetic Pulse systems, nets. According to Rear Admiral (ret) Massimo Annati[9] the Multi Frequency-Radio Frequency vehicle stopper could be operational in 2018 at the best.

Biochemical weapons are a particular case. According to Neil Davison: "while incapacitating agents have commonly been viewed as chemical weapons, biochemical weapons are also used to reflect the confluence of chemistry and biology in this area. Greater understanding of the biochemical processes in the body at the molecular level means that it is now more appropriate to

8 Massimo Annati, Non-Lethal Weapons, in: Military Technologie 11/2012, 49–53.

9 Massimo Annati, Non-Lethal Capabilities for Combat Vehicles, in: Military Technology 11/2013, 75–77.

think of a biochemical weapons spectrum rather than distinct chemical and biological weapons.... They share the characteristics of both. Their effects can range from incapacitation to death. They can act on a variety of physiological processes including blood pressure, temperature regulation and immune response...///The focus has long been on agents that depress or inhibit the function of the central nervous system."[10]

Biochemical weapons, or incapacitating agents (drugs), are technically feasible, but too dangerous and raise serious ethical concerns as they target the brain of the aimed persons. Their failure was demonstrated in 2002 during the theatre attack in Moscow, when many hostages were involuntarily killed and when the forces in charge of neutralizing the terrorists, shot the majority of them while unconscious. It happened in 23 October 2002, there were 800 hostages, 50 terrorists. At least 129 hostages were killed, and many survivors needed medical treatment.[11]

The second category includes the small "classical" short range operational systems more or less accepted on legal and ethical bases, except in cases of accidents. They include rubber bullets, flashbangs, flashballs, stun guns, tear gas, pepper spray and the TASER.

I include in this category the green dazzling lasers, not blinding, which have longer ranges (2,5 km), but remain individual weapons, used mainly at checkpoints to warn vehicles to stop. They could lead to permanent eye damages at close ranges.[12] According Massimo Annati,[13] the death rates in check points in Irak decreased from one a day to one a week after deployment of Green Lasers. The tactical utility is to determine the nature of the threat and to be a tool for escalation of force.

The third category includes long range high technology systems, with collective effects, which have proved their feasibility.

The first is the Long Range Acoustic device (US). According to Juliette Volcler[14] it has a 3000 m range, is very directional, with 2 functions: megaphone (music, voice) and alarm (continuous sound). At less than 5 metres, it could provoke a permanent deafness. Under 100 m, fleeing is mandatory. The system can either disseminate information, either being used as a weapon to saturate an adversary. It has been exported to Australia, Singapour, China, South-Korea. It was used by Georgia police against protestors in 2007.

10 Neil Davison, 'Non-Lethal' Weapsons, 106.
11 Cf. Neil Davison, 'Non-Lethal' Weapsons, 125.
12 Cf. Neil Davison, 'Non-Lethal' Weapsons, 152.
13 Cf. Massimo Annati, Non-Lethal Capabilities for Combat Vehicles, in: Military Technology 11/2013, 75–77
14 Cf. Juliette Volcler, Le son comme arme.

For Neil Davison,[15] LRAD can issue either a verbal warning with a capability to follow up with a deterrent tone to influence behaviour or determine intent.

There are several versions:

- LRAD 1000 has a circular dish (0,8 m diameter, 15 cm thick). The beam is 30° large. Behind the transmitter, the sound level is 40 DB below than in front. The range could be 500 m for voice, 1 km with tone (less than J Volcler estimation).
- LRAD 500 has ranges of 300 m for voice, 500 m for tone mode.

350 LRAD had been deployed by 2005, many in Irak for checkpoints, and for protecting ships or for maritime interdiction.

Stuart Casey-Maslen observes: "LRADs have reportedly been used in repelling pirate attacks off the coast of Somalia on a number of occasions. For instance, in November 2009, a security team aboard the motor vessel Maersk-Alabama responded to an attack on the vessel, 560 nautical miles off the north-east coast of Somalia, by using evasive manoeuvres, LRADs and small arms fire, causing the suspected pirates to break off their attack."[16]

But, according to Massimo Annati,[17] writes that the acoustic systems are often sensitive to the wind and not really efficient.

The second is the Active Denial System (ADS), working on the principle of directed energy. Massimo Annati indicates that the Active Denial System, products a millimetric wave (95 GHZ 100 kW), which penetrates 1/64 inches (0,3 -0,4 mm for Neil Davison) under the skin and cause a high feeling of hotness (45–55 degrees), without burning, in a few seconds. It was projected in Afghanistan, and brought back without being employed. Admiral M. Annati identifies 3 obstacles:

- It is an heavy system, with a bad mobility (2× 20 feet containers),
- As we will see later on, its acceptability by public opinions is low, it is painful for the targeted persons (but all weapons are at least painful) and could be considered as an instrument of torture,
- The preparation time is 16 hours (at least 2 hours for Georges Henri Bricet des Vallons).

15 Cf. Neil Davison, 'Non-Lethal' Weapsons, 195. 200.

16 Stuart Casey-Maslen, Non-kinetic Energy weapons termed 'non-lethal', 68.

17 Cf. Massimo Annati, Non-Lethal Weapons, in: Military Technologie 11/2012, 49–53.

According to Georges Henri Bricet des Vallons,[18] the ADS is sensitive to the meteorological conditions, rain in particular, loosing from 10 to 25% in efficiency.

As described by Stuart Casey-Maslen, the ADS emits a roughly two-metre-wide beam to a distance of 500 metres.[19]

And for Neil Davison,[20] it was firstly a US Airforce programme at the beginning of the 90s (research started as soon as the 80s to protect bases in repelling intruders, the main aim being to protect nuclear infrastructures). The short duration of exposure prevent the burns. The frequency was chosen as an atmospheric window for a good transmission in the air. It is the same technology as the anti material HPM. However the beam could damage the cornea.

The first public information was given in 2001 in an article titled "people Zapper".

In 2001 field tests were achieved on volunteers at 700 m ranges, (with up to 200 volunteers and 3500 exposures). A second generation was developed on HUMVEE in 2004 (ADS system 1).

The estimated range is up to 1 km; the beam can touch 3 or 4 grouped persons.

As said before, the critical factor is the time of exposure. The effects can vary from detection, pain, burns (second or third degree) even to death. During the tests, there were 6 blistering cases and 2 cases with 2nd degree burns requiring medical attention.

According to Altman the safe duration do not exceed a few seconds and depends from the intensity of the beam. But, according to the supporters, wounds on skin and eye will be avoided because the targeted persons will move out. However, these "targets" can be blocked by barriers or by the crowd.

It is said that the operator is able to see the beam and can control the duration. But the danger may come from repeated impulsions.

ADS modular system 2 was presented in 2007. There are now several other versions, with a portable one for the police (range 15 m, with an 8 cm diameter antenna, prototype level).

There are mixed information regarding the employment of the 100 kw system.

The last issue is the possible unknown effects, in particular on the brain. Although a 2004 NATO report established that tests on mice showed no cancer. That raises the common scientific issue of the limit of the precautionary principle.

---

18 Georges Henri Bricet des Vallons, expert en systèmes d'armes à létalité réduite.

19 Cf. Stuart Casey-Maslen, Non-kinetic Energy weapons termed 'non-lethal', 62.

20 Cf. Neil Davison, 'Non-Lethal' Weapsons, 166–174.

It depends on their employment, but both LRAD and ADS have difficulties to discriminate adversaries and innocent civilians.

To conclude this chapter, I would like to give the statement made by Thierry Jacob in the book of Pierre Thys:

> The absolute non lethal device do not exist and his research can be seen as the quest of the Grail, when we consider the uncertainty of the physiological reactions of the human targets. It is difficult to predict the emerging technologies in the near and medium terms. The chemical and kinetic technologies will remain probably the preferred ones. The true changes in the short term will be in the development of more adapted, compact systems with increased capacities. In the middle term, military will wait for rheostatic, gradable systems allowing to go from non lethal to lethal weapons. It remains a technical challenge but it will certainly raise many questions in terms of acceptability. Training will be more complex and detailed and will raise enormous problems in terms of responsibility.[21]

Legal Constraints

There are important, paradoxically more than on many lethal weapons, but they cannot be bypassed – circumvented. Law is Law. The main limits are the well known bans on chemical (1993) and biological (1972) weapons. A particularity is that chemical riot control agents used for law enforcement inside States are not forbidden. But they are forbidden as a method of warfare. The use of these agents in military crowd control operations is controversial. The US authorize them, the British not (as Australians and Canadians).

The UN General Assembly, in a resolution adopted in 1969 on the question of chemical and biological (bacterial) weapons, stated: "UNGA Declares as contrary to the generally recognized rules of international law, as embodied in the [1925 Geneva Gas Protocol], the use, in international armed conflicts of: "[a] any chemical agents of warfare – chemical substances, whether gaseous, liquid or solid – which might be employed because of their direct toxic effects on man, animals or plants".

There is a legal gap for Bio chemical weapons (drugs incapacitating), which are in the middle. But it is wise to consider them as chemical and biological; thus forbidden.

21 Pierre Thys, Les armes à létalité réduite, 51f.

Neil Davison writes: "the creeping legitimization of new biochemical weapons, as described by Perry Robinson, is seen as the greatest threat to the existing prohibitions on chemical and biological weapons and a contributions factor to what Wheelis and Dando have termed as the imminent militarization of biology."[22]

One important constraint is the 1980 Convention on Prohibitions or Restrictions on the Use of Certain Conventional Weapons which May Be Deemed to Be Excessively Injurious or to Have Indiscriminate Effects as amended on 21 December 2001. It is a strong limit, in particular for crowd control.

Generally speaking in any case, Law of armed conflicts forbid to target civilians.

There is the ban on blinding lasers (Protocol IV to the 1980 Convention on Certain Conventional Weapons, 13 October 1995). There is also the 1976 convention on the interdiction of the hostile use of technologies modifying the environment.

Stuart Casey-Maslen[23] develops also how Less Lethal Weapons (LLW) could be concerned by the international Human rights law, in particular the right to life, which can be in favour or against Less Lethal Weapons. They can be judged as unacceptable if they caused a death, even if it is exceptional. But, they would have been necessary if the use of classic weapons led to casualties. For example: "The European Court of Human Rights has specifically regretted the lack of availability of an alternative to lethal force to a State Party to the 1950 European Convention on Human Rights. In Gülec v. Turkey, the Court stated that: it goes without saying that a balance must be struck between the aim pursued and the means employed to achieve it. The gendarmes used a very powerful weapon because they apparently did not have truncheons, riot shields, water cannon, rubber bullets or tear gas. The lack of such equipment is all the more incomprehensible and unacceptable because the province of Sirnak, as the Government pointed out, is in a region in which a state of emergency has been declared,where disorder could have been expected."[24]

Stuart Casey-Maslen raises also the issue of the Right to liberty and security. "Less lethal weapons could be concerned if they prevent somebody from moving." And the right to protest: "This does not give the security forces the licence to use Non Kinetic Energy weapons unnecessarily or disproportionately, even if a protest is banned by the authorities." The last constraint is the right to

22 Neil Davison, 'Non-Lethal' Weapsons, 138.

23 Cf. Stuart Casey-Maslen, Non-kinetic Energy weapons termed 'non-lethal', 27.

24 Gülec v. Turkey, Judgment, 27. July 1998 (App. No. 54/1997/838/1044), § 71.

Health: "However, a challenge to certain Non Kinetic Energy weapons on the basis of their health effects, merits consideration."[25]

Stuart Casey-Maslen refers mainly to Law Enforcement situations but that could be extended to military examples. Lastly, the opponents to these types of weapons consider them as instruments of torture, or of cruel, inhuman, or degrading treatment or punishment. But there is no intent by the user to cause pain for getting an information of a confession, or for punishment; except in an illegal use, which is possible with many tools of the common life.

Lastly in this chapter, it could be worth to remind that policemen, gendarmes and soldiers have also the right to life and health, even if they are professionals accepting as part of their mission the risk to be killed or wounded. Their lives should not be endangered without strong reasons.

Public Opinion Effect

How will react medias and public opinions after showing people suffering pain at the TV is a major constraint facing commanders and politician wishing to employ less lethal weapons. That can be easily demonstrated by the controversies around the rare victims of the TASER or rubber bullets in law enforcement.

Public opinion reaction is a fact to accept. But it is the cost efficiency, the ethical issues and the legality of the system which should be taken as criteria of choice in the end, for the development and the employment of less lethal weapons.

Financial Aspects

The funding challenges are not the same as for big programmes on aircraft carriers, main battles tanks, missiles, nuclear weapons, jet fighters, etc. However, providing they cannot replace lethal weapons, they come in addition, in more and more tight budgets. Their cost appears then high, in particular if their operational value is not considered as essential. Data are not easy to find, but I got some elements:

According to Juliette Volcler,[26] Toronto Police bought 4 LRAD for 23,000 Euros for the 2010 G20, which is not very much. In 2004 New York police paid 25,000E each, in 2009 San Diego Police bought them 22,000E each.

25 Stuart Casey-Maslen, Non-kinetic Energy weapons termed 'non-lethal', 35.

26 Cf. Juliette Volcler, Le son comme arme, 119.

Neil Davison points out: "Up to 2005, ADS cost 51 millions dollars, including 9 millions to evaluate the effects on a human being. The 30 kw Silent Guardian version of the ADS could cost 10 millions dollars.

Non lethal weapons suffer from a lack of official funding. The US Joint Non Lethal Weapons annual budget is 50 millions de dollars, which is very few in comparison with the DOD budget (500 billions dollars). And the US Council of Foreign Relations considered that the need was 300 millions dollars (in 2004)."[27]

According to Georges-Henri Bricet des Vallons,[28] the 2009 budget of the US Joint Non Lethal Weapons Department (JNLWD) was 65 millions dollars.

But it is difficult to assess if the technical problems come only from the lack of funding, or if it is indeed the poor scientific and operational perspectives, as well as the legal and public opinion constraints which limit the funding, leading then to no technical improvement.

Costs of military equipment are difficult to assess. The best way is to consider the global cost of the programmes including development. Thus, the global cost of the RAFALE aircraft was estimated by the French Senate at more than 40 Billions Euros in 2011.[29] The cost by system depends greatly on the number built. For example the cost of a LECLERC main battle tank is estimated at 13 Millions Euros; a TIGER helicopter at 25 Millions Euros, a RAFALE aircraft at 65 Millions Euros.[30]

It is clear that Financial limits are important but not the main factor.

Advocacy and Oppositions

Obviously less lethal weapons can save live when they are considered as an alternative to the use of lethal force, or when it raises its threshold (Neil Davison). In asymmetric warfare or stabilization operations, in peace keeping missions, in the responsibility to protect situations, there are plenty of scenarios where less lethal weapons could save lives, keeping in mind that casualties remain possible: checkpoints, crowd control, guarding of installations, separation/interposition of belligerents, denial of an area, arrests of insurgents or terrorists. Less lethal weapons may mainly be useful also in self defence of units facing aggressive people or attacking crowds. In the Inflexion review

27 Neil Davison, 'Non-Lethal' Weapsons, 85.

28 Cf. Georges Henri Bricet des Vallons, expert en systèmes d'armes à létalité réduite.

29 www.usinenouvelle.com/article/les-senateurs-reevaluent-le-prix-du-rafale.N164290.

30 http://www.focus-defence.com/cout.html.

number 4 (December 2006), Brice Houdet describes such a situation when civilians including women and children attacked a unit near a village: the soldiers did not open fire, but the vehicles suffered a lot: broken windows, punctured tires. That could have led to the death of the soldiers or of civilians if the soldiers had opened fire. These types of situations appeared also in Somalia, in particular with armed opponents mixed within the population. If saving Lives is considered as the key ethical principle, who can oppose the use of Less Lethal Weapons when there is no other solution than the use of lethal force. Again, afterwards, it could be reproached to a military force not to have used Less Lethal Weapons.

However, opponents have good and valid reasons, to contest or to have concerns.

Firstly, Less Lethal Weapons can be a pretext, to appear attractive, for the industry, for the producers, or for the military supporters such as the famous colonel Alexander. "Rheostatic scalable weapons fall in this category. From the outset the US MOD stressed the requirement of a rheostatic capability. ... The first decade of the twenty first century has seen increasing emphasis on the integration of non lethal and lethal systems as well as continuing research and development towards individual weapon systems with variable effects ranging from non lethal to lethal. Clearly the less lethal terminology is becoming incompatible with the nature of many new weapons being developed under the banner on non lethal."[31]

Secondly, Less Lethal Weapons are a perfect tool to get compliance, for a political control. They are the perfect tool for a dictator to oppress or suppress freedom within its own population. The only way to avoid this critic is to tightly limit the export of these systems. But we all know it is difficult to implement.

Juliette Volcler observes in the conclusion of her book on acoustic weapons: "The reality is very disparate, badly matched, with fantasies and real devices. Both are instruments of the Power. We have today to prevent the confiscation of the sound for security and business reasons. If the Power intend to invest the life, we will try to escape this fact in the acoustic domain and elsewhere".[32]

As reported by Stuart Casey-Maslen, Less Lethal Weapons can be used to suppress rights to life, to Health or to basic freedoms such as the right to demonstrate.

As stated by Steve Wright declares in his article on: "So called 'non-lethal weapons" have featured regularly in human rights abuses since they first found a role in colonial times in crowd control operations... Security peacekeeping

31 Neil Davison, 'Non-Lethal' Weapsons, 7.

32 Juliette Volcler, Le son comme arme, 155.158.

packages often disguise agendas set by states, which demand pacification rather than justice. The very technologies and tactics used for coercive peacekeeping operations are designed to mask the level of violence being used. Tools to quash dissent are big business and the security apparatus is permeated by commercial interests aggressively marketing technical fixes for a wide range of social and political problems. BSSRS (1974) was the first NGO to realise that such technologies were being designed to appear rather than be safe and to identify their function as an apparent technical 'fix' for wider social and political problems. As such, names such as plastic bullets and teargas disguise the real effects of such weapons which include internal injuries, scalping, blindness, vomit induction and deaths (Omega 2000 and NIHRC 2003)."[33]

Thirdly, it can give to the soldier a false feeling of power, and increase the use of force, as he knows that he encounters less risk of causing death.[34] The opponent can have the same feeling and be more tempted to attack the force, knowing that he will not be killed. It is why the military leaders in particular wants always to have lethal force available. In comparison, lethal weapons may be more deterring. But looking at what is happening in the world may also make think of the contrary. Then, Less Lethal Weapons appear also as a new "High Tech" way for the developed countries to dominate the non developed ones. Using hostile crowds and the local population is indeed the way to bypass the advantage of the Western lethal systems. Less Lethal Weapon may also in fact just help the military to increase the lethality of their operations.

As reported by Stuart Casey-Maslen: "As part of a seemingly pre-planned massacre at a stadium in Conakry, Guinea, on 28 September 2009, it has been reported that tear gas was first fired into the political gathering from outside. This created a stampede, following which the security forces fired into the crowd."[35]

Another example: an acoustic system can oblige snipers to move (used perhaps by the US in Irak at Falloujah). But why not if this sniper is killing innocent civilians like in Sarajevo during the former Yugoslavian wars. Military commanders are right when they want to keep their freedom of action, in using Less Lethal Weapons as a complement, as an additional tool. Commanders do not want to be obliged to use them in some circumstances, or as a required step before using lethal systems. It is up to the local commander to assess the situation and take the best option. In this regard it is true that Less Lethal Weapons augment the complexity for the user, but if this user is correctly

33 Steve Wright, Violent Peacekeeping.

34 Cf. Mondo Diplomatique, 5. August 2000.

35 Stuart Casey-Maslen, Non-kinetic Energy weapons termed 'non-lethal', 52.

trained, it is manageable. Nevertheless we have to accept that there will be, under stress some errors. Pierre Thys has established this in scientific manner with a lot of data coming from police. But we must have more confidence in the Western trained soldier. That makes me remember what a US NGO member told me last year. In Kosovo he had been saved from a very bad situation by a young low rank soldier, who have taken the good decisions with a very cool manner. It is obvious however that the use of Less Lethal Weapons requires a high degree of training, and control by commanders and political authorities. But it is not a reason to abandon them.

Stuart Casey-Maslen describes in his article the statement of a US academic: "Pentagon's lack of interest and objections from humanitarian groups who worry that such weapons could cause permanent injuries and violate treaties such as the Chemical Weapons Convention. The perverse result of such criticism is that U.S. troops end up taking lives that might have been spared by such new technologies."[36]

Even Amnesty International, while expressing strong concerns, is not fully opposed to a Less Lethal Weapon such as the TASER (reported by Stuart Casey-Maslen) "At the same time, in the context of policing in the UK, a staff member of Amnesty International."[37]

UK has written specifically on the deployment of Tasers: "Amnesty International is not opposed to deployment of Tasers as an alternative to lethal force, nor does it seek a total ban on the device. However, Amnesty International is particularly concerned by the widespread deployment of a potentially lethal electro-shock weapon. That is when they are not restricted to deployment only the highest level of the force continuum, i.e. just below the point at which lethal force would be used. It should also be made clear here that the use of a Taser is clearly preferable to the deployment of a firearm as an alternative to lethal force."[38]

"Amnesty International has also stressed that Tasers should be used only by specially trained officers."[39] Again we speak about law enforcement cases, but that can be extended to military situations). The last thing I would like to notice is the fact that there could be a reluctance to the use of these weapons by the servicemen as non noble. It is no more the duel between knights, no more the loyal fight between adversaries who risks their lives and respect

36 Max Boot, The Struggle to Transform the Military.

37 Stuart Casey-Maslen, Non-kinetic Energy weapons termed 'non-lethal', 60.

38 Oliver Sprague, The Deployment of Taser Weapons to UK Law Enforcement Officials: An Amnesty International Perspective, 309.

39 Presentation by Angela Wright tot he May 2010 Meeting of Experts.

themselves (inflexions n 9 Jean-Paul Charnay p. 231). But there is no nobility at all to obliged to fire on civilians even hostile.

Conclusion

I will not give lessons as I am not in a responsibility position. I am not specially enthusiastic about promoting Less Lethal Weapons as I accept most critics. Neil Davison recommend scrutiny which is a good approach. Firstly I accept the vision given by Georges-Henri Bricet des Vallons: "The Non Lethal Weapon appears as a major concept in the post modern approach of conflicts. ... The non lethality theory introduces in the military action a bio-strategy, a techno strategy of the living, which is no more determined by the destruction of the enemy body but by a permanent control by and on the bodies."[40]

This new control on the bodies appears frightening, as it is unknown, while lethal weapons have been used for several thousands of years. Can we make the analogy with the Crossbow, which was initially forbidden in the Middle Age? I fully agree with François Bernard Huyghe: "Non Lethal Weapons are neither the utopia of some, neither the nightmare of others. More simply, they answer to a rational need of police and military forces: limit violence received or given to a necessary minimum. It is a moral principle as well as a principle of efficiency. But there is no violence without risk. No marvel of technology will take out the responsibility of the user, who will decide in addition in difficult circumstances (confusion, lack of information and time, disorder, stress). The user must be prepared technically, tactically and morally. The limit of all technical advance is in the responsibility of men who act on persons and not on things."[41]

Nevertheless I think there is a lack of confidence in the servicemen of the democratic forces. There will be rare accidents and mistakes but in most cases they will be able to take the good decisions. That does not mean they should not be controlled, for their good. Financing is not the real problem. Less Lethal Weapons will be funded if they are technically feasible, respect the international law and have a strong operational interest.

There are real technical difficulties: "The efforts to develop new non lethal weapons face some especially critical obstacles. During the last 10–15 years, we have witnessed dozens of technologies which offered potentially revolutionary

40 Georges Henri Bricet des Vallons, L 'arme non létale dans la stratégie militaire des Etats-Unis.

41 François Bernard Huyghe, les armes non létales, 125f.

results absorbing millions of dollars just for slowly and silently fading away as problems after problems arose. Military want increased ranges, which means increased energy, which means more risks of deaths or wounds, more weight, less mobility, etc...."[42]

But there is no absolute scientific obstacles, and such systems as LRAD and ADS prove that it is possible to develop "high tech" powerful Less Lethal systems. Legal issues cannot be bypassed and are an important constraint. However, there are opportunities to choose legal solutions. One key point is to assess the acceptable level of pain/suffering. Operational needs do not appear today sufficient to overcome the different constraints. If you consider the armed drones or the TASER, the strong critics do not prevent their use at a large scale. The pressure of the medias and the public opinions are a fact to face. But it is not a reason to abandon Less Lethal Weapons.

I am not sure that the classic "small" less lethal systems and munitions, such as rubber bullets or Green Lasers, will be sufficient for all situations. It seems more likely that, under strict conditions and control, in operations with a mandate of the UN Security Council, powerful long range less lethal systems could be useful in some circumstances, in particular when the military forces act close to the civilian populations, or are opposed to hostile crowds. At least, it is interesting to continue research and debate on the subject, for example in technical reviews.

Why not a fair dialogue between military experts, academics and even the defence industry? The basic assumption would be that these systems are really dangerous weapons, but aiming at, and having the capacity, to reduce casualties at the local and tactical level, served by "ethical warriors".

Bibliography

Annati, Massimo, Non-Lethal Weapons and Technologies Resources and Techniques and Lesson Learned, in: Military Technology 11/2012, 49–53.

———, Non-Lethal Capabilities for Combat Vehicles, in: Military Technology 11/2013, 75–77.

Bricet des Vallons, Georges Henri, L 'arme non létale dans la stratégie militaire des Etats-Unis. Imaginaire stratégique et genèse de l'armement, in: Culture et Conflits, automne 2007, 63–82.

———, expert en systèmes d'armes à létalité réduite, in: Review Défence et Sécurite International hors série, No. 12 (juin-juillt), 2010.

42 Massimo Annati, Non-Lethal Weapons, in: Military Technologie 11/2012, 49–53.

Boot, Max The Struggle to Transform the Military, in: Foreign Affairs, March/April 2005. https://www.foreignaffairs.com/articles/united-states/2005-03-01/struggle-transform-military.

Casey-Maslen, Stuart, "Non-kinetic-energy weapons termed 'non-lethal'; A Preliminary Assessment under International Humanitarian Law and International Human Rights Law" October 2010 http://www.geneva-academy.ch/docs/projets/Non-Kinetic-EnergyOctober2010.pdf (last access 23 June 2013).

Davison, Neil, 'Non-Lethal' Weapons, London 2009.

Houdet, Brice, review Inflexions No 4. 2006.

Huyghe, François Bernard, Les armes non létales (Que sais – je), Paris 2009.

Sprague, Oliver, The Deployment of Taser Weapons to UK Law Enforcement Officials: An Amnesty International Perspective, in: Policing 1(3) 2007.

Thys, Pierre, Les armes à létalité réduite, L'Harmattan 2010.

Volcler, Juliette, Le son comme arme, Paris 2011.

Wright, Steve, Violent Peacekeeping: The Rise and Rise of Repressive Techniques and Technologies; http://praxis.leedsmet.ac.uk/praxis/documents/Steve_violent_peacekeeping.pdf (last access 23 June 2013).

CHAPTER 13

A Dichotomy of Conflicting Duties

Jeff Montrose

> Militaries of true democracies now take great pains to minimize the deaths of innocent people.
>
> KARL MARLANTES[1]

Introduction

Over the last two decades as the clearly defined parameters of the Cold War have faded into history an array of new security threats have materialized. Among them is the increase in non-state actors' ability to wage conflicts, failed states, international terrorism, and transnational threats, just to name a few. Moreover, globalization, despite its many positive aspects such as increased global connectivity and technological advances, has also inflamed many old conflicts and accelerated new ones through negative aspects such as increasing social and economic disparities.[2] Transnational threats along with the ever increasing phenomena of globalization have created an array of complex national security challenges.

For the military this complex security environment and its new security threats represent significant challenges. The nature of warfare and threats to international security are changing; this is quite obvious to even the most casual observer. What is not so obvious is how state actors should deal with new threats and the role military force plays in dealing with them. Applying military force in response to new security threats is not necessarily achieving the desired goals it once did.[3] For the soldier this means that the range of task required to deal with these changing security threats is much broader and complex than that of previous generations.[4]

1 Marlantes, Karl. *What it's like to go to war*, (Atlantic Monthly Press, New York 2011) 254.

2 Swain, Ashok, *Understanding Emerging Security Challenges: Threats and Opportunities* (1st, Routledge, Milton park 2013) 2.

3 Gießmann, Hans J., 'Whither World Order? Challenges for Peace Studies' in Gießmann, Hans J., Kuźniar, Roman, and Lachowski, Zdzislaw (eds), *International Security in a Time of Change: Threats – Concepts – Institutions* (1st, Nomos, Baden-Baden 2004).

4 Krulak, Charles C, 'The Strategic Corporal: Leadership in the Three Block War' (1999) 28 1 *Marines Magazine* 28–34.

 | DOI 10.1163/9789004312135_014

The purpose of this paper is to describe the current dichotomy of a soldier's conflicting duties observed in contemporary conflicts. I will first explore how on the one hand the changing nature of warfare presents soldiers with a rather broad range of non-combat situations in which soldiers are required to execute tasks not traditionally associated with military operations. On the other hand soldiers are still required to execute traditional tasks, i.e. kill enemy combatants. To show this I explain how the traditional tasks of a combat soldier, which I define as kill-destroy, has expanded into a second sphere of duties which I call help-build. Next, I show how modern conflicts often create conditions under which these two mutually exhaustive duties collide and create situations that are at best extremely delicate and mentally taxing and at worst hold the potential for strategic fallout.

Conflicting Duties

Throughout the following pages I use the term soldier to mean those specific combat arms soldiers who are given the task of directly and repeatedly engaging an enemy force. In contemporary conflicts non-combat arms soldiers are quite often exposed to enemy contact, and combat is by no means unique to the infantry. Nonetheless, the primary task of non-combat arms soldiers is not to engage an enemy force directly. That is, they are not tasked to seek out the enemy and destroy them directly. Such tasks fall to combat arms soldiers, specifically the infantry and soldier. It can be argued that the infantry traditionally bears the brunt of warfare and subsequently will be exposed more often to the dichotomy of conflicting duties I describe in the following pages than soldiers in support roles. Thus, the term soldier throughout this paper refers to combat arms soldiers, but the situation which I described is not wholly unique to the infantry.

Kill-Destroy

The central task of a soldier has always been relatively straightforward. Whether one speaks of an ancient Assyrian soldier, a Greek Hoplite, a Japanese Samurai or an Army Ranger their primary task hasn't changed much in roughly 5000 years: to locate an enemy force and capture or kill it. The US Army's current tactical doctrine manual for infantry platoons and squads defines the task of the infantry as 'to close with the enemy, by means of fire and manoeuvre, in order to destroy or capture him, or to repel his assault by fire, close combat, and counterattack'.[5] As the manual clearly states, 'the infantry's primary role is combat.'

5 *Field Manual § 12.8 Infantry Rifle Platoon and Squad* (1st, Department of the Army, Washington, DC, 28 March 2007) 1–1.

In his book *Black Hawk Down* depicting the events of the 1993 Battle of Mogadishu, Mark Bowden sums up rather bluntly the primary role of the combat soldiers.

> Soldiering was about fighting. It was about killing people before they killed you. It was about having your way by force and guile in a dangerous world, taking a shit in the woods, living in dirty, difficult conditions, enduring hardships and risks that could – and sometimes did – kill you. It was ugly work.... and if things went to hell and you had to slug it out, then it was time to summon a dark relish for mayhem. Why be a soldier if you couldn't exult in a heart-pounding, balls-out gunfight?[6]

Therein rests the absolute central task of a soldier: to kill and destroy an enemy force. I label this primary and traditional role of a soldier simply as the kill-destroy role.

Help-Build

However, international security parameters have for various reasons changed over the last several decades and a consequence of these changes is that the role a soldier plays in the employment of military force has become significantly more complex. A new set of skills, apart from kill-destroy, are often demanded of soldiers to deal with these changes. Operations such as peacekeeping do not require soldiers to purposefully seek out an enemy force and engage them. Instead, such tasks revolve around 'monitoring cease-fires, separating hostile forces and maintaining buffer zones'.[7] Likewise, in humanitarian assistance or relief operations soldiers are 'increasingly involved in launching civilian-military projects, such as the building of bridges and schools or the distribution of aid'.[8] This new range of tasks which require a set of skills and knowledge which are distinct from the traditional skills demanded by the kill-destroy role, stands in opposition to kill-destroy and I label them simply help-build.

---

6 Mark Bowden, *Black Hawk Down: A Story of Modern War* (1st, Atlantic Monthly Press, New York: 1999) 24.

7 '50 Years of United Nations Peacekeeping Operations' (United Nations Department of Public Information 1998) <http://www.un.org/en/peacekeeping/sites/50years/2.htm> accessed 15 May 2014.

8 'Humanitarian Work is the Task of Aid Workers,' (Global Policy Forum 2006) <http://www.globalpolicy.org/component/content/article/176/31302.html> accessed 15 May 2014.

Military Operations other than War

The emergence of the new help-build role and the opposition it represents to kill-destroy did not, prior to the conflicts in Iraq and Afghanistan, present soldiers with a direct conflict between the two roles. Specifically, the operations which required soldiers to execute kill-destroy were almost always separated by time and space from missions that required help-build. To illustrate this I turn to a fictive Sergeant in the US Army who I will simply call Sergeant Smith.[9]

As a typical infantry soldier who enlisted into the US Army in the late 1980's Sergeant Smith could have easily participated in all three types of operations: combat, peacekeeping and humanitarian during his carrier. One of Sergeant Smith's first deployments could have been the 1989 US invasion of Panama and again perhaps the 1991 Gulf War. Although the duration of both Panama and the Gulf War operations were limited in comparison to the conflicts in Iraq or Afghanistan, Sergeant Smith would have still been exposed to the intensity and confusion of combat. A few years later Sergeant Smith could have deployed to Somalia or Haiti as part of an international humanitarian operation. After returning from Haiti Sergeant Smith would have then most likely served the first of several deployments to the Balkans, specifically Bosnia-Herzegovina and Kosovo, or even to the Sinai to participate in an international peacekeeping operation.

From the end of the Cold War until the post 9–11 conflicts in Iraq and Afghanistan, these three types of missions: combat, humanitarian, and peacekeeping, were separated through time and space. That is, apart from a very few instances the spectrum of tactical challenges presented by peacekeeping and humanitarian type missions did not involve actual combat. The so called Battle of Mogadishu in Somalia is a clear example where significant combat action was encountered by US forces during a humanitarian mission. However, the majority of the US soldiers engaged in the Mogadishu fire fight were from Ranger and Special Forces units, which were deployed to Somalia not to help-build, but to kill-destroy. No doubt many other peacekeeping operations involved the risk of combat like situations, but the risk was quasi-passive in nature. That is to say, for Sergeant Smith as a member of the US military, he was rarely the target of belligerents. The danger to the peacekeeping force came from being caught between and separating the warring parties and factions.

The US military subsequently drew a very clear line between the skills a soldier needed for combat (kill-destroy), and skills needed for operations which did not involve combat (help-build). These other non-combat missions were

9 I use the US military as an example due to my familiarity with that institution, but the concepts pertaining to this paper are by no means limited to soldiers in the US military.

shoehorned into a single category known as Military Operations Other Than War (MOOTW).[10] The U.S. Army defined some of these MOOTW as search and rescue, peacekeeping, humanitarian assistance and disaster relief, and counterdrug operations. The manual does explain that the nature of such operations can transition into hostilities, but little if any emphasis in the manual is given to kill-destroy tasks.

Despite the increased operational tempo throughout the 1990's with non-combat deployments to, among others, Somalia, Haiti, Bosnia-Herzegovina, Macedonia and Kosovo, for Sergeant Smith the majority of his training would have still been focused on the traditional role of kill-destroy. The reason being that non-combat operations and training took a back seat to the traditional tasks of kill-destroy.

> US Commanders must remember that their primary mission should always be to, prepare for, fight, and win America's wars. This is the most rigorous task facing any military establishment and requires nothing less than first priority when training and equipping forces.[11]

Thus, MOOTW represented the majority of military deployments in the US military during the 1990's but was seen as a secondary or contingency mission for US forces. Because combat operations and MOOTW remained separated by time and space, soldiers were rarely confronted directly with these two opposing roles.

The Three Block War and The Strategic Corporal

In 1999 the former Commandant of the US Marine Corps, General Charles Kurlak, observed the dramatic increase of US military forces to non-combat deployments and predicted that the fundamental change in the nature of future conflicts would force adversaries to adapt to asymmetric means to compensate for the disparity in the overwhelming conventional superiority of the US military power.

10 *Field Manual No. 100–7 DECISIVE FORCE: The Army In Theater Operations* (1st, Department of the Army, Washington, DC, 31 May 1995) Chapter 8.

11 Bonn, Keith E., Baker, Anthony, Guide to Military Operations Other Than War: Tactics, Techniques, & Procedures for Stability & Support Operations Domestic & International: Tactics, Operations, Domestic and International (1st, Stackpole Books, Mechanicsburg 2000) 2.

> The lines separating the levels of war, and distinguishing combatant from 'non-combatant,' will blur, and adversaries, confounded by our 'conventional' superiority, will resort to asymmetrical means to redress the imbalance. Further complicating the situation will be the ubiquitous media whose presence will mean that all future conflicts will be acted out before an international audience.[12]

In his article *The Strategic Corporal: Leadership in the Three Block War*, Kurlak depicts a fictitious scenario in which a squad leader is confronted with all three types of missions within the space of three adjacent city blocks: combat operations, peacekeeping, and humanitarian relief; meaning each city block represents one of the three different types of situations. The central idea of his concept is that leaders of modern small-unit operations must be prepared and trained to operate simultaneously in all three situations.

There has been a blurring of these three missions; a convergence onto one single battle space, presumably as General Kurlak predicted, within a three block area of a city. Today Sergeant Smith will experience a much different environment in Afghanistan and most likely in any other future military operation involving ground forces than he would have in the 1990's. Moreover, the strategic success of such mission 'may hinge on decisions made by small unit leaders, and by actions taken at the lowest level'.[13] The decisions Sergeant Smith makes on the battle field hold the potential for strategic success or failure and thus Kurlack coined the term strategic corporal.

The British General Rubert Smith made a similar observation that large scale war between state actors no longer exists, replaced by what he describes as war amongst the people. 'Civilians are the targets, objectives to be won, as much as an opposing force'.[14] Not only are contemporary conflicts fought amongst the people and over the people, but due to real time media coverage, they are also literally fought in our homes. 'We fight in every living room in the world as well as on the streets and fields of a conflict zone'.[15] Herein lies a significant factor in how Sergeant Smiths actions at the lowest tactical level can be rapidly amplified to the highest strategic level, namely through the CNN effect.

---

12 Krulak, Charles C, 'The Strategic Corporal: Leadership in the Three Block War' (1999) 28 1 *Marines Magazine* 28–34.

13 Ibid.

14 Smith, Rubert, *The Utility of Force: The Art of War in the Modern World* (1st, Vintage Books, New York 2005) 6.

15 Ibid 19.

Named after the first international television news channel, Cable News Network, which broadcasts 24-hours a day in real time, the CNN effect is the phenomena that the media profoundly influences the foreign policy and diplomatic decision process of a state. Because world events are easily broadcast live as they occur, the time which heads of state and policy makers have to react to those events has been significantly reduced. Concerning military operations Steven Livingston wrote that media coverage has 'the potential to undermine public support for an operation and erode troop morale on the ground.' In the end, the actions of Sergeant Smith, particularly actions which result in the accidental or unintentional killing of non-combatants, hold the potential to undermine 'perceived American credibility and resolve in the world'.[16]

Up until this point I have focused on the changing nature of warfare and the range of scenarios which often require modern soldiers to simultaneously execute both the traditional task of kill-destroy as well as the contemporary task of help-build in a single conflict zone. The situation for Sergeant Smith is exacerbated further by the CNN effect and it becomes even more difficult when we explore the issue deeper. Specifically, how Sergeant Smith's decisions are significantly influenced by his kill-destroy role in a scenario meant to help-build.

An Age Old Problem: The Individual in Battle

Although training and indoctrination can transform even the most unruly civilian into a disciplined soldier no amount of training will ever turn a soldier into a simple instrument of warfare. As Michael Walzer so wisely remarked, the trigger is always a part of the gun it is never a part the man.[17] It is precisely this individuality of the soldier, his subjectivity, which sets the ultimate limits on the battlefield, not his machines.

The subjectivity of the soldier can be viewed as two sides of a coin.[18] On one side is an innovative resource to the waging of modern war. This is the individual's ability to adapt to complex and rapidly changing situations and

16 Livingston, Steven, *Clarifying The CNN Effect: An Examination of Media Effects According to Type of Military Intervention Research Paper R-18* (1st, The Joan Shorenstein Center on the Press, Politics and Public Policy John F. Kennedy School of Government Harvard University, Cambridge 1997) 4.

17 Walzer, Michael, *Just and Unjust Wars: a moral argument with historical illustrations* (2nd, Basic Books, New York 1992) 311.

18 Warburg, Jens, *Militär und Seine Subjekte: zur Soziologie des Krieges* (1st, Transcript Verlag, Bielefeld 2008).

find creative means to deal with those changes; independent of their position within the hierarchy of the military.[19] This is the core concept of the strategic corporal. Battlefield situations can change so rapidly that traditional means of reporting information to higher headquarters, despite advances in technology, will be too slow to issue new directives and orders. Junior leaders must be competent to act according to their commander's intent. They must also know that they have freedom to deviate from those initial orders when the situation no longer meets the condition from which they were issued.

However, the other side of the coin is a source of friction. The soldier's reaction to events in combat creates a weak point in waging war and the friction starts with the human psyche.[20] Continuous exposure to extreme situations and events in combat such as killing and imminent death amplify emotions, not the least among them; fear, doubt and anger. Neither external influences such as training and counselling nor the soldier's self can completely prevent such extreme emotions from influencing their behaviour in combat.

In his widely published research of WWII infantry combat, S.L.A. Marshall discovered that only roughly 20 to 25 percent of US soldiers actually fired their weapons at enemy positions during battle. This was attributed to the human psyche's natural reluctance to kill other human beings; a rather straightforward example of the individual soldier creating a weak point in waging war. Marshall's study forced the U.S. military to adapt its training of soldiers, specifically rifleman, to overcome the individual's natural reluctance of killing. Pavlov like reflexive programming or conditioning desensitized recruits to the messy business of killing and by the end of the Korean War firing rate had increased to 55 percent, by Vietnam it was 90 percent.[21] Today's modern technology enables a military to train its soldiers on a wide variety of combat simulations, ranging from live ranges to life-sized video simulations. In the heat of battle it is expected that soldiers fire their weapons accurately and effectively and in essence the US military has done a well in overcoming a soldier's natural reluctance of killing another human being.

Today Sergeant Smith's may be sufficiently desensitized to overcome his natural reluctance to kill, but the immediate issue at hand for Sergeant Smith is that the enemy he will encounter is hardly if ever easily identifiable. Added

19 Keithly, David M. Ferris, Stephen P., 'Auftragstaktik, or Directive Control, in Joint and Combined Operations' (1999) Autumn, Parameters, 118–33.

20 Warburg, Jens, *Militär und Seine Subjekte: zur Soziologie des Krieges* (1st, Transcript Verlag, Bielefeld 2008).

21 Grossman, Dave, *On Killing: The Psychological Cost of Learning to Kill in War and Society* (1st, Back Bay Books., New York 1996) 35.

to this difficulty is that Sergeant Smith will be exposed to the extreme situations of combat for an extended period of time. The average deployment for Sergeant Smith to conflicts in Iraq and Afghanistan was 12 months with some deployments extended to 15 months.[22] Moreover, prolonged contact with such threats combined with physical strains such as pain, hunger and exhaustion will influence the emotions and behaviour of Sergeant Smith, often to the extreme. In his autobiography *Goodbye to All That*, Robert Graves a veteran of the First World War, remarked that after five months of fighting he had 'passed his prime.' Of his fellow officers he noted that at six months of combat an officer was 'still more or less all right.' At ten months he became a 'drag on the other company officers' and beyond one year 'he was worse than useless'.[23]

Kirson Weinberg's study of World War II combat veterans also found that after prolonged exposure to the extreme conditions of combat a soldier eventually becomes overwhelmed, and it is at this point that they are no longer able to 'formulate, enact, or complete a protective response.' A soldier may feel helpless and descend into a state of self-concern, focusing on measures of defence. His actions may become random and violent such as being 'trigger happy'.[24] The Roman philosopher Seneca attributed such actions to anger or what we might today call battle rage. He described it as a sweeping force from which there is no turning back, remarking that 'deliberation or second thought are cut off' as a downward course is set in motion; driven to the bottom by its own weight.[25] The desensitization to killing and the act its self play a central role in the breakdown of a soldier's psyche, and because the soldier has been given a license to kill does little to protect him from his own fears and stress of combat.[26]

The Switch

Memoirs and novels written by combat veterans are full of accounts of battle rage, and in its extreme cases it has commonly been excused as a brutal yet unavoidable reality of combat. Not least among these accounts is one from Guy Chapman's memoir where he tells the story of how a fellow officer recounts the

---

22 Tyson, Ann Scott and White, Josh, 'Strained Army Extends Tours To 15 Months' (Washington Post 12 April 2007) <http://www.washingtonpost.com/wp-dyn/content/article/2007/04/11/AR2007041100615.html> accessed 15 May 2014.

23 Graves, Robert, *Good bye to all that* (Revised, Cassell & Company Limited, London 1957) 152.

24 Weinberg, Kirson, 'The Combat Neuroses' (1946) 51 5 *The American Journal of Sociology* 472.

25 Cooper, John, Procopé, J. F., Seneca Moral and Political Essays (1st, Cambridge University Press, Cambridge, 2003) 25.

26 Jones, Edgar, 'The Psychology of Killing: The Combat Experience of British Soldiers during the First World War' (2006) 28 2 Journal of Contemporary History 236.

storming of a German trench in World War I. After the unit advanced into the trench an unarmed German officer attempted to surrender to a British sergeant, who 'half mad with excitement' took the surrendering officer's field glasses and then shot the man in the head. Chapman concludes the story with words that somehow carry a very uncomfortable truth about combat. 'I don't suppose he ever thought what he was doing' Chapman writes. 'If you start a man killing, you can't turn him off like an engine... He was probably half out of his head'.[27]

Roughly one hundred years later Sergeant Smith remains subject to the same exact human condition as that of the half-crazed British sergeant storming into a German trench. It is what I call the switch. It is the point where a soldier's ability to make moral and ethical judgments are influenced by emotional reactions to the point that the he is no longer capable of distinguishing right from wrong. Random and violent actions, the action of killing is 'switched' on and it cannot be easily 'switched' off. Battle rage, trigger happy, murder, call it what you will, the fact remains; Sergeant Smith is subject to the same physiological and emotional stress as soldiers in previous generations. However, several aspects make contemporary conflicts much more complex and stressful for Sergeant Smith.

As we saw earlier, Sergeant Smith has been sufficiently desensitized to overcome his natural reluctance to kill. On top of that his behaviour is influenced by extreme emotions brought on by the pressure of combat. Prolonged exposure to extreme situations, often up to 15 months added to multiple combat tours, amplify his emotions. The situation that makes this more sensitive for Sergeant Smith in say Iraq than it did for Guy Chapman in the trenches of the First World War, is that Sergeant Smith cannot readily and easily identify his enemy. To make matters worse, not only is the enemy unidentifiable, he is also indistinguishable from the civilian population as a whole. What's more, Sergeant Smith's two conflicting duties of kill-destroy and help-build have converged onto a single space. He is often required to help the civilian population within his duty of help-build, but at the same time he is told to kill-destroy certain groups within that population that he cannot readily identify.

When Good Soldiers Do Bad

Once Sergeant Smith reaches the point where the 'switch' is turned on, one needn't have much imagination or military experience to see the potential for disaster is immense. When it occurs, it will certainly be televised within days if

27 Chapman, Guy, *A passionate prodigality* (New edition, Ashford,Buchan & Enright, London 1985) 99–100.

not hours and will most likely hold some form of strategic consequence. However, one needn't turn to a fictive sergeant or address hypothetical situations as such events have already occurred in Iraq and Afghanistan.

So called checkpoint shootings such as the incident in Tal Afar, Iraq, where a family driving in a car failed to stop at a US checkpoint and soldiers opened fire. Both parents were killed in the shooting and their five children were injured.[28] Of course, such checkpoint shootings are by no means limited to the US military,[29] but they do represent a clear example of how the complex convergence of kill-destroy and help-build in a modern 'three-block' conflict can have deadly consequences. Such checkpoint shootings are rarely initiated by enemy contact though. Unclear and complex situations combined with stress can lead to situations where soldiers make deadly errors, such as shooting innocent passengers at a checkpoint late at night, but they are hardly attributed to battle rage. It is when soldiers are clearly acting within a kill-destroy frame that the potential for horrible events in a help-build situations are at their greatest. One such event did occur in November 2005 in Haditha, Iraq.

It was in the western province of Al Anbar in Haditha, Iraq, where the last vehicle in a patrol of US Marines was struck by an IED. The blast killed Lance Corporal Miguel Terrazas and seriously wounded two other marines.[30] Bing West wrote of the incident in *The Road to Haditha* and described the events after the IED blast as follows.

> Streaming video from an Unmanned Aerial Vehicle circling overhead showed a confused situation, with marines at various locations manoeuvring amid radio chatter indicating incoming fire. The remaining ten men in Terrazas's squad approached a car that had stopped nearby. When the five men inside started to flee, the marines shot and killed them. The platoon leader later reported that his men took fire from a nearby house. They assaulted first one house, and then a second. When the battle was over, fourteen Iraqi men, four women, and six children had been killed.[31]

28 'Checkpoints test US troops' rules' (BBC News 8 March 2005) <http://news.bbc.co.uk/2/hi/middle_east/4328579.stm> accessed e.g. 15 May 2014.

29 One example involving German soldiers in Afghanistan. Gebauer, Matthias, 'Tod am Checkpoint: Bundeswehr entschädigt Familie des afghanischen Opfers' (Der Spiegel 23 July 2007) <http://www.spiegel.de/politik/ausland/tod-am-checkpoint-bundeswehr-entschaedigt-familie-des-afghanischen-opfers-a-637647.html> accessed 15 May 2014.

30 McGirk, Tim, 'Collateral Damage or Civilian Massacre in Haditha?' (Time 19 March 2006) <http://content.time.com/time/world/article/0,8599,1174649,00.html> accessed 15 May 2014.

31 West, Bing, 'The Road to Haditha' (The Atlantic October 2006) <http://www.theatlantic.com/magazine/archive/2006/10/the-road-to-haditha/305230/> accessed 15 May 2014.

Most of the Marines involved in the killing had already served multiple deployments to Iraq, some were veterans of the fierce combat in Fallujah, and the conditions in Haditha were ripe for a disaster; armed men, who are trained to kill, exposed over an extended period of time to repeated enemy fire in an environment where the only characteristic to positively identify your enemy is 'military-aged males'[32] and a loved and likable comrade is killed by this unseen enemy. In an instant the 'switch' is turned on and it does not easily turn off. In such an environment one becomes overwhelmed and as Seneca wrote, a downward course is set in motion; driven to the bottom by its own weight.

Of those Iraqis killed in Haditha many were woken by the IED blast and subsequently shot while still wearing their pyjamas. The oldest Iraqi killed was 76, confined to a wheelchair and shot nine times. His elderly wife was killed as well. The youngest killed on that day was 3. After the initial blast, which killed Lance Corporal Terrazas not a single casualty from the Marines was taken. A lone AK-47 was found and 'no one has claimed that the rifle had been fired'.[33] The incident serves as a very tragic example of the convergence of kill-destroy and help-build. Soldiers, in this case US Marines, were sent to an area to help rebuild a troubled region of Iraq. Under duress, fear, anger, and a deadly cocktail of indescribable emotions, those young men caught in the confusion of modern combat did what they were trained to do; kill and destroy, with tragic consequences.

Conclusion

The moral and legal questions surrounding the use of military force by liberal democracies is nothing less than a Pandora's Box and at the tip of this confusing and complex environment rests the conviction that the unintentional killing or wounding of non-combatants is unacceptable. Although unintentional killing and so called 'collateral damage' can be limited by technological advances in weaponry, precision weapons alone cannot prevent unintentional killing. It goes beyond the weapon to the soldier who uses it. Soldiers, specifically those soldiers who are required to interact with a local population and when necessary, engage an enemy force, need to know what contemporary combat is like and most importantly know how they are expected to act.

32 Singer, Michael, 'The Killings in Haditha' (CBS 60 Minutes 15 March 2007) <http://www.cbsnews.com/news/the-killings-in-haditha/3/> accessed 15 may 2014.

33 Langewiesche, William, 'Rules of Engagement' (Vanity Fair November 2006) <http://www.vanityfair.com/politics/features/2006/11/haditha200611> accessed 15 may 2014.

The importance of training cannot be avoided. Just as S.L.A. Marshall's work revealed in WWII that American Infantrymen were not acting as expected, in this instance not firing their weapons at enemy combatants, it was with subsequent psychological training that their behaviour was 'corrected'. Whether such psychological training does more damage to a soldier or not is debate for another paper, but two facts remain. Firstly, the situation in which soldiers were not acting as expected was identified. Secondly, their training was adjusted so that their behaviour matched expectations – firing rates subsequently increased after new training was introduced.

War for contemporary soldiers such as Sergeant Smith may often resemble the intensity of combat that Marlantes experienced in Vietnam or Marshall saw in WWII, but a deployment to a contemporary crisis zone for Sergeant Smith is also in many ways significantly more complex than from the days of Marshall or Marlantes. The training Sergeant Smith and his peers receive must reflect the type of environment they will find themselves in so that they act in ways that are acceptable for western democracies. The first step is to acknowledge the situation; namely, a dichotomy of ethical duties exists in the contemporary 'battle space' between kill-destroy and help-build.

The potential for tragic consequences when these two duties collide goes beyond the tactical level where they occur and can have strategic impact. Thus, in the future, militaries should recognize this conflicting dichotomy of ethical duties and prepare their soldiers for it.

Bibliography

'United Nations Department of Public Information (ed.) 50 Years of United Nations Peacekeeping Operations' (United Nations 1998) <http://www.un.org/en/peacekeeping/sites/50years/2.htm> accessed 15 May 2014.

'Checkpoints test US troops' rules' (BBC News 8 March 2005) <http://news.bbc.co.uk/2/hi/middle_east/4328579.stm> accessed e.g. 15 May 2014.

'Humanitarian Work is the Task of Aid Workers,' (Global Policy Forum 2006) <http://www.globalpolicy.org/component/content/article/176/31302.html> accessed 15 May 2014.

Bonn, Keith E., Baker, Anthony, Guide to Military Operations Other Than War: Tactics, Techniques, & Procedures for Stability & Support Operations Domestic & International: Tactics, Operations, Domestic and International (1st, Stackpole Books, Mechanicsburg 2000) 2.

Chapman, Guy, A passionate prodigality (New edition, Ashford, Buchan & Enright, London 1985) 288.

Cooper, John, Procopé, J. F., Seneca Moral and Political Essays (1st, Cambridge University Press, Cambridge, 2003a).

Cooper, John, Procopé, J. F., Seneca Moral and Political Essays (1st, Cambridge University Press, Cambridge, 2003b).

Field Manual 3–12.8 Infantry Rifle Platoon and Squad (1st, Department of the Army, Washington, DC, 28 March 2007).

Field Manual No. 100–7 DECISIVE FORCE: The Army in Theater Operations (1st, Department of the Army, Washington, DC, 31 May 1995)

Gebauer, Matthias, 'Tod am Checkpoint: Bundeswehr entschädigt Familie des afghanischen Opfers' (Der Spiegel 23 July 2007) <http://www.spiegel.de/politik/ausland/tod-am-checkpoint-bundeswehr-entschaedigt-familie-des-afghanischen-opfers-a-637647.html> accessed 15 May 2014.

Gießmann, Hans J., 'Whither World Order? Challenges for Peace Studies' in Gießmann, Hans J., Kuźniar, Roman, and Lachowski, Zdzislaw (eds), International Security in a Time of Change: Threats – Concepts – Institutions (1st, Nomos, Baden-Baden 2004).

Graves, Robert, *Good bye to all that* (Revised, Cassell & Company Limited, London 1957) 368.

Grossman, Dave, On Killing: The Psychological Cost of Learning to Kill in War and Society (1st, Back Bay Books., New York 1996).

Jones, Edgar, 'The Psychology of Killing: The Combat Experience of British Soldiers during the First World War' (2006) 28 2 Journal of Contemporary History 229–246.

Keithly, David M. Ferris, Stephen P., 'Auftragstaktik, or Directive Control, in Joint and Combined Operations' (1999) Autumn, Parameters, 118–33.

Krulak, Charles C, 'The Strategic Corporal: Leadership in the Three Block War' (1999) 28 1 Marines Magazine 28–34.

Langewiesche, William, 'Rules of Engagement' (Vanity Fair November 2006) <http://www.vanityfair.com/politics/features/2006/11/haditha200611> accessed 15 may 2014.

Livingston, Steven, Clarifying The CNN Effect: An Examination of Media Effects According to Type of Military Intervention Research Paper R-18 (1st, The Joan Shorenstein Center on the Press, Politics and Public Policy John F. Kennedy School of Government Harvard University, Cambridge 1997).

Marlantes, Karl, *Was es heißt, in den Krieg zu ziehen*(Arche Verlag, Zürich 2013) 313.

Marshall, SLA, *Men Against Fire: The Problem of Battle Command* (Reprint, Peter Smith, Gloucester 1978) 213.

McGirk, Tim, 'Collateral Damage or Civilian Massacre in Haditha?' (Time 19 March 2006) <http://content.time.com/time/world/article/0,8599,1174649,00.html> accessed 15 May 2014.

Nadelson, Theodore, Trained to Kill: Soldiers at War (1st, Johns Hopkins University Press, Baltimore 2005) 208.

Singer, Michael, 'The Killings in Haditha' (CBS 60 Minutes 15 March 2007) <http://www.cbsnews.com/news/the-killings-in-haditha/3/> accessed 15 may 2014.

Smith, Rubert, The Utility of Force: The Art of War in the Modern World (1st, Vintage Books, New York 2005) 430.

Swain, Ashok, Understanding Emerging Security Challenges: Threats and Opportunities (1st, Routledge, Milton park 2013) 184.

Walzer, Michael, Just and Unjust Wars: a moral argument with historical illustrations (2nd, Basic Books, New York 1992) 361.

Warburg, Jens, Militär und Seine Subjekte: zur Soziologie des Krieges (1st, Transcript Verlag, Bielefeld 2008) 378.

Weinberg, Kirson, 'The Combat Neuroses' (1946) 51 5 The American Journal of Sociology 465–478.

West, Bing, "The Road to Haditha' ('The Atlantic October 2006) <http://www.theatlantic.com/magazine/archive/2006/10/the-road-to-haditha/305230/> accessed 15 May 2014.

CHAPTER 14

Conveying Ideas and Values in Education! Challenges in Teaching Military Ethics

Edwin R. Micewski

In view of human history and looking at what is going on in the world right now, one is tempted to ask whether ethics has ever been taught, indeed, can it even be taught? And if it can, what practical effect does it have, where does it show? What is the link between a possible ethical insight and its practical application in human activity? Because, after all, ethics attempts to connect norms and behavior, thus aiming at meaningful arrangement of human coexistence.

Does the source of morality lie in being and character, rather than in rationality and erudition? Or was Plato right already that immorality is simply ignorance, a lack of instruction and knowledge? Or, if morality constitutes a synthesis of both, what are the possibilities and limitations to ethical instruction? And what about ethics and ethical instruction in a social environment that features moral relativism and radical tolerance? When "anything goes", why ought we be moral after all and how could we possibly determine what is moral? Consequently, does individual moral responsibility perhaps exhaust itself by merely following the laws and abiding by the legal framework instituted by legislative institutions of society and state?

The challenges bedeviling the question of ethics and teaching ethics appear manifold and sheer limitless. They become even more intricate when it comes to the military world and the question of soldiering, where many argue that the nature of the organization with its strict hierarchy and implicit and unquestionable obedience leaves no room for individual freedom and morality, and thus renders the issue of ethics irrelevant.

These introductory remarks already hint at the intricate and most profound nature of ethics that defies easy and simple answers in the sense of a mere empirical and pragmatic approach. Ethics, like philosophy itself, does not represent a clearly defined and delimited subject area as most scientific disciplines do. This is why the ethicist as a practical philosopher, while instructing on terminology and the history of ideas of ethics, has to teach and foster how to think and judge properly rather than conveying a closed doctrine or a certain school of thought. Ethics touches upon the deepest grounds of being human and cannot be grasped without proper foundation in ontology and

 | DOI 10.1163/9789004312135_015

philosophical anthropology, thus necessitating comprehensive metaphysical reflection. This is consistent with Immanuel Kant's dictum: "[…] pure philosophy (metaphysics) must precede; without it there can be no moral philosophy at all." (I. Kant, Grounding for the Metaphysics of Morals, Preface [390]). Consequently, the area of political and military ethics cannot be grasped without proper foundation in comprehensive political and military philosophy.

If humans are free to act, then the subject of ethics is the reality of human acting as it 'ought' to be. Ethics represents an ideal science that considers proper acting in the modality of theoretical reasoning, and is thus clearly distinguished from any concrete and practical ethos. This distinction points at the essential methodological difference between the two major approaches of how to teach ethics: Should ethics be taught on the basis of comprehensive grounding in abstract theory, or should it be promoted by a pragmatic ethos-approach that features empirical examples and draws recipes for ethical behavior from experience and historical precedence? The latter approach attempts to minimize any intellectualization of ethical instruction and features the concept of virtue ethics and character building by following the principle that ethics should be "caught" rather than "taught".

While examples and illustrations always help to understand theoretical concepts and norms, a mere pragmatic focus neglects the truly metaphysical and thus philosophical nature of the subject matter of ethics. Only the comprehensive foundation of ethics will potentially generate a self-reliant individual morality that allows for responsible decisions under circumstances that are unique and are not covered by precedent and case study. The methodological reduction to case examples and discourse studies might generate workable results on an interim and superficial level, however, at the cost of forfeiting the qualitatively profound comprehension of ethics. Due to its ubiquitous tendency to control individual behavior and tie it to established rules and regulations, the military organization generally features the pragmatic approach and it will require concerted and determined efforts to overcome these limitations.

If we put the pragmatic approach to teaching ethics with its attempt to provide prescribed recipes for moral behavior in a broader cultural context, we encounter the calamitous path political modernity has walked as it undertook the attempt of ethicizing human existence and terminating individual morality. Individual morality was dissolved into collective ethics, thus reducing personal and individual responsibility to compliance with precepts and regulations that were considered reasonable and whose retention was acknowledged as desirable. The "moral law within myself", true morality as it were, of which

Immanuel Kant had spoken, was replaced by an ethical code and personal responsibility was decreased to the level of either abiding by, or breaking, socially and organizationally accepted rules and regulations. While everybody acknowledges the conceivably positive impact of this modus operandi on human coexistence, nobody can equally deny that the mere subordination of one's responsibility to norms and customs certainly does not do justice to the full potential of the moral Self.

In the armed forces the modernist approach condenses to the inescapable commitment to unquestioning obedience and to the essentially literal compliance with military orders and Rules of Engagement (RoE). Ultimately, this means to wait around and do nothing if the required or desired order is outstanding or arrives belatedly. Srebrenica and Rwanda are but two examples that made the disastrous consequences of this attitude and understanding visible to the whole world.

What we are dealing with here is not insubordination or selective obedience, but the fact that fully responsible behavior cannot ultimately be tied to laws and regulations alone. In most difficult and challenging situations responsible behavior and potentially successful outcome can only be achieved if the moral consciousness of one's Self can be brought to bear in full measure.

In order to underscore individual and personal moral responsibility, which man can only find before himself and his own conscience, the philosopher Emanuel Lévinas posits: "The I always has one responsibility more than all the others" (E. Lévinas, Ethics and Infinity. Pittsburgh, 1985, p. 101).

Only by way of proper ontological instruction we become aware that the final moral responsibility is bigger and more powerful than any ethical or legal norm. Man is not moral because of society or their occupational environment; because of those he is only ethical or lawful. To be moral means that man is fundamentally relegated to his own Self and thus, to his own freedom. This is also true for the soldier and military officer.

What I am aiming at here is the ontologically important difference between morality and legality, the human possibility to act ex lege, outside of the law or, to speak with Immanuel Kant, in a moral-juridical realm. This circumstance is not unproblematic, most certainly not in the military organization where functional efficiency often depends on the swift and frictionless execution of orders and instructions; however, the denial or negation of this antagonism can prove disastrous in many cases. To not allow for covering this particular aspect of moral philosophy in ethical instruction sets the stage for failure and diminishes the scope of responsible behavior in situations where autonomous decisions of ethical relevance are needed.

Ethical instruction has to take into consideration that any possible ethically relevant situation is specifically genuine and unique. Thus, moral obligation should never become habitualness as routine in ethics, as again Kant makes clear, always holds the risk to lead to the inhumane. Ethical education, therefore, while providing comprehensive philosophical background, has to foster and cultivate the capability, but also the courage, to come to autonomous and self-reliant moral conclusions and ethical decisions.

Military Ethics, as every other sector of applied ethics, should ideally be based on normative ethics as it investigates the supreme principles of the morally good and right that should guide human actions. Considerations in that vein from ancient philosophy up to contemporary theories should enable students to grasp the scope and significance of these core dimensions of moral philosophy. Thus equipped and readied the subject area of military ethics can be tackled as the normative criteria are being applied to all ethically relevant challenges the world of soldiering and military life potentially holds ready. Aside from ethical aspects of everyday duties, the bulk of instruction has to focus on questions of the application of political and military force, in other words, the criteria for ethically legitimate use of military force and the maintenance of the moral integrity of the individual soldier. By dealing with Just War Theory the basic political (ius ad bellum) and military (ius in bello) responsibilities can be grasped and brought into historical and contemporary contexts. In addition to the morally responsible behavior of soldiers in wartime and combat, military ethics has to touch upon the specific liabilities of military officers and leaders in view of their particular command authority. A third area of military ethics has to cover the social ethical challenge arising from the embedment of the military organization in the societal environment of (post) modern open and democratic statehood. This latter part of military ethical instruction aims at enhancing the intellectual and social competence of soldiers, particularly of officers, to adequately represent the military vis-a-vis society and state, citizens and politicians and argue patterns of legitimacy and military authority.

Yet, military ethics cannot be properly tackled unless another pragmatic precondition has been conveyed, namely the purpose of armed forces and the military establishment and its distinct organizational culture in contexts of national and international policies. To put through political interests as an instrument of politics and under the primacy of policy in exceptional circumstances by “management and application of violence” (Samuel Huntington) shapes the organizational character of military formations. The preparation of military personnel to deal with the essential elements of war and armed conflict as normatively outlined by Carl von Clausewitz – danger, exertion, uncertainty, and chance – has to be viewed in conjunction with what resided at the core of any military identity, especially of officers and military leaders, namely the most philosophical and existential question of how potentially killing and getting killed can be justified. This 'metaphysical kernel' of the nature of the military can never change and constitutes the substantial distinction of military professionalism to other forms of occupational activities. How this organizational culture and the inherent military ethos can be upheld as well as legitimized in (post) modern societal environments represents a challenge that rounds off the scope of military ethical instruction.

There should be no doubt that the subject matter of military ethics, at least for military leadership personnel, ought to be based upon comprehensive military-philosophical education. The cultivation of an informed ethical consciousness is the objective of military ethical instruction that requires an all-encompassing approach and cannot be achieved by providing action recipes and historical examples alone. However, ethical behavior and proper moral decision-making cannot be the result of constant reasoning over concepts such as the categorical imperative or theories on justice, fairness, courage and the like either.

Military ethics, therefore, as ethical instruction in other walks of life for that matter as well, has to aim at creating an inner temperament, an inclination of the will, a sense for what is morally right and proper rather than imposing standardized procedures, whose imitation might not provide suitable solutions. This moral disposition will allow for good judgment and appropriate ethical decision-making in unique and unprecedented circumstances.

While it is appropriate to draw a distinction between the process through which ethics is taught, and the content taught, a correlation exists between these two. This has become particularly evident in the approach to ethics introduced here.

CHAPTER 15

Sound Moral Psychology behind Ethics Education

Florian Demont

Ethics is a philosophical discipline.[1] Nevertheless, ethics is often taught – especially in armies and in civil life – by non-philosophers and to people with little training in philosophy. It is therefore not surprising that what is taught under the label "ethics" and how it is taught sometimes lacks the conceptual rigor and coherence characteristic of a philosophical discipline. A consequence of this is that in some courses views within and about ethics are taught which rest on dubious or even incoherent conceptual grounds. That is, however, not the only pitfall in ethics education. A second problem is that moral judgment is a complex phenomenon comprising different intuitive and conscious processes which are sensitive to social and other contextual constraints.[2] It is therefore probable that a pure armchair approach in philosophy, which neglects state of the art moral psychology, soon finds itself tangled up in speculations too far removed from empirical facts to be applicable in the real world.

1 To keep things simple, I shall not distinguish between ethics and morality, fully aware that such a distinction is important in other discussions.

2 Strictly speaking, there is a third problem in ethics teaching. Some scholars (like D. Parker & P. Greener, 'Ethics Research: Moral Psychology and its Promise of Benefits for Moral Reasoning in the Military' in David Woycheshin (ed), *Military Ethics. International Perspectives* (Canadian Defence Academy Press 2010) still advertise an approach to teaching ethics which depends on a view of moral psychology that neglects intuitive processes to a significant degree. Such views have, of course, become untenable since the findings of James Blair, 'A cognitive developmental approach to morality: Investigating the psychopath' (1995) 57 *Cognition* 1; Jonathan Haidt, 'The emotional dog and its rational tail: A social intuitionist approach to moral judgment' (2001) 108 *Psychological Review* 814; J. Haidt & C. Joseph, 'Intuitive ethics: How innately prepared intuitions generate culturally variable virtues' (2004) 133(4) *Daedalus* 55; Shaun Nichols, 'Norms with feeling: Toward a psychological account of moral judgment' (2002) 84 *Cognition* 221; Shaun Nichols,*'Sentimental rules: On the Natural Foundations of Moral Judgment'.* (OUP 2004); D.A. Pizarro & P. Salovey, 'On being and becoming a good person: The role of emotional intelligence in moral development and behavior' in Joshua Aronson (ed) *'Improving Academic Achievement: Impact of Psychological Factors on Education'* (Academic Press 2002); P. Rozin, L. Lowery, S. Imada & J. Haidt, 'The CAD triad hypothesis: A mapping between three moral emotions (contempt, anger, disgust) and three moral codes (community, autonomy, divinity)' (1999) 76(4) *Journal of Personality and Social Psychology* 574; Kees Van den Bos, 'On the subjective quality of social justice: The role of affect as information in the psychology of justice judgments' (2003) 85 *Journal of Personality and Social Psychology* 482.

 | DOI 10.1163/9789004312135_016

This does not mean that philosophy and empirical science pursue exactly the same ends with exactly the same methods, but that philosophy forges, examines and changes conceptual frameworks which are suited to the natural world.

In what follows below I shall begin with an account of moral decision-making which is sensitive to intuitive and conscious processes while also allowing for social and other contextual influences. The account stems from moral psychology and is therefore based on empirical fact. I shall then draw attention to some conceptual problems and argue that revision is required to make it philosophically acceptable. In a subsequent part, a different (and more specific) account of moral judgment will be introduced to complement the original account of decision-making. The result will be an account of moral decision-making which has a much wider scope of applicability.

The account of moral decision-making under discussion below is the *Interactional Dual-Process Model of Moral Decision Making* (IDP) developed by Seiler, Fischer and Ooi. It is designed to explain decision-making when faced with moral dilemmas. I shall argue that the account is not satisfying because it features a view of moral perception which is not conceptually watertight. I propose to fix this by adopting part of John Mikhail's account of moral perception. The upshot will be that the resulting account – the *Extended Dual-Process Model of Moral Decision Making* (E-IDP) – promises to explain all sorts of moral judgment (not just moral dilemmas).

IDP and Its Conceptual Weakness

The *Interactional Dual-Process Model of Moral Decision Making* (IDP) developed by Seiler, Fischer and Ooi has five components, which they call "aspects". Here are these five aspects with the official descriptions:

1 *moral perception*: the individual perceives the inherent moral conflict of the eliciting situation
2 *internal dual-process*: the individual undergoes the internal dual-process of reasoning and intuition
3 *moral judgment and decision*: the individual achieves a moral judgment and decision
4 *post hoc reasoning*: the individual undergoes a post hoc reasoning process to further support or adjust his or her previously made judgment
5 *social interaction*: the individual's social interaction with others during and after the problem-solving process influences his or her internal dual process to reach a more elaborated or new moral judgment and decision.

It is not necessary that a decision-making process starts with the first aspect and then proceeds to the next up to the fifth aspect. IDP is therefore not meant to be a model of a five-step process. Aspects 2, 4 and 5 interact in a loop: a final decision (aspect 3) is reached through a complex internal process of reasoning and intuition which changes with post hoc reasoning and social interaction. Of course, post hoc reasoning and social interaction do not always play a significant role (for example in extreme situations where quick decisions are necessary) and their influence varies with the task at hand and the situation.

From a philosophical point of view, the presentation of IDP in Seiler, Fischer & Ooi has a serious conceptual weakness. They claim to present a "comprehensive moral decision-making framework", but they do not. Aspect 1 focuses on an "inherent moral conflict of the eliciting situation" and hence the model only deals with moral conflicts and not with all sorts of moral judgment.

But there are other questions concerning the formulation of aspect 1. What does "inherent" mean in this context? The formulation suggests that the moral conflict is part of the situation. But moral conflicts can stem from different sources. There might be a difference between what an individual perceives and what is the case. There might also be a conflict between different values the individual has: in a military context, there is often a conflict between obedience or loyalty on the one hand and some other value – and such conflicts are not at all inherent in the situation, but they are part and parcel of the values that the individual has. The important point here is purely conceptual: if we insist that there is such a thing as a moral conflict inherent in a situation, then we would be driven to hold that the situation elicits a conflict between two values within one system – and even though such cases might be possible, they are certainly not common enough to serve as paradigmatic cases for a comprehensive moral decision-making framework.

Let me spell this out in detail. If moral values are to be more than mere opinion, they have to be general and objective. By "general" I mean that they should guide judgment and action in different situations and for different people. By "objective" I mean that there must be a difference between merely thinking one has firm grasp of a value (when judging and acting) and actually firmly grasping that value (when judging and acting). So, if a moral conflict is inherent in a situation and the conflict is brought about (as we should suppose) by conflicting values, which are general and objective, then the conflict cannot be inherent in the situation, but the conflict must be inherent in any value-system which contains the two values. Therefore, if the concept of moral perception – as conceived of by Seiler et al. – makes any sense, it presupposes a system of values which has two incompatible values and it presupposes that there are situations which elicit precisely that conflict. Charitable interpretation demands that this is along the lines of what they have in mind. But it is also clear that such cases of moral perception are exceptional and that they cannot serve as a stable footing for a comprehensive moral decision-making framework. The upshot is that we have to revise the conception of moral perception. What alternatives do we have?

Toward an Extended Version of IDP

I have introduced IDP and I have argued that it builds on an inacceptable account of moral perception. The questionable idea was that there are situations which elicit inherent moral conflicts. No matter how one tries to make sense of "inherent moral conflict", a conception of moral perception which builds on very specific conflicts along the lines insinuated by Seiler et al. cannot provide a stable footing for a comprehensive moral decision-making framework. Fortunately enough, that conception of moral perception is not essential to IDP and it can be replaced by a more suitable conception of moral perception which can feed into a dual-process of reasoning and intuition.

John Mikhail has a conception of moral perception which explains how we represent events and process them for moral judgment. That conception of moral perception is a model of intuitive processes which draws on insights from Chomskian linguistics.[3] Here is how it works: first, specific events are represented; second, a temporal and a causal order between the events is established; third, all effects are labelled as good or bad. Consider an example to make this more clear:

1 Assume we have available descriptions of three events such as '*X* throws *Y* off a foot bridge', '*Y* prevents a train from hitting 5 innocent people' and '*X* kills *Y*'.
2 Then follows a temporal and causal ordering of the events: first, *X* throws *Y* off the foot bridge (event 1) and that causes *Y*'s death (event 2) and *Y*'s preventing a train from hitting 5 innocent people (event 3).
3 After that, the effects are labelled. As only events 2 and 3 are effects, they are the only events that are labelled: event 2 is bad (*Y* dies) and event 3 is good (5 innocent people are saved).

3 Compare Demont 'John Mikhail on Moral Intuitions' (2013) 7 *Kairos: Journal of Philosophy & Science,* where I have argued that Mikhail has an interesting model of how we represent events in order to prepare moral judgment, but that he cannot explain how we decide what we ought to do, because moral oughts cannot be the result of intuitive processes à la Chomsky.

Note that labelling events as good or bad does not yet establish what one ought to do. Whatever I ought to do is, if it is the result of a rational internal process of moral decision-making, something of which I am conscious that I ought to do it. The labelling Mikhail is talking about is, however, part of an intuitive process which remains unconscious. The results of the intuitive process, the labelled events, feed into the internal process of moral decision-making, where it is combined with information from memory and, if the circumstances are right, information from social interaction and inferences provided by post hoc reasoning.[4]

So, the alternative conception of moral perception generates descriptions of events which are put into temporal and causal order. They are then labelled good or bad.[5] This process of moral perception is completely intuitive and, therefore, largely unconscious. The result is a representation of an event as good or bad which then becomes available for reasoning within the internal dual-process of IDP. Memories, inferences and maybe other labelled events from moral cognition are compared and possible outcomes of decisions are thought about consciously. Moral values and estimated probabilities of the different outcomes are then combined to derive what one ought to do.[6] A moral ought, on this view, is the result of applying a moral value (which is general and objective) to a likely outcome.

At this point, external factors such as social interaction and post hoc reasoning (adducing new inferences and maybe new evidence from perception and memory) influence thought about possible outcomes, their probability and what values to apply to them. When a decision is reached, because the process has reached one best solution or because circumstances demand it, moral decision-making is completed.

The result is an extended version of IDP, called, E-IDP, which does not depend anymore on a conceptually inacceptable view of moral cognition.

---

4 I surmise that social interaction and inferences provided by post hoc reasoning do overlap considerably and remain on a linguistic level (Florian Demont, *Rules and Dispositions in Language Use* (Palgrave 2014)). But whether my account of rule-following fits here remains to be seen.

5 The process is presented in John Mikhail, *Elements of Moral Cognition. Rawls' Linguistic Analogy and the Cognitive Science of Moral and Legal Judgement* (CUP 2011), Ch. 6. The labeling is based on innate principles for classifying events in to good ones and bad ones.

6 The way it is presented here, a detailed story may draw on Bayesian decision theory or on ranking-theory (see Wolfgang Spohn, 'A Survey of Ranking Theory' in F. Huber & C. Schmidt-Petri (eds) *Degrees of Belief* (*Synthese Library 342*) (Springer 2009) 185, for a suitable ranking-theory). Given details of how moral perception works precisely and of what account of a moral value we choose, empirical adequacy remains to be established.

With Mikhail's alternative account of intuitive processes and my sketch of how this process feeds into conscious processes, E-IDP has the potential to be developed into a comprehensive moral decision-making framework, which is conceptually sound and accords with empirical facts.

Conclusion

IDP was originally designed as a psychological basis for teaching ethics at the Military Academy at ETH Zurich, where it was successfully implemented in the military ethics-education of the Swiss Armed Forces.[7] Given its success, it seems a good idea to strengthen its virtues by, first, furnishing it with a better conception of moral perception and, second, thereby widening its scope through changing its focus from a model for a very specific kind of dilemmas to a more comprehensive framework that has the potential to deal with all sorts of moral decision-making. E-IDP, as sketched above, must still be fleshed out, but given that it virtually preserves all of IDP's virtues, it is reasonable to expect that it can be developed into a framework which is state-of-the-art by conceptual and empirical standards. What I have hoped to show here is that there is scope for improving a good moral psychology for ethics education into a more comprehensive one.

7 The positive impact of that ethics-education has been documented by S. Seiler, A. Fischer & S. Voegtli, 'Developing Moral Decision-Making competence: A Quasi-Experimental Intervention Study in the Swiss Armed Forces' (2011) 21(6) *Ethics & Behavior* 452; S. Seiler, A. Fischer & Y.P. Ooi, 'An interactional dual-process model of moral decision making to guide military training' (2010) 22(4) *Military Psychology* 490.

CHAPTER 16

Legitimacy of Military Deployments Especially in Asymmetric Conflicts

Hartwig von Schubert

Under the title *Legitimacy of Military Deployments* I will address the following four topics:

- The background and origin of global modernization as well as asymmetry and human rights ethics
- The long way to an international legal order (international law or law of nations)
- The ethics of law sustaining force in international and non-international armed conflicts
- Ethics in combat as the core issue of professional military ethics

Global Modernization and the Ethics of Humankind

To understand the global asymmetry between a set of stable and prosperous states and numerous unstable and even failing states we have to understand the socio-historical process of global modernization. Global modernization is derived from two ancient origins. One is the occidental ancient philosophy; the other is the oriental monotheistic religion. Both merge in the amalgamation of western Hellenism and eastern monotheism in the roman empire in the wake of the constantinian shift. This extraordinary encounter of two strong and independent cultures and their dynamic and conflict-ridden fusion over centuries laid the basis for the European expansion since the 15th century and Europe's unique role as the watershed in the global modernization processes.

What is the essential *philosophical* and what is the essential *monotheistic* impulse to modernity? Aristotle, who invented the word "ethics", advises his audience of young intellectual Greek noblemen to each make his individual choice out of a broad variety of empirically given ways of life. He himself proposes what he calls the *bios theoreticos* as being supreme: a spirit and attitude of prudent deliberation in every possible sense, including scientific – although not yet experimental – research. But let us note carefully who is excluded: women, children, slaves and all non-Greek cultures. By analogy he discusses

 | DOI 10.1163/9789004312135_017

more than 50 empirical constitutions governing Greek cities and settlements in an attempt to find out which constitution is the most successful. What I essentially want to point out is the method of his thinking, rather than the content: the method is "scientific" in the sense that he starts with empirical data, considering both the perspectives of the individual as well as political life. The historical influence of this empirical approach and the distinction made between individual and political ethics on the occidental path towards modernity cannot easily be overestimated. Nevertheless it took centuries to overcome the much more influential monistic neo-platonic heritage. It was Albertus Magnus in the 12th century who realized the potential of the Aristotelian method, after it had been rediscovered by Arab scholars like Al-Kindi, Al-Farabi, Ibn-Sina (Avicenna) and above all Ibn-Ruschd (Averroes).

This, however, is only one half of the entire story. The other ancient source of modernity is the evolution of the monotheistic religion within the ancient orient. The cultural heritage of two small kingdoms on the Syrian/ Phoenician isthmus – that of northern "Israel" and that of southern "Juda" – only survived first the Assyrian invasion and later the Babylonian one, and the following deportation, because they were able to incorporate the documents and visions from the times of their relative independence into the "holy scriptures" of a religious association without land, without a capital city, without a temple, and without a royal dynasty, but with a resulting even stronger literal and spiritual dedication to the "eternal law of God" as a constant alternative to the changing laws of human kings and princes, who came and went: we are talking of Judaism, later complemented by Christianity and Islam! Witnessing the rise and decline of the kingdoms and empires of Aram, Assur, Babel, Persia, Hellas and Rome the Jewish scholars in their settlements in Palestine, Mesopotamia and Northern Africa, came to the conclusion that there must be a power behind the powers, a kingdom behind the kingdoms, one God behind the Gods of the Nations (e.g. Psalm 82).

This tradition transcended the ethnic borders of Judaism, when the teachings, and even more, the passion of Jesus of Nazareth became the founding narrative of a "new people of God", which then included anybody from any ethnic, cultural or social background. Thus the essential contribution of the monotheistic tradition to modernity is the "universalization" of the cultural, historical and moral conscience. The classical document is the word of the Apostle Paul – please remark the difference to Aristotle: "There is neither Jew nor Greek, slave nor free, male nor female, for you are all one in Christ Jesus" (Gal 3, 28).

Due to the so called "dark age" of the barbarian migration towards the Mediterranean basin in the 4th and 5th century there was only one branch of further cultural evolution, where the late antique amalgamation of occidental philosophy and oriental religion survived. It was, in political terms, a rather weak branch, where a plurality of political powers allowed none of them to effectively control the progress of philosophical and theological doctrines. As we look upon the three cultures, which followed the decline of the Mediterranean ancient civilization – Greek Byzantium, Arab Islam and the Latin kingdom of the Franks (*Francia, Imperium Francorum*), it is only the latter where the ancient science tradition experienced a sustainable revival. It needed a few hundred monasterial scriptoriums and a few dozens of universities, and we do not find these around Alexandria, Ephesus and Byzantium, nor around Baghdad, Cairo or Cordoba, but at places like Bologna, Paris, Cracow, Heidelberg, Oxford, Prague, Salamanca, and Uppsala. Again: it was not at all greater intellectual strength, but the lack of a strong political centre, that channelled the "West" towards the evolution from scholasticism to renaissance and reformation, and the victory of experimental natural science over Aristotelian doctrines, and from there to the age of enlightenment, and finally towards the industrial revolution with all its splendour and misery. Please note: we should be very careful not to think of the "western" concept of "modernity" as in any respect superior to any other cultural pattern, it simply became enormously attractive to the rest of the world.

Thus, Point No. 1: we just need to realize that *so far any culture on this planet sooner or later chooses to enter what we might call the "scientific" approach to reality.* And, from the very beginning, this approach was universal in its methodological challenge (e.g. mathematical), even if not yet universal then in its cultural implementation.

Point No. 2: it took another cultural impulse – the oriental monotheistic religion – to also *universalize history and ethics* and to open the view towards a concept of one "humankind". If there would be enough space here, it would be worthwhile to show how, for example during the times of scholasticism (Thomas Aquinas) and the enlightenment (Immanuel Kant), both often contradictory traditions – the scientific philosophical and the monotheistic religious tradition – claimed universal recognition and thus had to be matched with each other. Thus I come to the following conclusion: the universalization and globalization of the scientific and industrial revolution will only be a blessing, *if humankind learns to respect itself as one legal community, and not divided into friends and implacable enemies.* It needed hecatombs of victims of religious fanaticism, of cultural arrogance, of nationalistic zeal, of relentless industrialization and modernization, which led the peoples of the world in the year 1948 to the conclusion that was laid down in a Universal Declaration of Human Rights, constituted in respect of all of humankind a…

1 *Duty to protect*, by giving every individual the guarantee of the Rule of Law (national und international);
2 *Duty to respect*, by giving every individual a fair chance to participate in public issues, which in the long run tends towards democracy (electoral rights and parliamentarism);
3 *Duty to fulfil*, by giving every individual a fair chance to participate in economic, social and cultural welfare.

The Long Way to an International Legal Order

This rather deep historical insight gives us the necessary background to now understand what is at stake when we now concentrate and discuss armed mass violence under the concept of the "Duty to Protect". The relevant traditional theory is known as the "Just War" doctrine. It has some origins in Aristotle, first being developed by Cicero, integrated by Augustine into Christian teaching, and systematically explained by Thomas Aquinas. Its basic idea is to submit the use of force up to the use of military force to the rule of law. It places the use of massive military violence under the authority of political power. Cicero just wanted the republican senate to keep control over the republican troops and their powerful generals – as we know, it was in vain. His idea was to use military force as means of punishment and sanctioning, which a judge on the basis of a fair trial imposes upon the delinquent. Thus this concept worked as long as the Roman Republic and later Empire, with its *ius civilis,* provided a broad legal framework, which half a millennium later was adopted by the Christian papacy, together or in competition with the "Imperator", as the only supranational institutions serving as supreme "judges" in international affairs in the medieval age. This framework broke apart with the Reformation, as papal *sacerdotium* and imperial *regnum* became themselves parties amongst others, which in the early 17th century brought the end of the *ordo christianum* in the west. The religious divide of Europe led to an era of brutal religious civil wars. The Westphalian peace from 1648, after the Thirty Year's War in central Europe, put an end to the religious slaughter and – further on lacking an international "judge" – constituted the principle of non-interference in internal affairs together with the concept of national sovereignty, including the sovereign right of warfare. The ideal of "Just War" had become obsolete, as in an anarchic world of states any sovereign authority could now claim its case to be "just", lacking a judge to proclaim a final sentence. With the French revolution in 1798 the dynastic perception of sovereignty up to that point turned into the sovereignty of the people, at a time when Europe, in a wave of massive industrial and colonial ambition, expanded into the width and lengths of the natural environment and over the entire globe.

In fact it was the Russian Czars Alexander II and Nicolas II. who after the Crimean War, one of the first industrialized wars, invited Europe's main powers to come to The Hague from 1864 to 1907 and conclude a "Law of Armed Conflict" based on interstate consensus. Unfortunately it took another, now global war, the Thirty Year's War from 1914 to 1945 to teach humankind the vital necessity of what the philosopher Immanuel Kant ironically called "Eternal Peace" and in the year 1945 declared:

- the fundamental *prohibition of violence* laid down in the UN Charter Article 2.4, with only the two exceptions
- of the natural right of self-defence (Art. 51)
- and the use of force in a system of collective security (Art 39ff.) under the mandate of the Security Council.

Beware: self-defence is only meant as a provision until the responsible system of collective security stands in. And systems of collective security are not so much intended to protect against external attacks. The systems are based on the mutual assurance, that the members protect each member against the attacks of another member. The system functions like a multinational legal community including an institutional body serving as the long missing international "judge". In the year 1945 – three hundred years after 1648 – a weak supranational authority again appeared on the horizon of history. Not before the year 1989 with the end of the confrontation between the blocks the Security Council began to work. Since then many other mechanisms for international crisis management started with some impressive results: the number and intensity of wars on the planet decreased down to about 50% in the two decades after the fall of the Berlin wall. Do we now stand at the brink of an era of "Just Peace"? Have the nations of this earth really for all times decided to abolish war as a means of interstate politics? And don't we still suffer the huge burden of domestic "intrastate" violence? Nothing is safe, and war might easily raise its head again. The idea of law as conceived by Kant may at least minimize the threat of war: law is "the sum of the conditions under which the arbitrariness of the one with the arbitrariness of the other according to a universal law of freedom can be combined together". It works quite well within stable states, it may work between stable states, but does it work in the case of weak states? The LOAC has been developed for international armed conflicts, how can it be adopted for non-international or internal armed conflicts?

The Demands of the Ethics Law-Sustaining Force

Following the idea of law and the advent of international bodies for passing legal judgements, the demands of any legal judgement and of the ethics of law-sustaining force are the following:

1 Authorization (*legitima potestas*)
Only *responsible, independent and non-partisan* bodies are authorized in specific conflicts to legislate (p. legislatoria), to make judgments (p. iusticiaria) and to enforce them (p. rectoria).
2 Justification (*causa iusta*)
Only the proven violations of an *indispensable condition of freedom* are the grounds for and reasons to pass a law, make and enforce a judgment.
3 Right intention (*recta intentio*)
Only the right to be able *to pursue legitimate free interests* needs to be protected and restored by passing judgment and enforcement of the decision reached.
4 Proportionality (*proportionalitas*)
Only that coercive measure is legitimate, which is *suitable, adequate and necessary* in order to protect the indispensable conditions of the freedom of all concerned.

Aren't these the demands of the old Just War doctrine? Why publish them under the new title? Do we have to redesign them for post-heroic societies, again trying to seduce them by subliminally legitimizing the scourge of war? Is it more than a rhetorical artifice? Not at all. First: these demands simply lead us to the principles, any normative judgement passed on the actions of rational beings must fulfil: impartiality, independence, freedom, suitability, adequacy and necessity. And second: The vision behind these demands is essential; it is not any more the logic of the self-empowerment of states to wage wars but of the vision of global peace, based not on totalitarian ideology, but on an international legal order which respects the individuality of local legal orders. No state can anymore pass directly from "justice" to "war". Everybody has to address and respect the authority of the international legal order, which lays in between. The more humankind closes ranks in the Global Village, the more the concrete vision of an international legal order is vital for the survival of humankind; there is just no alternative. The Westphalian order of sovereign states will stay on, but enriched and valued by systems of collective security, otherwise war again show its ugly face to humankind in the struggles lying ahead of us.

The actual financial crisis is an impressive example. Concerning financial power, the international community still has to develop global regulatory mechanisms equivalent to those already existing in the case of the use of military force. The credibility of the "Western" civilization stands and falls with the success of this vision. Every single deployment of military force has to be assessed according to all of these norms. Of course these norms lay out the ideal optimum. Any real scenario will fall short in this or that respect, but with the help of these norms we are able to identify areas needing continual improvement. Certain "middle principles" or criteria such as the need for authorization by the Security Council may serve as one finite approximation to the infinite "ideal principles". If the Council fails, a local system of collective security may stand in its place.

Core Issue: Ethics in Combat

We now have the needed foundation to consider the concept of Law in Armed Conflict (LOAC; also International Humanitarian Law IHL) and its ethical implications. Based on the legal revolutions of 1907 and 1945 the IHL now meets most of the required norms.

LOAC distinguishes between specific types of conflict: international or non-international armed conflict, internal armed conflict, instability below the level of armed conflict, stable statehood with "normal" social crises. For each of these cases LOAC offers a specific set of regulations and rules in The Hague and the Geneva Conventions, in National Criminal Law, Emergency Law, Human Rights Conventions, Military Technical Agreements, and Status of Force Agreements.

The LOAC as the actual set of wartime regulations says that in an International Armed Conflict (IAC) in accordance with Art. 51 or Art. 39ff of the UN-Charter, combatants (= military personnel authorized by UN member states) are allowed: (a) to destroy legitimate military targets, and (b) to weigh the destruction of legitimate military targets versus the protection of civilians. Only excessive collateral damage is seen as a war crime! By analogy, in a Non-international Armed Conflict (NIAC), combatants are allowed to fight "persons who without permission take a direct part in hostilities" as respecting their duty to protect civilians. Thus we have to acknowledge that this concept differs entirely from the concept of International Human Rights Law (IHRL), where nobody has (a) a right to combat or (b) the right to weigh one human life against another human life. To make it clear: the LOAC is a major concession to the brutal fact of collectively organised and armed violence, and although we should certainly not be too proud of it, it nevertheless serves as a second barrier against the total outbreak of industrialized aggression amongst human beings, it at least brings a minimum of order into the chaos and nightmare of war. It meets the demands of legitimate authorization, of permissible causes, right intentions and of proportionality and discrimination.

All needed regulations have mainly been developed to regulate military operations in IAC's and only to some small extent also in NIAC's. Thus the combatant and his political master have to pay regard to the very specific type of regulations according to the specific type of operation in the very specific type of conflict: there is another set of rules for long distance strikes to gain air supremacy in IAC's, another set of rules for ground operations in order to establish territorial rule, again very different approaches in a dynamic and complex theatre of full spectrum operations in NIAC's aiming for the stabilization of territorial rule against insurgents, partisans and terrorists and – last not least – again there are very different rules of engagement according to IHRL for national guards, gendarmeries and police forces, who have to execute state rule under peace conditions or conditions which at least show a trend to peaceful normality.

All these options come together in a nutshell within a dynamic and complex theatre of full spectrum operations in asymmetric scenarios. From one minute to the next the soldier has to change from escalation to de-escalation and back again to escalation. To train a soldier to cope with combat stress to a degree that enables him to (a) select proportional means (b) identify permissible causes (c) recognize the various legitimate authorities on all levels from village elders to international headquarters is an enormous challenge. Here we speak of the "strategic corporal", who is only able to do his job, if his superiors did theirs and clean up the mess caused by national egoisms and caveats in multinational deployments. This is the core issue of military ethics! Without those capacities we do not need discuss ethics in combat, because there simply would not be a consistent set of Rules of Engagement (RoE), nor a stress resistant subject to implement them in action.

The selection and training of mentally, physically and technically competent military experts is the precondition of the moral education of the individual conscience as well as the development of a constant ethical reflexion within the military professions. The goal is the ability for controlled armed escalation and de-escalation including a carefully suspension of the inborn inhibition to kill and the external cultural prohibition to kill. This includes the provision of simulated combat conditions and the training in the use of weapons, "drilling", which is then completed by intensive training in the entire range of specific proportionate means against the potential hostile attack. The main resources to match these standards are trust in task and equipment, solidarity in the small combat group, restricted periods of deployment, a clear concept of the enemy, a professional briefing in the general care, aftercare and therapy in case of trauma, and after a killing: investigation by a public prosecutor to meet the legal requisitions of the vital respect for human life.

These ethical standards we owe not only to civilians and the enemy but first of all to our own troops: the significant lower rate of posttraumatic stress disorders in the UK (4%) and Germany (2%) compared to the US (25%) is an indicator of the benefit of the application of high ethical standards in the military education and training in the European Armed Forces, including a set of Soldiers Virtues according to the demands of law-respecting use of force:

1 Legitimate authorization: command und professional responsibility
   a Initiative, faithfulness and clarity in command
   b Forthrightness in facing up to all consequences
   c Serving as a convincing role model
   d Careful recognition of legitimate authorities on all levels

2 Viable justification: assessment and evaluation of the situation
   a Solidarity with all in need of protection
   b Sober assessment of the enemy's intentions

3 Conscientious and responsible intentions: assessment and evaluation of the goals
   a Reliability in ensuring all necessary protective measures
   b Loyalty to the intended legitimate order

4 Proportionality in action: means and methods
   a Fortitude as a combination of courage, prudence und readiness to make sacrifices in respect to one's own danger and that of comrades
   b Moderation in the choice of effective, required and adequate means to achieve the intended goals

The LOAC gives the broad legal framework; the troops have to fill it – even in asymmetric warfare. They have to transfer impartiality, independence, freedom, suitability, adequacy and necessity into dynamic and complex theatres of full spectrum operations in asymmetric scenarios. The chief of a local Pashto tribe might be a better partner in terms of impartiality than many officials of the central government. The RoE's of local commanders should allow them to draw their judgements on scene.

Bibliography

Agamben, Giorgio (2002): Homo Sacer. Die souveräne Macht und das nackte Leben, Frankfurt Main.

Aird, Enola et al. (2002): what we're fighting for. A letter from America, Washington: http://www.washingtonpost.com/wp-srv/nation/specials/attacked/transcripts/justwar_letter020102.html.

Alexy, Robert (1996, 2001³): Theorie der juristischen Argumentation, Frankfurt a.M.

Anselm, Reiner (2006): Von der theologischen Legitimation des Staates zur kritischen Solidarität mit der Sphäre des Politischen, in: *Unger, Tim* (2006, Hrsg.): Was tun? Lutherische Ethik heute, Hannover, 82–102.

Arendt, Hannah (2011): Eichmann in Jerusalem. Ein Bericht von der Banalität des Bösen. Mit einem einleitenden Essay und einem Nachwort zur aktuellen Ausgabe von Hans Mommsen, München/Zürich.

Balke, Friedrich (2009): Figuren der Souveränität, München.

Beestermöller, Gerhard (1990): Thomas von Aquin und der gerechte Krieg. Friedensethik im theologischen Kontext der Summa Theologiae, Köln.

Beestermöller, Gerhard/Haspel, Michael Trittmann, Uwe (2006, Hrsg.): "What we're fighting for…". Friedensethik in der transatlantischen Debatte, Stuttgart.

Benz, Arthur (2004, Hrsg.): Governance. Regieren in komplexen Regelsystemen, Wiesbaden.

Biehl, Heiko (2012): Einsatzmotivation und Kampfmoral, in: Leonhard, Nina/Werkner, Ines-Jacqueline (2012², Hrsg.): Militärsoziologie – Eine Einführung, 447–474.

Bielefeld, Ulrich/Bude, Heinz/Greiner, Bernd (2012): Gesellschaft – Gewalt – Vertrauen. Jan Philipp Reemstma zum 60. Geburtstag, Hamburg.

Bothe, Michael (2013): Das Internationalen Komitee vom Roten Kreuz und die Weiterentwicklung des Rechts des nicht-internationalen Konflikts, in: Weingärtner, Dieter/Krieger, Heike (2013, Hrsg.): 11–22.

Braun, Johann (2001): Rechtsphilosophie im 20. Jahrhundert. Die Rückkehr der Gerechtigkeit, München.

Braun, Megan/Brundstetter, Daniel R. (2013): Rethinking the Criterion for Assessing CIA – Tagreted Killings: Drones, Proportionality and *Ius Ad Vim*, in: Journal of Military Ethics 12/2013/4, 304–324.

Brugger, Winfried/Neumann, Ulfried/Kirste, Stephan (2008, Hrsg.): Rechtsphilosophie im 21. Jahrhundert, Frankfurt am Main.

Brunkhorst, Hauke (2012): Legitimationskrisen. Verfassungsprobleme der Weltgesellschaft, Baden-Baden.

Buckel, Sonja/Christensen, Ralph/Fischer-Lescano, Andreas (2009²): Neue Theorien des Rechts, Stuttgart.

Bundesverfassungsgericht (2012): Plenarentscheidung des Bundesverfassungsgerichts zum Einsatz der Streitkräfte im Inneren „Luftsicherheitsgesetz"; Pressemitteilung Nr. 63/2012 vom 17. August 2012; Beschluss vom 3. Juli 2012, Karlsruhe.

Canaris, Claus-Wilhelm/Larenz, Karl (2007[4]): Methodenlehre der Rechtswissenschaft, Berlin.

Cassirer, Ernst (1923, 1953[2], 1994[10]): Philosophie der symbolischen Formen I/II/III, Darmstadt.

Cassirer, Ernst (1946): The Myth of the State, New Haven.

Dreher, Eduard et al. (2011[27]): Strafgesetzbuch, München.

Duchrow, Ulrich/Liedtke, Gerhard (1972, Hrsg.): „Schalom – Der Schöpfung Befreiung, den Menschen Gerechtigkeit, den Völkern Frieden." Eine biblische Arbeitshilfe zum Konziliaren Prozess. Stuttgart.

Durand, Béatrice (2007): Rousseau, Stuttgart.

Ehs, Tamara (2014): Welt ohne Gericht. Die stets vertagte Völkerrechtsrevolution, in: Blätter für deutsche und internationale Politik 2014/4, 65–72.

Engisch, Karl (2010[11]): Einführung in das juristische Denken, Stuttgart.

Evangelisches Kirchenamt für die Bundeswehr (2009, Hrsg.): Friedensethik im Einsatz, Gütersloh.

Falge, Christiane (2011): The Global Nuer: Transnational Livelihoods, Religious Movements and War, Oxford.

Frau, Robert (2013): Entwicklungen bei der gewohnheitsrechtlichen Einbindung nicht- staatlicher Gewaltakteure, in: *Weingärtner, Dieter/Krieger, Heike* (2013, Hrsg.): 23–54.

Frau, Robert (2014, Hrsg.): Drohnen und das Recht. Völker- und verfassungsrechtliche Fragen automatisierter und autonomer Kriegführung, Tübingen.

Gareis, Bernhard/Varwick, Johannes (2014[5]): Die Vereinten Nationen: Aufgaben, Instrumente und Reformen, Stuttgart.

Gauck, Joachim (2014): Eröffnung der 50. Münchner Sicherheitskonferenz, Berlin: http://www.bundespraesident.de/SharedDocs/Reden/DE/Joachim-Gauck/Reden/2014/01/140131-Muenchner-Sicherheitskonferenz.html; zuletzt besucht am11.05.2014.

Geismann, Georg (1974): Ethik und Herrschaftsordnung. Ein Beitrag zum Problem der Legitimation, Tübingen.

Gemeinsame Konferenz Kirche und Entwicklung (1997 ff.): Rüstungsexportbericht der GKKE, Bonn.

Gensichen, Hans-Peter et al. (1983): Art. Frieden I-V, in: TRE 11, Berlin/New York, 599–646.

Geyer, Klaus (1972b): Literaturbericht zu Arbeiten aus dem Bereich der neutestamentlichen Wissenschaft, in: *Liedtke, Gerhard* (1972, Hrsg.): 187–199.

Gillner, Matthias (2014, Hrsg.): Kollateralopfer, Baden-Baden.

Grimm, Dieter (2009): Souveränität. Herkunft und Zukunft eines Schlüsselbegriffs, Berlin.

Großmann, Andreas (2004): Im Bann des Leviathan. Hobbes, Carl Schmitt und die Folgen, in: Internationale Zeitschrift für Philosophie 1/2004, 15–27.

Grote, Rainer/Marauhn, Thilo (2006, Hrsg.): The Regulation of International Financial Markets, Cambridge.

Habermas, Jürgen (1996), "Kants Idee des Ewigen Friedens – aus dem historischen Abstand von 200 Jahren", in: Die Einbeziehung des Anderen. Studien zur politischen Theorie, Frankfurt/Main 1996, 192–236.

Habermas, Jürgen (2001): Kommunikatives Handeln und detranszendentalisierte Vernunft. Stuttgart.

Habermas, Jürgen (2009): Politische Theorie. Philosophische Texte: Studienausgabe, Band 4, Frankfurt.

Hankel, Gerd (2011): Das Tötungsverbot im Krieg. Ein Interventionsversuch, Hamburg.

Haspel, Michael (2002): Friedensethik und Humanitäre Intervention: Der Kosovo-Krieg als Herausforderung evangelischer Friedensethik, Neukirchen-Vluyn.

Herdegen, Matthias (2013[12]): Völkerrecht, München.

Hoerster, Norbert (2006): Was ist Recht?, München.

Höffe, Otfried (1983, 2007[7]), Immanuel Kant, München.

Höffe, Otfried (2003): Politische Gerechtigkeit. Grundlegung einer kritischen Philosophie von Recht und Staat, Frankfurt a.M.

Höffe, Otfried (2010): Thomas Hobbes, München.

Hofmann, Ekkehard (2007): Abwägung im Recht, Tübingen.

Hörnle, Tatjana (2011): Straftheorien, Tübingen.

Huber, Wolfgang (1972): Literaturbericht zu Arbeiten aus dem Bereich der systematischen Theologie, in: *Liedtke, Gerhard* (1972, Hrsg.): 200–216.

Hüning, Dieter (2005, Hrsg.): Der lange Schatten des Leviathan. Hobbes' politische Philosophie nach 350 Jahren, Berlin 2005.

Institut für Theologie und Frieden (1984, Hrsg.), Bibliographie Theologie und Frieden, Köln.

International Committee of the Red Cross (2008): Interpretive Guidance on the Notion of Direct Participation in Hostilities under International Humanitarian Law, in: International Review of the Red Cross (90) 4/2008, S. 991–1047.

Jacoby, Sigrid (1997): Allgemeine Rechtsgrundsätze. Begriffsentwicklung und Funktion in der Europäischen Rechtsgeschichte, Berlin.

Kaufmann, Arthur/Hassemer, Winfried/Neumann, Ulfrid (2010[8], Hrsg.): Einführung in Rechtsphilosophie und Rechtstheorie der Gegenwart, Heidelberg.

Kelsen, Hans (1934): Die Technik des Völkerrechts und die Organisation des Friedens, in: Zeitschrift für öffentliches Recht 2/1934, 240–255.

Kersting, Wolfgang (2009[4]): Thomas Hobbes zur Einführung, Hamburg.

Kindhäuser, Urs et al. (2013[6], Hrsg.): Strafrecht Allgemeiner Teil, Baden-Baden.

Kirste, Stephan (2010): Einführung in die Rechtsphilosophie, Darmstadt.

Körtner, Ulrich H.J. (2003): „Gerechter Friede" – „gerechter Krieg". Christliche Friedensethik vor neuen Herausforderungen, in: ZThK 100/2003, 348–377.

Kramer, Ernst A. (2010³): Juristische Methodenlehre, München.

Krause, Joachim (2010): Multilateralisierung der Verantwortungslosigkeit. Humanitäre Katastrophen unter Bedingungen kollektiver Sicherheit, in: *Gerber, Doris/Zanetti, Veronique* (2010; Hrsg): Kollektive Verantwortung und internationale Beziehungen, Berlin, 295–318.

Krieger, Heike (2010): Deutschland im asymmetrischen Konflikt. Grenzen der Anwendung militärischer Gewalt gegen Taliban-Kämpfer in Afghanistan, in: *Weingärtner, Dieter* (2010, Hrsg.): 39–59.

Krishnan, Armin (2012): Gezielte Tötung. Die Zukunft des Krieges, Berlin.

Kühn, Manfred (2004): Kant: Eine Biographie, München.

Liedtke, Gerhard (1972a, Hrsg.): Frieden-Bibel-Kirche, Stuttgart/München.

Liedtke, Gerhard (1972b): Israel als Segen für die Völker, in: *Liedtke, Gerhard* (1972, Hrsg.): 65–74.

Liedtke, Gerhard (1972c): Literaturbericht zu Arbeiten aus dem Bereich der alttestamentlichen Wissenschaft, in: *Liedtke, Gerhard* (1972, Hrsg.): 174–186.

Lüder, Sascha Rolf (2013): Die Weiterentwicklung der zivil-militärischen Zusammenarbeit im Rahmen der Neuausrichtung der Streitkräfte, in: *Weingärtner, Dieter/Krieger, Heike* (2013, Hrsg.): 199–214.

Luhmann, Niklas (1987³): Rechtssoziologie, Opladen.

Marauhn, Thilo (2005, Hrsg.): Recht, Politik und Rechtspolitik in den internationalen Beziehungen, Tübingen

Marschall, Stefan (2005): Parlamentarismus. Eine Einführung, Baden-Baden.

Mensching, Günther (2000): Jean-Jacques Rousseau zur Einführung, Hamburg.

Montenbruck, Axel (2011): Zivilreligion. Eine Rechtsphilosophie II. Grundelemente: Versöhnung und Mediation, Strafe und Geständnis, Gerechtigkeit und Humanität aus juristischen Perspektiven, Berlin.

Müller, Friedrich/Christensen, Ralph (2002⁸): Juristische Methodik, Bd. 1, Grundlagen, Berlin.

Müller, Rolf-Dieter (2005): Der letzte deutsche Krieg 1939–1945, Stuttgart.

Münkler, Herfried (2001): Thomas Hobbes, Frankfurt M.

Münkler, Herfried (2006): Der Wandel des Krieges. Von der Symmetrie zur Asymmetrie, Weilerswist.

Naucke, Wolfgang/Harzer, Regina (2005⁵): Rechtsphilosophische Grundbegriffe, München.

Naumann, Klaus (2008): Einsatz ohne Ziel. Die Politikbedürftigkeit des Militärischen, Hamburg.

Naumann, Klaus (2013): Der blinde Spiegel. Deutschland im afghanischen Transformationskrieg, Hamburg.

Obermaier, Frederik (2004), Der totalitäre Aspekt in den staatsgründenden Vertragsvereinbarungen bei Hobbes und Rousseau, München.

Perlitt, Lothar (1972): Israel und die Völker, in: *Liedtke, Gerhard* (1972, Hrsg.): 17–64.

Pfordten, Dietmar von der (2011): Rechtsethik, München.

Picht, Georg/Huber Wolfgang (1971): Was heißt Friedensforschung?, Stuttgart, München.

Piketty, Thomas (2014): Capital in the Twenty-First Century, Boston Mass.

Rat der Evangelischen Kirche in Deutschland (2007): Aus Gottes Frieden leben – für gerechten Frieden sorgen. Eine Denkschrift des Rates der Evangelischen Kirche in Deutschland, Gütersloh.

Rengier, Rudolf (2012⁴): Strafrecht Allgemeiner Teil, München.

Roehl, Klaus F. (1999): Praktische Rechtstheorie: Die deontischen Modalitäten, in: JA 1999/7, 600–605.

Rohde, Joachim (2001): Die Entwicklung des deutschen Rüstungsexportes in den 90er Jahren. Ergebnisse der vier wichtigsten internationalen Statistiken (SWP-Studien 2001/S 12), Berlin.

Römelt, Josef (2006): Menschenwürde und Freiheit. Rechtsethik und Theologie des Rechts jenseits von Naturrecht und Positivismus, Freiburg.

Rüthers, Bernd/Fischer, Christian/Birk, Axel (2011⁶): Rechtstheorie. Begriff, Geltung und Anwendung des Rechts, München.

Schlichte, Klaus (2012): Der Streit der Legitimitäten. Der Konflikt als Grund einer historischen Soziologie des Politischen, in: Zeitschrift für Friedens- und Konfliktforschung 1/2012/1, 9–43.

Schlotter, Peter/Wisotzki, Simone (2011, Hrsg.): Friedens- und Konfliktforschung, Baden- Baden.

Schmidt, Rolf (2010⁹): Strafrecht Allgemeiner Teil, Grasberg.

Schmitt, Carl (1938): Der Leviathan in der Staatslehre des Thomas Hobbes. Sinn und Fehlschlag eines politischen Symbols, Hamburg.

Schörnig, Niklas (2014): Die neue „westliche Kriegführung" wirft mehr Probleme auf als sie löst, in: *Werkner, Ines-Jacqueline* (2014, Hrsg.): Friedensgutachten 2014, 224–236.

Schubert, Hartwig von (2011): Afghanistan und die Tugend strategischer Geduld, in: *Bayer, Stefan/Gillner, Matthias* (2011, Hrsg.) Soldaten im Einsatz. Sozialwissenschaftliche und ethische Reflexionen, Berlin, 43–64.

Schubert, Hartwig von (2013): Die Ethik rechtserhaltender Gewalt, Opladen, Berlin, Toronto.

Schubert, Klaus/Klein, Martina (2011⁵): Das Politiklexikon, Bonn.

Schütz, Christoph (2013): Die Ingewahrsamnahme nicht-staatlicher Kämpfer im nichtinternationalen bewaffneten Konflikt, in: *Weingärtner, Dieter/Krieger, Heike* (2013, Hrsg): 83–99.

Schwacke, Peter (2003⁴): Juristische Methodik, Stuttgart.

Schwerdtfeger, Johannes/Lienemann, Wolfgang (1986): Art. Frieden, EKL3 I, Göttingen, 1372–1382.

Seelmann, Kurt (2010[5]): Rechtsphilosophie, München.

Soëtard, Michael (2012): Jean-Jacques Rousseau. Leben und Werk, München.

Steck, Odil Hannes (1972): Jerusalemer Vorstellungen vom Frieden und ihre Abwandlungen in der Prophetie des Alten Israel, in: *Liedtke, Gerhard* (1972, Hrsg.): 75–95.

Steiger, Dominik (2013): Nicht-staatliche Gewaltakteure im Fokus des Sicherheitsrats der Vereinten Nationen, in: *Weingärtner, Dieter/Krieger, Heike* (2013, Hrsg.): 55–82.

Stiftung Wissenschaft und Politik/German Marshall Fund of the United States of America (2013): Neue Macht – neue Verantwortung. Elemente einer deutschen Außen- und Sicherheitspolitik für eine Welt im Umbruch, Berlin, Washington.

Stolzenberg, Jürgen (2007, Hrsg.): Kant in der Gegenwart, Berlin.

Strub, Jean-Daniel (2007a): Wofür steht das Konzept des gerechten Friedens? Replik auf Hans-Richard Reuter, in: *Strub, Jean-Daniel, Grotefeld, Stefan* (2007, Hrsg.): 191–207.

Strub, Jean-Daniel Grotefeld, Stefan (2007b, Hrsg.): Der gerechte Friede zwischen Pazifismus und gerechtem Krieg, Paradigmen der Friedensethik im Diskurs, Stuttgart.

Stümke, Volker (2009): Folter; in: *Evangelisches Kirchenamt für die Bundeswehr* (2009, Hrsg.): 249–256.

Stümke, Volker (2014): Der Umgang mit Macht und Machtlosigkeit, in Vorbereitung.

Taureck, Bernhard H.F. (2009): Jean-Jacques Rousseau. Mit Selbstzeugnissen und Bilddokumenten, Reinbek.

Thiel, Winfried (2005): Aspekte des Friedens im Alten Testament, in: *Thiel, Winfried* (2005, Hrsg.): Gedeutete Geschichte. Studien zur Geschichte Israels und ihrer theologischen Interpretation im Alten Testament, Neukirchen-Vluyn, 107–120.

Thyen, Hartwig (1972): Zur Problematik einer neutestamentlichen Ekklesiologie, in: *Liedtke, Gerhard* (1972, Hrsg.): 96–173.

Vesting, Thomas (2007): Rechtstheorie. München.

Vitzthum, Wolfgang Graf/Proelß, Alexander (2013[6], Hrsg.): Völkerrecht, Berlin, Boston.

Walzer, Michael (1977, 2006[3]): Just and Unjust Wars, New York.

Walzer, Michael (1982): Gibt es den gerechten Krieg?, Stuttgart.

Walzer, Michael (2003): Erklärte Kriege – Kriegserklärungen – Essays, Hamburg.

Walzer, Michael (2006): Arguing about War, Yale.

Weber, Quirin (2011): Parlament – Ort der politischen Entscheidung? Legitimationsprobleme des modernen Parlamentarismus, Basel.

Weinberger, Ota (1989): Rechtslogik, Berlin.

Weingärtner, Dieter (2010, Hrsg.): Die Bundeswehr als Armee im Einsatz, Baden-Baden.

Weingärtner, Dieter/Krieger, Heike (2013, Hrsg.): Streitkräfte und nicht-staatliche Akteure, Baden-Baden.

Weiss, Wolfgang (2001): Allgemeine Rechtsgrundsätze des Völkerrechts, in: Archiv des Völkerrechts 39/2001, 394–431.

Welzel, Hans (1962[4]): Naturrecht und materiale Gerechtigkeit, Göttingen.

Wessels, Johannes/Beulke, Werner (2012[42]): Strafrecht Allgemeiner Teil, Heidelberg.

Wieland, Josef (2007[5])*: Die Ethik der Governance, Marburg.*

Wilkens, Erwin (1987): Art. Frieden, EStL3I, Stuttgart, 999–1007.

Wisotzki, Sabine (2013): Notfalls mit Gewalt? Globale Gerechtigkeit und die Rechtfertigung militärischer Intervention, in: Zeitschrift für Frieden und Konfliktforschung 2/2013/1, 98–129.

Zangl, Bernhard (2009): Auf dem Weg zu internationaler Rechtsherrschaft?, Frankfurt M.

Zangl, Bernhard/Zürn, Michael (2003): Frieden und Krieg. Sicherheit in der nationalen und postnationalen Konstellation, Frankfurt M.

Ziolkowski, Katharina (2008): Gerechtigkeitspostulate als Rechtfertigung von Kriegen. Zum Einfluss moderner Konzepte des Gerechten Krieges auf die völkerrechtliche Zulässigkeit zwischenstaatlicher Gewaltanwendung nach 1945, Baden-Baden.

Ziolkowski, Katharina (2010): Gerechtigkeitspostulate als Rechtfertigung von Kriegen. Zum Einfluss moderner Konzepte des Gerechten Krieges auf die völkerrechtliche Zulässigkeit zwischenstaatlicher Gewaltanwendung nach 1945, in: *Weingärtner, Dieter* (2010, Hrsg.): 23–38.

Zippelius, Reinhold (2011[6]): Rechtsphilosophie, München.

Zippelius, Reinhold (2012a): Juristische Methodenlehre, München.

Zippelius, Reinhold (2012b): Das Wesen des Rechts. Eine Einführung in die Rechtstheorie, Stuttgart.

CHAPTER 17

Attitudes of Military Academy Cadets on Code of Honour of the Serbian Army

Zoran Jeftic, Vanja Rokvić and Svetlana Stanarevic

Introduction

The modern officer corps is a professional group; a modern military officer is a professional.[1] Huntington is but one of the authors who highlighted the uniqueness and difference of the modern officer to warriors from previous eras. Every profession, and especially the military one, demands in addition to high professional standards, no less than a high ethical value system. Frequently, a given profession develops its own code of honour, which is partly based on total cultural tradition of society, and partly based on the specific requirements of the profession concerned.[2] Thus, judicial ethics adopted the virtue of justice, medical ethics are based on the ideas of humanism, and religious ethics are based on spiritual love, and in military ethics adopted the military honour.

The importance of ethics and morality is emphasized by Anthony E. Hartle in his book, *Moral issues in military decision-making*. He writes that professional ethics serve at least three purposes: '(1) they protect other members of society against abuse of the professional monopoly of expertise; (2) they "define the professional as a responsible and trustworthy expert in the service of his client"; and (3) in some professions they delineate the moral authority for actions necessary to the professional function but generally impermissible in moral terms'.[3]

The topic of this article concerns the development of the Code of Honour in Serbia; we will review pertinent attitudes of the students of the Serbian Military Academy about the Code of Honour of the Army of Serbia.

1 Samuel P. Huntington, *The Soldier and the State The Theory and Politics of Civil-Military Relations*, (Belknap, Press of Harvard University Press, 1985), p. 9.

2 Војни информатор мај-јуни 2000, Генералштаб Војске Југославије.

3 Anthony E. Hartle, *Moral issues in military decision-making,* (2nd rev ed, University Press of Kansas,2004), p. 31.

 | DOI 10.1163/9789004312135_018

The Case of Serbia

A momentum for reform in the Republic of Serbia was launched after October 2000, and more specifically for the Ministry for Defence in 2003. Until 2006, reform was mainly associated with creating an environment for organizational changes. This, in turn, achieved the newly integrated organization of the Ministry for Defence (2004), and subsequently, the new structure of the General Staff and the Army of Serbia (2006–2007). This process was, however, burdened by political differences which concerned both the perceived speed as well as the quality of the reforms.[4] By 2010, the National Security Strategy, Defence Strategy, Law on Defence and Army, was adopted. The Army of Serbia became subsequently professionalized (2010), the military education was reformed, the University of Defence as well as new concept of military health care were developed and established, resources for emergency response were integrated. Additionally a number of other tasks necessary to establish a coherent and orderly system of defence were implemented.

The new organisational environment raised a number of issues that were not cast in regulations. Thus, a need emerged for a new ethical value system as well as a modernisation of the code of conduct for the members of the military. Existing regulations were not fully able to cover the ethical conduct of members of the military. The Army subsequently received a request for the codification of conduct and ethical standards in the modern Serbian Army.

Viewed from a historical perspective, a document detailing a Code of Honour did neither exist within the Republic of Serbia until 2010 nor within the states that, like Serbia, constituted the former Socialist Republic of Yugoslavia. Until the Second World War, Serbia (Yugoslavia) has developed the privileged status of the officer corps, and the cult of loyalty to the king as a wartime commander, and in the period of socialism, until the disintegration of Yugoslavia (1991) and to Josip Broz Tito.

Although soldiers' oaths are not part of the Code of Honour, some of its aspects can be identified in the oaths of the Principality of Serbia, The Kingdom of Serbia and Kingdom of Serbs Croats and Slovenians and the Kingdom of Yugoslavia during the socialist period. The oath of soldiers in particular brought out a number of problems, since it referred to the period of the Socialist Federal Republic of Yugoslavia, which contained a provision and protection of the constitutional

4 Occasional disputes arose in 2007 and 2008 in order to 2009. There was an open disagreement with Minister of Defence and Chief of General Staff of the Serbian Army, which as a result had a succession of Chief General Staff by the president.

order and socialist homeland.[5] Under the 1992 Constitution jurisdiction is given to the Yugoslav Army to defend constitutional order.[6] This provision has continued the tradition of socialist Yugoslavia whose constitutions contains provisions on the military as defenders of the constitutional order.[7]

The Code of Honour of the Army of Serbia

The Law on Defence[8] provided for the adoption of a Code of Honour of the Army of Serbia in the form of a bylaw. It is a moral code aimed at influencing the behaviour of members of the Serbian Armed Forces. The Ministry of Defence, as the responsible authority for the Code, has engaged a number of experts from outside the Ministry,[9] to assist in the drafting thereof. This has resulted in a short and plain text which is embedded in the value system of society, and which is appropriate to the Army's circumstances and needs.[10] During the drafting of the Code of Honour, the experience of foreign armies was used, as well as codes of professional associations and unions.

The Code of Honour is not based on a penal system; it basically has a moral responsibility, pertinent in cases of non-compliance. However, this approach does not exclude the possibility that a member of the Army, in case that he violates the Law and the Code, may also be legally responsible.

The basic idea is that the application of the Code of Honour is a phase in a development; it is not a process which has reached its conclusion. Compliance

---

5 The oath reads: 'I (name) do solemnly pledge to defend the independence and constitutional order, sanctity and integrity of the Socialist Federal Republic of Yugoslavia, and that I will keep and develop brotherhood and unity of our peoples and nationalities. I will always conscientious and disciplined fulfil the obligations and duties of counsel of his self-socialist homeland and be ready to fight for her freedom and honour, not wishing to give this fight and your life!'.

6 The Constitution of the Federal Republic of Yugoslavia, FRY Службени гласник, 1/92, Article 133, "Federal Republic of Yugoslavia have an Army to defend sovereignty, territory, independence and constitutional order."

7 Јефтић, Роквић, Младеновић, „Цивилно-војни односи", Београдски универзитет, Факултет безбедности , Београд, 2014, стр 71.

8 Law on Defence of the Republic of Serbia was adopted in 2007.

9 In the preparation of the document were included representatives of the Faculty of Philosophy, Serbian Academy of Sciences and Arts, Institute for Contemporary History of Serbia, and the Ministry of Religious Affairs of the Republic of Serbia.

10 Code of Honour of the Serbian Armed Forces is available on:http://www.vs.rs/content/attachments/Kodeks_casti_pripadnika_Vojske_Srbije.pdf.

with its provisions is achieved primarily through command, training, control, and, most importantly, the everyday educational work of the superiors. In other words, the aim is on the educational component, although this does not exclude the possibility of finishing the Code of Honour and introducing institutions such as courts of honour.

The Code offers in a systematic manner a number of general moral principles of the military profession, its core values and standards of conduct of members of the SAF directing them to act in accordance with basic social and professional values and standards that can be achieved only through the personal responsibility of the Army of Serbia. The Code is a valuable Serbian military tradition of the SAF and should act under the Constitution, laws, military regulations and norms of international humanitarian law.[11]

The Code of Honour defines the moral principles of the military profession, core values and norms of behaviour, common to all members of the Army of Serbia. For the first time, there have been especially elaborated Codes of Honour for different categories of members of the Serbian Army and the officers, non-commissioned officers, soldiers, military officials and military service employees.

In accordance with the general moral principles, the Code of Honour defines the basic values of the military profession and by their acceptance a member of the Army of Serbia is obliged to turn them into his own virtues.[12] The core values for the members of the Serbian Army are: loyalty to the Fatherland, professional dedication, loyalty, courage, discipline, solidarity, humanity, dignity, sacrifice, and respect.[13] In addition, the norms of behaviour have also been defined in relation to the members of the Army of Serbia as an integral part of the Code of Honour.[14]

---

11 Code of Honour of the Serbian Armed Forces – General Provisions , p. 2.

12 Basic as they are not the only ones, but for the members of the Serbian Armed Forces are primary, because they express the essence of the professional military ethic.

13 Code of Honour of the Serbian Armed Forces – General Provisions, p. 2.

14 With Fatherland he is in a covenant relationship and unconditionally defends it; respects, preserves and defends the state and military insignia and wears his uniform of the Army of Serbia in a dignified way, in the service and beyond; when executing combat missions: force is used only as necessary; treats humanely the captured enemy soldiers and civilians, especially the elderly, women and children; does not allow the war materiel entrusted to him come into the possession of the enemy in proper condition , in case of capture refuses to cooperate when it is contrary to legal norms and provisions of the Code of Honour; do not accept an act of treason, never leaves in trouble the other member of the Army of Serbia; respects the personality and diversity; does not curse, does not insult and does not speak in a derogatory way about values sacred to others; he is dedicated to

Attitudes of Military Academy Cadets

There have been very few studies related to the views of the professional members of the Serbian Army and the cadets of the Military Academy concerning the Code of Honour. The study, which was conducted in November 2012 in the context of 'Military culture', had as its theme the examination of the attitudes of the male and female cadets on significant aspects of military culture. Among these was the set of variables classified as the conceptual basis of the Code of Honour of the Army of Serbia. The questionnaire was composed of 61 questions of which 11 referred to the Code of Honour, and in which was required the assessment of the level of agreement with each of the offered statements in the range of 1 to 5 (completely disagree, mostly disagree, undecided, mostly agree, completely agree).

The carried sample included 282 male and female cadets, of which 69.1% of respondents were male and 30.9 female. The study included cadets from all four years of study; more specifically: 23.8% in the first year: 28.7% in the second year, 23.4% in the third year and 24.1% in the fourth year of study. Differentiated by type of neighbourhood they came from, the cadets' sample included 56% from urban areas, 14.2% from suburban areas, 12.8% from small towns and 17% from rural areas. This reflects the structure of the population of the Republic of Serbia in general.

The requested attitudes were related to the following:

1 The military ideal of SAF's is loyalty the homeland Serbia.
2 Members of SAF professionally and responsibly perform their duties regardless of the difficulties and dangers.
3 Members of SAF consciously fulfil their obligations respecting the Constitution, laws and military regulations.
4 The behaviour of members of SAF contributes to the development of mutual trust and unity.
5 Members of SAF do not use more force than is necessary to overcome the enemy.
6 Members of SAF enhance the reputation and the trust that members of the Army have among the citizens.

---

the military profession and lives in accordance with its values; he also seeks to: control his behavior, is relaxed and calm, and is unswerving in his battle with himself, the enemy and the elements of the nature; holds a given word, is self-critical, self-righteous, truthful, tolerant, humble, trustworthy and open; personal interests he harmonizes with common ones; is not wicked, vain, vindictive, surly, arrogant, boastful and overbearing, does not flatter and does not defame others; is a moral role model for all members of society.

7 Members of SAF are willing to sacrifice for the sake of the homeland, without expecting a reward.
8 Members of SAF value and respect the sanctity of others (people, cultures, groups etc.).
9 Members of SAF help other members of the SAF in all circumstances when he needs help.
10 Members of SAF always ready to face the (risk to themselves) uncertainty, danger and evil.
11 Members of SAF always take fair and reasonable decisions regardless of the severity of the situation in which it is located.

The Analysis of the distribution of responses according to variables shows that gender does not reveal significant differences: men and women demonstrate a high degree of agreement.

As for the type of neighbourhood from which cadets originate, statistically significant differences can be observed between respondents from the city and from the countryside. The respondents from the city have higher scores on those variables listed. Also a statistically significant difference was observed between respondents coming from suburban areas and towns (taken together) and respondents coming from villages: respondents from suburbs and towns have higher scores on the variables.

An explanation for this outcome remains a topic for thought and further research. Perhaps the reason lies in the fact that those respondents who come from the city in large numbers entered the Military Academy for the love of the military and, with it, for its value system. Respondents who come from the countryside have socio-economic reasons as their primary reason for their enrolment into the Military Academy, and less authentic commitment to the military as such, including its essential characteristics.

The motives of cadets to apply for admission to the Military Academy thus reveal a variety of views. The results from the study show that the love of uniforms and weapons is the strongest motive which guided the respondents, to be followed by socio-economic reasons, adventure, righteousness and family tradition.

When it comes to the Code of Honour, the study also finds that there is a statistically significant difference between those respondents whose only motive for enrolment into the Military Academy is the love for uniforms and weapons, in comparison to those respondents whose only motives are poverty and poor socio-economic conditions of life. Specifically, respondents who enrolled in Military Academy for the love for uniforms and weapons have a distinct Code of Honour with respect to the other. The situation is similar when comparing the Code of Honour among the respondents who were motivated by poor socio-economic conditions and those in the military service part of a family tradition, and Code of Honour is more pronounced in those respondents who entered MA to continue the family tradition.[15]

Conclusion

Code of Honour is a morally binding document. It had to avoid various ideological and political obstacles, while it had to offer a clear connection between tradition on the one hand, and a message for the future, on the other. The adoption of the Code of Honour and its entry into force is only the first step in codifying the behaviour of members of the Serbian Armed Forces.

Respecting the military hierarchy, the Code of Honour has also been developed for officers and non-commissioned officers, soldiers, military officials and military service employees. Recognizing the importance of all human resources of the Army of Serbia, but also their specificity, the integral part of the Code also contains special standards of conduct for each of them.

Military Academy cadets aş future leaders in the military, should complete their education with clearly defined and adopted values. Therefore, the study of universal military culture and within it value parameters of military honour is urgent need of our time.

The results which offered the research in December 2012. They indicate satisfactory level. Some results suggest a relatively high percentage of neutral responses. Moreover, cadets of the first year students had higher scores on the value scale than cadets of senior years – a point which should be the subject of further research in order to eliminate the causes of it.

Certainly it can be expected that the reinforcement of the Code of Honour contribute to the improvement of the moral profile of the Serbian Army and the Military Academy cadets, and become a permanent dimension of cadets personality.

15 Possible answers are: socio-economic reasons, family tradition, adventure; someone made him, righteousness, and love of uniform power.

Index of Names

Index of Subjects

Printed in the United States
By Bookmasters